— THE SAGA OF THE —

PONY EXPRESS

JOSEPH J. DI CERTO

D1455361

Mountain Press Publishing Company
Missoula, Montana
2002

Cover art: Map of Pony Express route by
William Henry Jackson, courtesy Pioneer Village

Maps by Tony Moore, Moore Creative Designs

Library of Congress Cataloging-in-Publication Data

Di Certo, Joseph J.
    The saga of the Pony Express / Joseph J. Di Certo.
      p. cm.
    Includes bibliographical references (p.) and index.
    ISBN 0-87842-454-7 (cloth : alk. paper) — ISBN 0-87842-452-0
(pbk. : alk. paper)
      1. Pony express—History. 2. Postal service—United States—
History—19th century. I. Title.
HE6375.P65 D533 2002
383'.143'0973—dc21
                                      2002070923

Mountain Press Publishing Company
P.O. Box 2399 • Missoula, MT 59806
406-728-1900

— THE SAGA OF THE —
PONY EXPRESS

SAN FRANCISCO,

APRIL 19, 1860.

Expresses.

*To my precious Nina,
one of God's greatest gifts to me*

CONTENTS

ACKNOWLEDGMENTS

WITH THE MOST sincere gratitude, I would like to express my appreciation to the following people and organizations:

Dominick Di Certo, who helped to organize the manuscript

The Fort Laramie Historical Association

Ms. Jackie Lewin, St. Joseph Museum, who was always there for me when I needed information

Chad Wall, Nebraska State Historical Society

Ms. Aimee Klask, a very cheerful helper

Mr. and Mrs. David Bagley, for their wonderful generosity in providing me with some great photographs

Dean Knudsen and Valerie Naylor, at Scotts Bluff National Monument, for their incredible generosity in providing me with a large number of W. H. Jackson illustrations

Tami Lambert, at the Patee House Museum

Sally Pike, at the St. Joseph, Missouri, Chamber of Commerce, for service above and beyond the call of duty in providing photographs

Mr. Al Mulder, at Utah Cross Roads, for going out of his way to find some much needed photographs

Gwen McKenna: What can I say? I saved the best for last. Her incredible devotion to her work, her sincere interest in the project, her uncanny attention to detail, and her unbounded patience with the author are the real power behind the book. A very heartfelt thanks to a great editor.

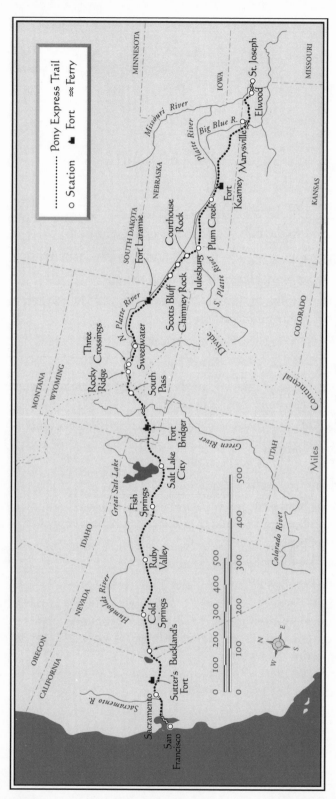

Overview of the Pony Express Trail

INTRODUCTION

M OST PEOPLE ARE astonished when they learn that the Pony Express lasted a mere eighteen months—from April 1860 to October 1861. The larger-than-life image of this heroic undertaking and its impact on American frontier history create the impression that this enterprise existed for at least several decades. This misconception is understandable considering the indelible imprint the drama of the Pony Express has burned in the American imagination.

It is right and fitting that the Pony Express hold such a prominent place in our nation's heritage. Its length of service should not be the measure of its greatness; rather, the Pony Express should be judged by its contribution to the development and stability of a nation in crisis, and by the magnitude of the courage, persistence, endurance, and dedication of the men and women that kept it going under the most challenging conditions.

Yet while the name of the Pony Express is well known to Americans, its full story is not. The Pony Express story might be called a historical iceberg: most people are vaguely familiar with the image of brave young riders racing from station to station, carrying mail across the wilderness, but the full, fascinating epic has been hidden beneath the surface for decades. The story unfolds not only in the vast expanse of the American West, but also in the glittering mansions of our nation's capital. It involves not only the sturdy riders whose word and honor were held above all else, but also opportunists and scoundrels, congressmen and senators, even a president, whose words were as malleable as a campaign promise. Its creation came against all odds, and its existence changed the West forever.

The Pony Express was important to America in a myriad of ways. First, and most obviously, it filled an urgent need of its time. By 1860, the citizens of California were no longer willing to remain cut off from their families and friends back East, or from the news of the nation. The Pony Express, if only for a short time, connected California and much of the rest of the West with the motherland, and in doing so it solidified the bond and confirmed the West's identity as part of the United States.

The Pony Express was a product of its times, not only in its purpose but in the sheer daring of its inception and execution. The sense of bravado that permeated mid-nineteenth-century America was apparent in the Pony Express riders, of course, but less apparent was the financial bravado of its creators and investors. Arthur Chapman, author of *The Pony Express* (New York: Putnam, 1932), notes:

> The "Pony," as it was soon affectionately called, was one of the outward expressions of a certain business audacity, which was common at the time. Men in the whirl of frontier activities seldom stopped to figure the costs. Mines were paying—the wealth of the new, raw West was inexhaustible. Fantastic schemes lost all aspect of distortion. Men plunged, and, if they lost, were game in defeat. The Pony Express could not have been born in any other era.

In writing this book, I have attempted to re-create for the reader the story of this legendary mail-delivery service, in which a group of young riders risked their lives to carry crucial messages across nearly two thousand miles of hostile wilderness. I have also worked to place this exciting story in the context of its prevailing social and political milieu, in an effort to help the reader fully appreciate the significance of the Pony Express in its times. The early chapters of the book provide a brief overview of the development of the major cities on the East Coast and of the tensions between whites and Native Americans on the western frontier. Most importantly, these first chapters explain the conditions that made rapid mail-delivery service to California critical.

Later chapters discuss the service itself, the men who created it, and the men who provided it. They provide a brief history of the great western freighting company Russell, Majors & Waddell and its heroic commitment to establish the Pony Express in a seemingly impossible short period of time. Stories of extraordinary adventures and death-defying rides by fearless young riders are also graphically described in these chapters. The final chapter reveals the factors that led to the demise of the service. In short, this book presents not only the story of the Pony Express, but also the world of the Pony Express.

In attempting to re-create the world of the Pony Express, I was often stymied by a lack of information and by inaccurate or conflicting information. Complete records and detailed descriptions of the events were not always kept, and the ravages of the Civil War destroyed some of the records that did exist.

For example, substantiating the existence of certain Pony Express relay stations and identifying their official names was often daunting and sometimes fruitless. Several stations on different sections of the trail had the same name, and many stations had different names at different times—East Canyon Station in Utah, for instance, was also referred to as Dixie Hollow, Dixie Creek, Big Mountain, Dutchmann's Flat, Bauchmann's, and Snyder's Mill. Some relay stations existed for only a short period and were subsequently replaced by other stations. There was also much conflicting data regarding distances between relay stations and other details. Even the location of the Pony Express Trail itself varies from one document to another.

In spite of the difficulty in untangling and clarifying the facts about this fascinating chapter of American frontier history, much scholarly work has been done over the past few decades. This work has enabled me to set before you this spectacular drama of courageous, determined, and unselfish pioneers of the Pony Express and their invaluable contribution to our nation.

To this day, the stories of the brave riders who rode around the clock carrying the U.S. Mail across the wilderness remind us that the settlement of the West was made possible by people of great character and foresight, many of whom were ready to make the supreme sacrifice for their country.

— 1 —
AN EVOLVING NATION

THE BOLD IDEA of men on horseback riding in relays across nearly two thousand miles of wilderness did not occur to someone out of the blue. It was created to fill the urgent demand for timely mail service to the rapidly expanding population in the West. Yet simply recognizing this crying need was not enough to create the Pony Express. Its execution required men of supreme courage, unquestioning dedication, and extraordinary vision. These appeared at the right time and the right place in the persons of William Russell, Alexander Majors, and William Waddell. Yet before we investigate this particular 1860 innovation, we must look at the seeds from which it grew.

With the turn of the nineteenth century came an air of anticipation worldwide, a stirring of new political and social developments. In Europe, Napoleon in his seemingly unstoppable exploits crossed the Great St. Bernard Pass, defeating the Austrians and going on to conquer Italy. Two years later (1802) he proclaimed himself President of the Italian Republic. These actions led many Europeans to flee their homelands, some of them finding sanctuary in the newly formed United States.

America at this time was a kaleidoscope of rapidly developing industries and social activities, a nation experiencing political, social, and commercial growing pains. Cities were getting bigger and more crowded. Industries were expanding. Transportation and communications were developing at high speed, and people were moving west. Extreme political views were evolving.

In 1800, the offices of the U.S. government were moved from Philadelphia to Washington, D.C., newly platted on a parcel of land independent of the laws of individual states. Its inhabitants comprised 2,464 free citizens and 623 slaves. But the winds of political change were blowing strong as the government prohibited further import of slaves from Africa in 1808. It generated additional upheaval when it declared war

5

against Britain in 1812. The war resulted in great devastation, as Britain burned the city of Buffalo and much of Washington, D.C.

But in spite of national crises, the opening decades of the nineteenth century also saw positive developments. New technologies never ceased to amaze U.S. citizens. Word spread in 1807 that in London, streets were being lit with a lamp that burned gas from the ground, and by 1822 the new streetlamps were burning in Boston. In 1809 a fellow named Louis Braille invented a system by which blind people would be able to read. A printing press run by steam was printing the *London Times* in 1814, and in 1815 the U.S. Navy was operating its first steam-powered warship, the U.S.S. *Fulton*. Three years later another steam-driven ship, the *Savannah*, was the first to cross the Atlantic Ocean.

As the century went on, new inventions continued to come fast and furiously. An Italian fellow named Volta figured out a way to hold electricity in a container called a battery. A young civil engineer, Robert Fulton, assembled the first boat that could operate underwater—he called it a submarine. A most practical invention saw the light of day in 1827 when John Walker introduced an ingenious little stick covered with sulphur chemicals that, when rubbed against a rough surface, burst into flames. These "friction matches" were a boon to both the housewife and the frontiersman.

On the East Coast, big cities such as Boston, Philadelphia, and New York were flourishing. By 1800 the population of New York City reached an "astounding" 60,000, and by 1810 there were 7,239,881 citizens residing in the United States. Large numbers of new shops (many of them built by John Jacob Astor, considered the richest man in the nation) featuring ready-made goods, from stationery to clothes, were springing up almost daily. Some of the more exclusive shops boasted the "latest styles of Paris," attracting to their doors wealthy and fashionable shoppers. Previously, fine clothes had to be ordered from the great shops of Paris and London or were custom-made.

Before the Industrial Revolution, the poorer classes had made their own clothing—some women even weaved their own cloth. But now, large-scale manufacturing was beginning to change this. Because of the large volume, the prices for garments were significantly reduced, while the quality improved. A whole new industry known as "retail" evolved to market the goods.

In addition to providing goods, these new retail shops also created many employment opportunities. Jobs as clerks, salespeople, store managers, accountants, stockers, janitors, and a myriad of other entry-level and skilled positions became available. With these jobs adding to the hundreds of factory jobs in the cities, the United States seemed destined to be the most prosperous country ever known.

Meanwhile, urban dwellers clamored for indoor plumbing. By 1800 there were about two thousand indoor baths in Philadelphia alone. As with clothing, manufacturers introduced ready-made furniture that could be bought "on the spot" and carried away. It was even possible to buy ready-made houses, which were shipped as far away as Texas.

American cities saw innovations in social and leisure activities as well. Enticing city residents out for an evening's entertainment were theaters featuring music, ballet, and dramatic productions. Any time of day, one might stop off at one of the fancy ice cream parlors that had recently opened. For those who sought more excitement, there was plenty to be had at the newly established horse-racing tracks. Or, one could merely enjoy the simple pleasures of a meal at a new "quick lunch" restaurant.

By 1860 in Washington, D.C., gas lamps had been installed along the avenues, in government offices, and even in some private homes. Congress granted permission for sewer pipes to be laid throughout the city, and some streets were paved with cobblestones. Large horse-drawn buses ran with a reasonable frequency, making travel across the city very convenient. For the first time signs were placed on lampposts to identify streets, and a new ordinance required that every home and commercial building display its address number.

This whirlwind of change was not restricted to the cities. The once remote, pastoral life on the farm was also being caught up in the flurry. Henry Clay and other inventors introduced new, mechanized farm equipment. People could see the latest machines and learn about new methods of farming at periodic gatherings called farm fairs.

Early nineteenth-century America also saw expanding vistas. When explorer Thomas Walker discovered the Cumberland Gap through the Appalachian Mountains in 1750, he opened the inland south to settlement, and America's westward expansion began. But these early settlements were only a foreshadowing of the expansion to come. In 1803 the United States would secure the biggest single land acquisition in its history, and it would devote the next hundred years to its assimilation.

When the United States was founded, the huge, uncharted expanse of North America from the Mississippi River to the Stony (Rocky) Mountains, between New Orleans and the Canadian border, belonged to France. In 1762 France ceded this vast area, collectively called

Louisiana, to Spain, which was of no great consequence to the American settlers. But in 1800 events in Europe began to have an impact on the new nation. On October 1, Napoleon Bonaparte secretly induced a very hesitant King Charles IV of Spain to return Louisiana to France. The news did not sit well with President Jefferson. Napoleon was not to be trusted; to have him in control of America's western border and of the port of New Orleans was disturbing.

Knowing that France was having serious financial difficulties and was facing an imminent renewed war with England, Jefferson sent envoys to try to pressure Napoleon into selling them New Orleans by threatening a U.S. alliance with England. Much to the envoys' amazement, the French emperor sold them the entire Louisiana Territory. Its 828,000 square miles doubled the size of the United States.

Shortly after acquiring Louisiana, Jefferson sent an expedition led by William Clark and Meriwether Lewis to explore and map the uncharted new territory and to seek out a possible water route to the Pacific, opening the way to eventual settlement. Meanwhile, the pace of change in the states east of the Appalachians continued to accelerate over the next several decades. As new railroad and telegraph lines went in, citizens eagerly migrated across the country up to the frontier boundary of the United States, western Missouri. In only twenty years, between 1840 and 1860, the railroads expanded at an incredible rate, adding 27,700 miles of new track, mostly in the Northeast. And all along the railroad, wherever there was a station, towns sprang up and grew.

Adding to the national growth was a surge of immigrants, the majority coming from Europe, in the first half of the century. Between 1825 and 1850, more than two million immigrants came to the United States: ten thousand came in 1825; more than twice that number immigrated in 1830; and in 1849, a massive flood of three hundred thousand immigrants arrived. The growth in the American population was nothing less than staggering, expanding from four million in 1790 to twenty-three million in 1849.

For many, the eastern United States was becoming too crowded, and there was no longer enough land available for people who wanted to farm. Americans and immigrants began to migrate even farther west. The West, which by the 1840s meant all the land to the Pacific coast, held allure beyond its ample land for homesteads. Since the days of the mountain men, the West represented adventure and freedom.

Reaching destinations west was not easy, however, especially hauling a wagonful of possessions. While east of the Missouri River were abundant stagecoach lines, riverboats, and rail lines, it was a totally different story for anyone wanting to travel west. To reach the Pacific coast, a traveler had only two choices: by sea or by his own means overland.

The ocean voyage risked rough seas and possible shipwreck. Ships heading to the Pacific coast left from one of the eastern seaports, such as Boston, New York, or Charleston, then sailed down the coast and around Florida. From there, a ship took one of two routes. It could make a long journey across the Caribbean Sea, along the coast of South America, around Cape Horn, and back up the western coast of South America to California, a grueling eight-week journey. The other option was to take a shortcut and sail to the insect-infested Isthmus of Panama, where there was a good chance of dying of malaria. From there, the voyagers had to ride pack mules to the opposite shore and board another ship to continue to California. Neither choice was appealing, and boat travel to the West Coast was understandably light.

The other choice of travel to the West was overland by wagon train. Travelers had to provide their own wagons and teams, which generally carried their things while they themselves walked. This option meant a four- to six-month journey through treacherous wilderness, across seemingly endless plains, and over mountains. Along the way, there was the ever-present threat of Indian attacks or early winter storms. Whether by sea or overland, the trip west required great courage and determination, but thousands of Americans felt it was worth it for the promise of a better life.

The first major portion of the West to be settled was the Oregon Territory. Until 1846, this huge area was jointly owned by the United States and Britain. Through the powerful Hudson's Bay fur trading company, Britain had dominated the region economically for the first few decades of the nineteenth century. As late as 1839, there were still only one hundred Americans living in the Oregon Territory.

However, word about the rich soil, rushing rivers alive with fish, and vast forests of prime timber slowly drifted east, and "Oregon fever" began to spread. Suddenly the rush was on to reach the Promised Land. By 1843 there were fifteen hundred Americans living in Oregon Territory, and by 1859 the territory boasted about fifty thousand emigrants from the states.

California also became a destination for U.S. emigration. This vast territory along the West Coast, which belonged to Mexico until 1848, had long been settled by Spanish missionaries. This land of "never-ending sunshine" had an excellent climate for growing all sorts of crops, and

By 1859, Oregon Territory boasted about fifty thousand inhabitants. Many wagon trains gathered at Westport Landing and other Missouri River crossings in Independence, Missouri, the starting point for the long journey to the West Coast. (Painting by W. H. Jackson.) —Courtesy Scotts Bluff National Monument

settlers in ox-drawn covered wagons came by the hundreds to start farms. But it was an unforeseen event in the northern California hills that caused the population to explode from a few thousand to tens of thousands almost overnight.

On January 24, 1848, just before the United States signed a peace treaty with Mexico, a man named James W. Marshall discovered gold at a place called Sutter's Mill, in the Sacramento Valley. News of the find drifted east, and within a year, gold fever was reigning unchecked. Prospectors arrived in California by the thousands, by land and by ship from all parts of the world. In 1849 more than forty-five thousand adventurers, mostly men, crossed the Sierra Nevada in search of riches.

In a surprisingly short time, major cities had developed in California and Oregon, their citizens anxious for eastern products and the latest news, especially news of the growing conflict between the Northern and Southern states. The country was being torn apart over the issue of slavery.

Following the 1848 gold discovery in California was a mad rush of prospectors to the West Coast. Soon demand grew for better communications with the East. —Courtesy California State Library

At first the government tried to work around the issue. Congress passed the Compromise of 1850, which stated that, among other things, the territory of California would be admitted as a free state, and the territories of New Mexico and Utah would have no regulations regarding slavery. One of the resolutions, the Fugitive Slave Act, required the U.S. government to help capture and return runaway slaves. In the end, however, the law settled very little.

Several years before the Pony Express came into being, things really started to heat up. Violence and murder occurred on both sides. In 1855, the famous Dred Scott case, which argued that slave Dred Scott became free when his owner took him into free territory, lost before the Supreme Court, creating further tension between the North and the South. In October 1859, abolitionist John Brown and twenty-one followers captured an arsenal in Harpers Ferry, West Virginia, and a fierce

A cartoon bitterly attacking Democratic presidential candidate Franklin Pierce for endorsing the Compromise of 1850 and pledging to enforce the Fugitive Slave Act.
—Courtesy Library of Congress

battle erupted. Brown was later hanged, becoming something of a martyr for the Northern cause. Although the political leaders in the North insisted that they had nothing to do with the Harpers Ferry tragedy, the Southern states reacted with extreme resentment. These hostile feelings of the Southern states were clearly reflected in the words of Georgia's Alfred Iverson: "Disguise the fact as you will, there is an enmity between Northern and Southern people that is deep and enduring, and you can never eradicate it—never! . . . We are enemies as much as if we were hostile states."

By 1860, the United States was consumed by this grave crisis. News-making events were occurring rapidly and needed to be reported to the people in California and Oregon. To fulfill this urgent need, the Pony Express was born. Within days, western residents were informed of the dramatic, historic developments as they unfolded.

NOVEMBER 6, 1860
ABRAHAM LINCOLN WINS THE PRESIDENTIAL ELECTION

DECEMBER 20, 1860
SOUTH CAROLINA DISSOLVES ITS UNION WITH THE UNITED STATES

DECEMBER 27, 1860
SOUTH CAROLINA STATE TROOPS CAPTURE A FEDERAL NAVAL SHIP

DECEMBER 30, 1860
SOUTH CAROLINA STATE TROOPS SEIZE
THE U.S. ARSENAL IN CHARLESTON

JANUARY 9, 1861
MISSISSIPPI SECEDES FROM THE UNION

JANUARY 19, 1861
GEORGIA SECEDES FROM THE UNION

JANUARY 23, 1861
TEXAS SECEDES FROM THE UNION

JANUARY 26, 1861
LOUISIANA SECEDES FROM THE UNION

FEBRUARY 18, 1861
JEFFERSON DAVIS INAUGURATED AS PROVISIONAL
PRESIDENT OF THE CONFEDERATE STATES OF AMERICA

APRIL 12, 1861
CONFEDERATE ARTILLERY FIRES ON FORT SUMTER

The act of aggression at Fort Sumter, off the coast of Charleston, South Carolina, marked the official beginning of the Civil War. While citizens thoroughout the states received this historic news via telegraph and stagecoach, the anxious throngs on the West Coast would receive word through the gallant, dedicated service of the Pony Express riders.

— 2 —

AMERICA IN TURMOIL

IN JANUARY 1860, one of the major concerns of the U.S. government was ensuring that the state of California and other western states would remain in the union. Their gold and other natural resources, as well as their military stores and equipment, would be of great value in the event of a civil war.

In the West, opinions about the impending war and the western territories' place in it were mixed. In a Fourth of July sermon at Sacramento Congregational Church in 1856, Reverend Charles Edward Pickett, predicting an eventual dissolution of the Union, encouraged a discontinuance of California's relationship with the eastern states and strongly supported the concept of an independent Pacific Republic. Surveyor William H. Brewer, who had come west in 1860, fiercely opposed this idea, a view shared by many westerners. In a journal entry of April 26, 1861, Brewer wrote:

> [T]here are many desperadoes who would do anything, hoping to gain personally in any row that might arise, but the masses feel that their only safety is in the Union. Without protection, without mails [the Pony Express was operating at this time] what could California be? A "Republic of the Pacific" is the shurest [sic] nonsense. A republic of only about nine hundred thousand inhabitants, less than a million, spread over a territory much larger than the original thirteen states, scattered, hostile Indians and worse Mormons on their borders—what would either sustain or protect such a country? And the people feel it.

The fear of a California secession was not without foundation. Much of the population of California, as well as that of Oregon, had come from Southern states or were sympathetic to slavery. In fact, 40 percent of Californians had come from slave states, and others, though born Northerners, hated blacks. In fact, in the 1850s Oregon voted to ban all blacks (slave or free) from the territory, and such a vote had almost been successful in California.

Out of the fifty-three newspapers in California, an overwhelming forty-six of them took an editorial stand against Abraham Lincoln. The influential *San Francisco Herald* and the *Los Angeles Star* supported the idea of California taking sides with the Confederate states. Editorials became so vehemently anti-Lincoln, in fact, that the federal government banned one particularly contentious paper, the *Expositor*, from the U.S. Mail. As a result of this decision, anti-Union plots sprang up throughout the state, and tempers ran hot. Two incidents, one involving two state legislators and the other a former chief justice and a state senator, resulted in fatal duels. Eventually, in late 1861, California implored General George Wright, Commander of the Department of the Pacific, to send troops to the San Joaquin Valley to maintain the peace.

California's pro-Confederacy contingent was still in the minority, but it numbered many powerful and influential people, including its U.S. senator, William Gwin. There was also the Spanish-speaking community that constituted a dissatisfied, conquered group, eager to regain dominance. In other regions, numerous Indian tribes saw an opportunity to drive out the white settlers as the two factions killed each other off.

The intensity of Confederate sympathy in California was manifested in a bill submitted by Senator Gwin to the state legislature. It called for the establishment of a separate state government consisting of the six southern California counties. The bill passed both houses and was signed by Governor Latham in April 1859. The six counties then had a popular vote and also passed the bill, which was then sent to Washington, where it languished for lack of action.

Many of the fears of the federal government concerning the proslavery influences in the western regions were soon realized. There were individuals who supported the Southern cause at high levels, not only in the legislature, but also in the military installations in all parts of the country. John Floyd, then Secretary of War, deliberately arranged to send Colonel William W. Loring, an ardent secessionist, to head the War Department in New Mexico Territory in 1861. Meanwhile, during a brief period in 1860 and the first half of 1861, the secessionist organization Knights of the Golden Circle managed to dominate most of the crucial strategic positions in San Francisco, including the arsenals, the mint, the navy yard, and many of the local army posts. The prize to be won from the conquest of the West was great. It involved, among other things, a number of important military installations including Forts Fillmore, Bridger, Wise, Craig, Thorn, McLane, Buchanan, and Breckenridge.

A cartoon harshly critical of Jefferson Davis and the Confederacy, and of outgoing president Buchanan's ineffective administration. Secretary of War John B. Floyd, who was accused of misappropriating government funds, is shown raking coins into a sack. —Courtesy Library of Congress

Threats to the Union came throughout the West. On February 18, 1861, General David E. Twiggs blatantly turned over all the property under his command in Texas to the Confederate Army. Southern leaders hoped this act would be repeated by other officers sympathetic to their cause. On June 5 of the same year, in Virginia City, Nevada, a group of secessionists raised a rebel flag. General E. V. Summer, Commander of the Department of the Pacific, immediately ordered federal troops to Fort Churchill. They seized the arms of a rebel militia company of four hundred men, a quarter of whom were fully armed. In August, secessionists held a huge rally in New Mexico Territory, where they declared that Arizona was ready to join the Confederacy and elected a delegate to the Confederate Congress.

By late summer of 1861, the political crisis in California was reaching its climax. So intense were concerns for the security of the state that on September 17, 1861, based on reports of a secessionist rebellion in

southern California, General Summer ordered the first California infantry and cavalry to the area. Later, additional federal troops were sent
in to prevent the South from invading California and to aid the Union
soldiers in driving out Confederates from Arizona and New Mexico.

Throughout this period of terrible anxiety, the Pony Express delivered desperately awaited information about the pending conflagration
in half the time of the stagecoach. Twice each week, riding around the
clock through rain and snow, the riders arrived with the mail. The feelings of the Californians regarding this mail service were best expressed
by the words of Hubert Howe Bancroft:

> It was the pony to which every one looked for deliverance; men prayed
> for the safety of the little beast, and trembled lest the service should
> be discontinued . . . after all, it was to the flying pony that all eyes and
> hearts were turned. . . .

3

BIRTH OF A DREAM

IN 1859 AND 1860, as the Civil War approached, rebel sympathizers spread a great deal of propaganda among the people of California and the other western states. The government needed to provide its western citizens with the latest factual information to counter it. West of St. Joseph, Missouri, the flow of information from the East was an infrequent trickle. Could a fast, dependable mail route be established across the wilderness?

Mail to San Francisco was sometimes carried by steamship, either around the southern tip of South America and up the West Coast—an extremely long and hazardous voyage—or through the malaria-ridden Isthmus of Panama, at least a twenty-eight-day journey and usually much longer. Yet overland travel across the desolate terrain west of the Missouri was dangerous and unreliable, so transportation of mail by ship appeared to be the most practical, if not the most economical, solution.

In March 1847, Congress passed a bill to construct five steamships for the express purpose of delivering mail to the West Coast. This project was placed under the direction of the Secretary of the Navy, who in turn issued ten-year contracts for mail service to the West Coast to two companies. One would take mail from the Atlantic states and New Orleans to the Pacific coast, and the other would deliver it to other western points once it arrived from the East. The East Coast contract was awarded to a company headed by Arnold Harris, and the West Coast contract to the company of A. G. Sloo. The total payment was $199,000 annually for monthly mail service. In April 1848 William H. Aspinwall took over the contract from Sloo and established the Pacific Mail Steamship Company, assuming the responsibility for mail delivery in the coming fall.

The first of the five mail ships was the *California*, which sailed out of New York Harbor on October 6, 1848, heading for the West Coast by way of Cape Horn. Because of the lack of rapid mail service, the crew of

The S.S. California *was built to carry mail from the East Coast to the West Coast. With its first voyage, however, came an unexpected development.*
—Courtesy San Francisco Maritime National Historical Park

the *California* had not yet heard about the gold strikes at Sutter's Mill, so when the ship docked at Callao, Peru, two and a half months later, they were astonished by the large number of gold seekers wanting passage to California. At one port the *California* was overwhelmed when four hundred would-be prospectors crowded aboard and settled into quarters designed for no more than one hundred passengers. By then, the talk of gold had affected everyone. When the ship landed in San Francisco, not only did the passengers disembark, but the entire crew dashed madly off the ship and straight to the goldfields, with little thought of the fate of the mail the ship was carrying.

Another example of the problems of coast-to-coast mail delivery arose after the creation of Utah as a territory in September 1850. The news was dispatched by steamship to San Francisco, and from there a private messenger headed east across the Sierra Nevada to Salt Lake City. This important news finally arrived at its destination about four months later, in January 1851.

However, as slow as they were, steamships did carry large volumes of mail and other printed matter, and soon the citizens of San Francisco eagerly looked forward to their arrival. So much so, in fact, that when a ship was expected, someone would remain on watch on Telegraph Hill, searching the horizon for the first sign of a steamer. Once sighted, a signal, easily seen by the general populace, was sent by semaphore hand signals. So familiar did the citizens of San Francisco become with the semaphore signals that during an evening performance of a tragedy in a local theater, when an actor standing on the stage with his arms outstretched uttered, "What does this mean?" the audience shouted out, "A side-wheeled steamer!" bringing a roar of laughter.

This seabound postal service was also a very expensive system. It ended up costing the government more than $700,000 each year while it received a little more than $200,000 in postage. In other words, they were losing about half a million dollars a year for a slow mail service. Meanwhile, most of the people in the West were exasperated with dreadfully stale news. Even after a railroad had been completed across the Isthmus of Panama in January 1855, the steamship delivery was inadequate. Many western residents had traveled cross-country to get there, they reasoned, so why couldn't an overland mail service be established? Surely it could not be any slower than ship-delivered mail.

The first try at overland mail service to the West Coast came in 1851 when two enterprising men, George Chorpenning and Absalom Woodward, signed a contract with the U.S. government to carry mail between Sacramento, California, and Salt Lake City, Utah, by way of the Carson Valley. The contract called for monthly delivery. In hopes of establishing a regular mail route, they arranged to have some crude stations erected along this desolate stretch of country.

Meanwhile, on the eastern end of the route, a man named Samuel H. Woodson was carrying mail between Salt Lake City and Independence, Missouri. He had begun a monthly stagecoach service on July 1, 1850, receiving a fee of $19,500 per year for four years from the government. During those four years, mail service was satisfactory, although sometimes late or damaged due to bad weather.

On May 1, 1851, Chorpenning left Sacramento with a horse loaded with about seventy-five pounds of mail and arrived in Salt Lake City fifty-three days later. The delay was due to deep snowdrifts in the Sierra Nevada, which substantiated the prevalent notion that a central mail route was impractical during winter months. In November 1851 Woodward led a group of four men from Sacramento with mail loaded on mules, which led to the expression "jackass mail." The Woodward party never arrived at Salt Lake City, nor was anything heard from them. In the spring, their remains were found; they had been massacred by an Indian war party.

Word of this incident quickly spread, making it almost impossible for Chorpenning to hire another crew. In late 1852 Chorpenning delivered some mail on his own. His sense of dedication won him a second contract with the government in April 1854. However, this time the route from Salt Lake City headed almost due south, through Utah into Nevada Territory and finally on to San Diego, California. The mail to San Francisco would then be taken north through California. The southern route was more reliable in winter than a direct route west to northern California.

By 1858 Chorpenning had a contract to establish a central overland mail route between Salt Lake City and Placerville, California, near San Francisco. This time, instead of mules, he used stagecoaches to carry mail as well as passengers. The new route, often called Egan's Trail after Howard Egan, who developed the route, went south of the Humboldt River, with stations approximately every twenty miles, at such points as Rush Valley, Deep Creek, Ruby Valley, Smith's Creek, and Buckland's Station.

Chorpenning's funding from the government was slow to arrive and ultimately inadequate. Establishing the new line cost Chorpenning's company about $300,000; his government subsidy was to be $180,000, later reduced to $160,000, then to only $80,000. It was not long before Chorpenning's financial losses became extensive, and by 1860 he was forced to annul his contract with the Postal Service.

While Chorpenning foundered, a new southern mail route was established on September 15, 1857, after the government signed a six-year contract with the Butterfield Overland Mail Company. The Butterfield Company was an organization of four great express companies: Adams; American; National; and Wells, Fargo & Company. When the Butterfield line started operation, the company had assembled eight hundred employees, one hundred Concord stagecoaches, and a thousand horses and mules. The route, called the Butterfield or Oxbow Route, started in St. Louis, Missouri, and headed south to Little Rock, Arkansas, through El Paso, Texas, then west through Yuma, Arizona, and Los Angeles, California, and north to San Francisco, for a total distance of twenty-seven hundred miles.

The line's feasibility was about to be tested when the first two stage-coaches started on the long trip—one heading west from St. Louis, the other heading east from San Francisco. The westbound coach reached San Francisco on October 10, several hours ahead of its twenty-five-day schedule. The eastbound coach pulled into St. Louis on October 9, forty-four hours ahead of schedule.

The Butterfield service was better than the steamship mail, but it was still not very fast. And, of course, there were times when the mail would not make it through at all, with hostile Apache, Comanche, and Kiowa often encountered along the route. Another problem with the Butterfield line was that the route passed through states that were sympathetic to the Confederacy. With the serious threat of a civil war brewing, it would not be the best route for the U.S. Mail to follow.

These concerns would prove to be well founded when in 1861, after the start of the Civil War, Southern troops in Texas practically destroyed the Butterfield Overland Mail line. The rebels burned the stage station at Syracuse, Missouri, and most of the railroad bridges west of St. Louis. Soon all Butterfield stagecoaches were halted, and mail service along the route was never resumed. Even so, the Butterfield Company maintained its exclusive right to carry the U.S. mail to San Francisco, and the government continued to make full payments; it even paid the company $50,000 to cover the loss of its stock.

With the Butterfield route in jeopardy, the alternate, central route seemed preferable for mail service. This was the historic trail the pioneers took across the plains, through the Rocky Mountains, and over the Sierra Nevada to California. But it was a long, extremely hazardous journey. The failure of Chorpenning's company and others supported the viewpoint that a dependable mail service along the central route would be nearly impossible, as did the stories of horror and terrible suffering of pioneers and others who made the trek. The tragic fate of the Donner party, a group of emigrants stranded in the Sierra Nevada during a blizzard and reduced to cannibalism to survive, left an indelible impression on the American psyche regarding cross-country travel in winter.

Other stories, less well known but every bit as tragic, also abounded and reinforced the notion that the central overland route to California was nothing less than a death trap in the winter. One of these, the terrible Mormon handcart disaster of 1856, in which the death toll soared far above that of the Donner party, left a particularly vivid impression on the public. In this incident, two of five parties of Mormon emigrants pushing handcarts, the Martin and Willie companies, set out late for their journey to Salt Lake and were caught in bitter early-winter storms in Wyoming. More than two hundred of the original one thousand Mormons died of starvation or froze to death.

In spite of these horror stories, by 1860, with tensions between the North and South ready to explode, the need for a fast central-route mail service was urgent. This need gave birth to the radical idea of the Pony Express. Perhaps one strong man on a horse could make it through the harsh weather and rough terrain that had devastated emigrant families.

The Pony Express was not the first system to use a horse relay over a great distance. The first recorded horse relay was established by Genghis Khan, the great Chinese conqueror. According to reports by Marco Polo, his riders rode between stations situated about twenty-five miles apart. A single rider, using many fresh horses, carried messages as far as three hundred miles in a single day. Even in the United States, the system of a horse relay had been in use for several decades before 1860. Between 1825 and 1830, newspapers used horse relays between New York and Boston to gather news. The difference between these earlier relay deliveries and the Pony Express's task was that the former covered distances of a couple of hundred miles under fairly civilized conditions, while the Pony Express would have to provide dependable mail delivery over nearly two thousand miles of treacherous wilderness.

There is a great deal of controversy over who originated the idea of the Pony Express. As far back as 1849, a visionary named Henry O'Rielly proposed to Senator Stephen A. Douglas of Illinois a plan to construct a telegraph line between St. Louis and California. The telegraph had already been in common use in eastern cities for several years by then. The senator presented the proposal to Congress, who rejected it as impractical. Three years later O'Rielly devised an ingenious system to support his transcontinental telegraph plan: to build a series of small stockades, each manned with about twenty soldiers, at intervals of approximately twenty miles, to shelter telegraph crews while the line was under construction. In the meantime, mail could be relayed between stockades by two or three soldiers, providing a daily mail service across the continent. In effect, O'Rielly proposed a Pony Express mail system.

In April 1852 Senator Douglas presented a bill that included O'Rielly's proposal to the senate, and for a while it looked as through it would pass. In the end, however, more pressing demands took precedence, and the bill was defeated. But the issue of a transcontinental telegraph line remained active for the next decade.

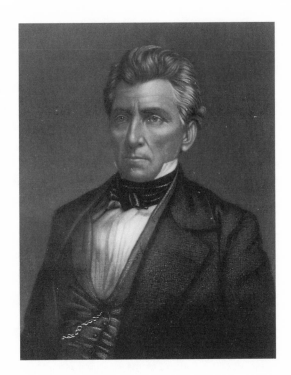

William M. Gwin, senator from California, is one of the many men sometimes credited with conceiving the idea of the Pony Express. —Courtesy California Historical Society

Some credit the idea for the Pony Express to a man named B. F. Ficklin, then general superintendent of the huge freighting and stage company of Russell, Majors & Waddell. According to some sources, he and California's United States senator William M. Gwin were traveling on horseback from San Francisco to Washington, D.C., in 1854 when Ficklin described his idea of a relay of horse riders carrying the mail from St. Joseph, Missouri, to Sacramento, California, in ten days. In January 1855 Gwin introduced a bill to finance Ficklin's system, which would be a weekly service across the frontier along a central route, at a rate of no more than $500 per trip. The bill was eventually killed.

Credit for the idea might go to William H. Russell, who was forever considering new business ventures. In his *Personal Reminiscences*, Charles R. Moreland, in charge of Russell, Majors & Waddell's headquarters in Leavenworth, Kansas, writes that Russell had thought about a horse-back relay system and discussed the concept with John B. Floyd, the secretary of war, in early 1858.

Writing in the *Lexington Missouri News* on August 22, 1888, Russell, Majors & Waddell employee John Scudder stated that in the winter of 1859 in Salt Lake City he, William Russell's partner A. B. Miller, and other employees began to work out the details of a horse relay network between Sacramento, California, and St. Joseph, Missouri, to deliver mail in twelve days. According to the story, in December 1859, after requesting further details about their plan, Russell told them to begin making preparations for the Pony Express.

The list of possible originators includes one other man, Frederick A. Bee, a partner in the Placerville, Humboldt & Salt Lake City Telegraph Company. Bee reportedly approached a number of owners of San Francisco newspapers in the mid-1850s with an exciting proposal. He asked them to help finance a horseback relay system that would deliver mail between the Missouri River and Sacramento, California, where there was a telegraph line to San Francisco. His proposal was rejected.

Regardless of who came up with the idea first, by 1860 the concept had supporters, and William Russell was chosen to develop it. In January 1860 Russell met with Senator Gwin, who was enthusiastic about the idea of a central overland-route mail service. The successful establishment of such a service would certainly add to Gwin's stature in Washington and make him more popular with his constituency in California. Russell, for his part, knew that if his company could make the system work, it would lead to a very lucrative government contract, perhaps an exclusive one to deliver all government mail to California. Then and there, he committed to establishing the Pony Express. But the contract would require the mail service to start at the beginning of April, a very short time to do a great deal of work.

Russell raced back to Leavenworth to confer with his partners. To his surprise, Alexander Majors and William Waddell did not like the idea at all, pointing out that such an undertaking would be extremely expensive and undoubtedly unprofitable. Russell argued that a government mail contract would secure their future, but they were still not convinced. Finally Russell admitted that he had already committed the company to the project. That settled the argument. The name of Russell, Majors & Waddell was one of the most respected in the country. They would never go back on their word, even if it meant losing money. Besides, it was perhaps their patriotic duty to help improve communication between the East and the West. So with their usual energy and professionalism, the three men plunged into the task of setting up the Pony Express.

4

THREE MIGHTY VISIONARIES

THE SEEMINGLY IMPOSSIBLE task of creating and implementing a two-thousand-mile system of horse-changing stations for cross-country mail delivery fell to three men whose personalities could hardly have been more different: William H. Russell, Alexander Majors, and William B. Waddell. Their names would come to represent one of the boldest business enterprises in American history.

Of the three, William Russell had the highest social pedigree, being a lineal descendant of Lord William Russell, who on July 21, 1683, was beheaded for his participation in a plot against King Charles II. About a hundred years later, one of Lord Russell's descendants, Benjamin Russell, came to America and settled in Burlington, Vermont, where he married Betsy Ann Eaton, daughter of a general and statesman. Their youngest son, William, married Betsy Ann Hepburn, who died a few years after their marriage. He then married her younger sister, Myrtilla, who bore him two children, a girl and a boy. The son, William Hepburn Russell, was born on January 31, 1812.

Young William never got to know his father, who died in 1814 while serving as a land commander in the War of 1812. Two years later, Mrs. Russell married Oliver Bangs, who had also served in the war. Although the records are not clear, Bangs apparently acquired a position at the Iowa Indian Agency and moved his family to western Missouri in the late 1820s.

In 1824, sixteen-year-old William set out to seek his fortune in the small town of Liberty, Missouri. Handsome, optimistic, and intensely ambitious even at that young age, William Russell knew what he wanted and started his career early. After acquiring experience as a merchant clerk in one of the stores in Liberty, Russell moved on to the mercantile firm of James Gull and Samuel Ringo.

In early 1830 Gull and Ringo sent Russell to work in their store in Lexington, Missouri, the most prosperous town in western Missouri.

Lexington was a retail and wholesale center for a large area both north and south along the Missouri River. Russell was very energetic and eager to learn the mercantile business, and he applied himself to his duties, which included bookkeeping, letter writing, collecting bills, reviewing invoices, as well as sweeping the floor at night and making the fire in the morning.

At the age of twenty-three, Russell married Harriet Elliot Warder, the daughter of Reverend John Warder, a rather unusual man who built his own church on his farm near Liberty and preached whatever he pleased. Since the Baptist minister was also an important land owner in the community, the marriage, which took place on June 9, 1835, gave the ambitious young Russell the social recognition he desired.

In 1837 Russell helped organize the Lexington First Addition Company, in which he purchased five shares of stock. Although Russell did not know him at the time, his future partner William Bradford Waddell, five years his senior, was also a stockholder in the company. Eventually Russell, with his increasingly aggressive business style, purchased controlling interest in the First Addition Company. In 1837 he left the employ of Gull & Ringo to open his own dry goods store in partnership with James S. Allen and William Early.

This store ultimately failed, closing in 1845, but in the meantime Russell had formed a partnership with James H. Bullard, and their store proved successful. Soon Russell was enjoying the rewards of a highly profitable enterprise and bought a number of properties in town, as well as three thousand acres of rich farmland in Lafayette and Ray Counties.

By the time he was in his mid-thirties, William Russell was a wealthy and socially successful man, with close friends in the upper echelons of business and government. He was always seeking new and bigger opportunities, and in 1847 he looked west. The great wilderness was not quite void of civilization. There were a number of military installations, and Santa Fe was a burgeoning town in Mexican territory. These places required supplies, which, because they had to be transported over long, arduous, dangerous trails, were scarce. Russell saw the potential to make a great deal of money. So Bullard and Russell, teaming up with E. C. McCarty of Westport, Missouri, assembled a large wagon train filled with merchandise and set out for Santa Fe along the famous Santa Fe Trail. The venture was so profitable they sent a bigger train out the following year.

Russell determined that he could make even more money hauling goods for the army to far-flung western posts. In 1848 Russell established a new partnership, this time with James Brown, and sent a large supply train to Colonel S. W. Kearny's military installation on the Santa Fe Trail.

Of course, Russell never accompanied these rough-and-tumble expeditions himself. He was a man of intelligence and gentility, certainly not one to ride the hot dusty trail or snap a bullwhip. Although he had a quick temper when his judgment was challenged, he remained always the New England gentleman in speech and manner. Dinner in his home was a formal affair, and he always appeared in a well-tailored black suit. The closest he came to roughing it was making a trip across the plains in the cushioned cab of a large Concord coach.

In 1850 business was so good that Russell and Brown took on another partner, John S. Jones of Pettis County. The new outfit hauled 600,000 pounds of military supplies down the Santa Fe Trail on that year's delivery. And that was only the beginning—there were many other forts in the wilderness that needed vast amounts of supplies.

With business success firmly in his grasp, Russell aspired to climb higher up the social ladder. But in order to do so, he had to adopt the

William Russell
—Courtesy St. Joseph Museum

strong proslavery sentiment of many of the citizens of Missouri. He became a vocal supporter of the movement to make neighboring Kansas a
slave state, and he became treasurer of the Lafayette County Emigration Society, which provided aid to new proslavery settlers.

In keeping with his new social status, Russell built a twenty-room
mansion on a large corner plot in Lexington, at South and Fourteenth
Streets. He spared no expense in filling the home with the finest fur-
nishings. As his prominence grew, he continued to expand his activities,
helping to establish the Lexington Mutual Fire & Marine Insurance
Company and to found the Lexington Female Collegiate Institute. By
the time he was forty years old, Russell had an imposing amount of
money, property, social status, and political clout.

Russell was also a distinguished member of the Lexington Baptist
Church, which is where he became acquainted with William Waddell.
In 1851 Russell joined the firm of Morehead, Waddell & Company as a
full partner. A year later Morehead died, and the company became known

William Waddell
—Courtesy St. Joseph
Museum

as Waddell & Russell. Four years later the partners merged with their arch competitor, Alexander Majors, to form one of the most famous freight enterprises in the history of the West: Russell, Majors & Waddell.

As Russell was the opportunist and gambler of the trio, William Bradford Waddell was the stabilizing force. He preferred to remain in the background, "behind the counter," taking care of the everyday nuts and bolts of the business. Not that he was timid in nature—quite the contrary. He never hesitated to pursue a promising opportunity.

Waddell's family tree had its roots in Scotland, where John Waddell, William's grandfather, was born. As a youngster of eleven, John was apprenticed to a man named Carter, who brought him to the then frontier region of the New World, Fauquier County, Virginia. At thirty-three, John Waddell married Elizabeth Green and went on to father seven children. His youngest, John, married Catherine Bradford, a descendant of the very prominent governor William Bradford of Plymouth Colony. The couple's first son, William Bradford Waddell, was born on October 14, 1807.

William was only five years old when his mother died. Two years later, his father married Sarah Crow, and the next year he moved the family from Virginia to the sparsely developed territory of Kentucky, one of the main thoroughfares for settlers who were headed to the western frontier, Missouri.

At seventeen, William Waddell left his comfortable home in Kentucky to satisfy his wanderlust. Seeking adventure and fortune, he found only backbreaking labor in the lead mines of Galena, Illinois. This dirty, tedious work did not suit his ambitious plans, so he kicked the dust from his boots and headed for the bustling metropolis of St. Louis. There he found employment as a clerk in the retail store of Berthoud & McCreery. It was his first taste of business—a labor of the mind, with real potential for financial success.

After a while, Waddell returned to Kentucky and worked as a store clerk in the town of Washington, but he did not stay long at the job. He went back to his father's farm and spent some time working as a farmhand. There he met a beautiful young lady named Susan Byram, who came from a wealthy family. Their wedding brought Waddell a handsome dowry, which enabled him to open a small dry goods store in Mayslick, Kentucky, a few years later.

Waddell had an excellent head for business, and the store prospered. Yet he was restless—he remembered the long trains of freight wagons he had seen heading out of St. Louis to remote parts of the frontier, and he knew there was money to be made. In the mid-1830s, he sold the business, packed up his family's belongings, and moved to Lexington, Missouri.

With the money he made selling his business in Mayslick, Waddell was able to build a store right on Lexington's busy waterfront, near Jack's Ferry. Things went well, and within a short time he had built a luxurious home across the street from his new friend, William Russell. After several successful years in business, Waddell built a larger, all-brick store and warehouse. Along with Russell he helped establish the Lexington First Addition Company and the Lexington Mutual Fire & Marine Insurance Company. He also helped finance a party of miners' trip to the goldfields in California.

In the late 1840s and early 1850s, Waddell's career was moving fast and furiously. In 1852 he and Russell created Waddell & Russell. One of their first activities was to deliver a wagon train of supplies for the army to Fort Riley in 1853. While this was not a major business venture, it was significant, as it was their first experience in freighting. In a few years fate would bring the third partner, Alexander Majors, into their merging paths of destiny.

Majors, the rugged ramrod of this extraordinary collaboration, was one of the great uncelebrated heroes of nineteenth-century America. Unlike Russell and Waddell, Majors came from a dirt-poor farm family—hard-working, plain-talking folks totally dedicated to the tenets of Christian living and a genuine work ethic. He grew up on the Missouri frontier in a one-window log cabin his father built.

Majors's grandfather, also named Alexander, had served as a foot soldier with General George Washington and was present when Cornwallis surrendered at the end of the Revolutionary War. The elder Majors raised a family in North Carolina, where his son Benjamin was born in 1794. In 1800 the family moved to Franklin, Kentucky, for its ample space and rich soil. There Benjamin grew up and married a tall, beautiful Irish woman named Laurania Kelly, whose father had also fought in the Revolutionary War. They named their firstborn Alexander, after Benjamin's father.

In 1820 Benjamin Majors packed a prairie schooner with all his family's belongings, and with his wife and three children, the family dog, and the livestock, he headed for western Missouri, the farthest territory of the frontier. Even before they arrived, little Alexander experienced a good dose of adversity. On the way west, the family's wagon suddenly went out of control, and Alexander's father had to throw the

Alexander Majors
—Courtesy Alexander
Majors Historical House

boy and his younger brother out of the racing vehicle, then he jumped out after them. It was a close brush with death.

Shortly after this mishap, Alexander's mother slipped off the wagon, hurting herself badly. Several months after they settled in their new homestead, she died of her injuries, leaving six-year-old Alexander to help his father run the farm. Guided by his father's solid sense of family and deep religious belief, the young boy met the challenge.

Life on the frontier was hard. Just after the Majors family had settled, a cloud of voracious grasshoppers, stretching nearly from horizon to horizon, descended on the area. The Majors and their neighbors watched helplessly as their late crops were devoured within twenty-four hours. Six years later, an awesome cyclone ripped its way through the area, destroying nearly every structure in its path. For young Alexander, these events provided stark lessons in survival.

At the age of thirteen, Alexander had to take on the full responsibility of the farm and the family when his father, along with twenty-four other settlers, made a long journey to the Rocky Mountains to search for silver. The boy carried the burden for nearly five months. Meanwhile, his father's group was attacked by Indians and nearly died of starvation on their way home across the desolate prairie, without having found an ounce of silver.

In 1834 Alexander Majors married a neighbor's daughter, Catherine Stalcup, and built his own house on a small piece of land his father gave him. The couple had several daughters and a son. In May 1846 Majors served in a detachment of more than a thousand Missouri volunteers sent to fight the Mexican troops at Chihuahua. Majors was wounded during one fierce battle. His detatchment was on the verge of being overwhelmed when reinforcements arrived and turned the tide.

Upon returning home after the war, Majors realized that with only the limited income of a small farm, he would have to find a way to make more money to support his growing family. In 1846, on top of tending his crops and raising his family, Majors began hauling neighbors' crops to market in Independence, Missouri, and trading with local Indian tribes. So successful was this extra activity that he decided to go into

Alexander Majors began his freighting career by hauling supplies along the Santa Fe Trail. (Painting by W. H. Jackson) —Courtesy Scotts Bluff National Monument

business full-time. He borrowed money and bought five more wagons and seventy-eight head of oxen.

In 1848 Majors received a contract to haul supplies from Independence to Santa Fe, a distance of eight hundred miles, most of which passed through hostile Indian territory. The small train of freight wagons started out on its maiden journey on August 10, 1848, rather late in the season for starting such a trip. After braving the threat of Indian attacks, storms, holdups, and other disasters, ninety-two days later the party returned with all hands safe and a profit of $1,500. More surprising, the trip was made in record time and immediately established Majors's reputation among the other freighting firms. No doubt word of this success reached the ears of Waddell and Russell.

While on the trail, Majors, an extremely devout man, observed the practice of resting on the Sabbath, an uncommon habit among hard-driving wagon bosses. He even handed out small leather-bound Bibles to his employees, and he wrote out a pledge to be taken by every man he hired:

> While I am in the employ of A. Majors, I agree not to use profane language, not to get drunk, not to gamble, not to treat animals cruelly, and not to do anything else that is incompatible with the conduct of a gentleman. And I agree, if I violate any of the above conditions, to accept my discharge without any pay for my services.

Majors's Christian principles served him well. In his autobiography, *Seventy Years on the Frontier*, he wrote:

> I will say to my readers that, had I had the experience of a thousand years, I could not have formulated a better code of rules for the government of my business than those adopted, looking entirely from a moral standpoint. The results proved to be worth more to me [financially] than that resulting from any other course I could have pursued, for with the enforcement of these rules, which I had little trouble to do . . . gave me control of the business of the plains and, of course, a wide-spread reputation for conducting business [with] a humane plan.

Not all Majors's trips went smoothly. In June 1850, on their way to Santa Fe, Majors and his freighting team camped by a stream not far from Santa Fe. They unyoked the oxen for the night, and the next morning, a number of them were missing. Majors found the trail of the oxen along with the hoofprints of Indian ponies. Though unarmed, he took off after them. Emerging from a small forested area, he came upon the thirty-four missing oxen, and just a short distance away were six armed

Indian men. To the warriors' utter astonishment, the lone white man charged the oxen, rounded them up, and drove them out.

On the way back, a larger band of warriors headed by the chief of the same (unnamed) tribe confronted Majors. About twenty-five Indians surrounded him and the herd. For some reason the chief decided to talk to Majors rather than kill him. Majors held his ground and finally agreed that the Indians could take one ox. Amazingly, the chief agreed to the deal and allowed Majors to leave with the rest of the herd. Had Majors lost the thirty-four oxen, the wagon train would not have been able to proceed, costing him and his men a lot of money.

Majors's freight company continued to grow. In 1851 he received a large government contract, requiring him to expand his train to twenty-five wagons and three hundred oxen. Two years later his work order multiplied fourfold—Majors took on one hundred wagons, twelve hundred oxen, and 120 men to carry supplies to Fort Union. When he returned, he was a wealthy man with a highly respected reputation as one of the best freighters in the business. His company was stiff competition for Russell and Waddell. In 1854 the pair did not win any bids for major government contracts, but it was a banner year for Alexander Majors.

Up until that year, government freighting contracts were awarded to various companies for relatively small shipments. But military activities on the frontier had increased dramatically, mostly because of the great flow of emigrants moving west crossing the wilderness and the new stagecoach lines being established, so beginning in 1854, the government awarded a single, enormous contract covering a two-year period. Only a very large company could compete. In 1858, for example, the supplies to Utah alone weighed more than sixteen million pounds and required over thirty-five hundred wagons.

William Russell realized that his company could not handle assignments of that size, so he and Waddell approached Alexander Majors with a proposal. If their two companies were to merge, they could form a giant organization that could easily monopolize the freighting industry in the West. To make the business even more profitable, they would establish a new payment system whereby they would charge per hundred pounds per mile rather than charge by weight alone. On December 28, 1854, the three men signed an agreement to form Russell, Majors & Waddell—the company that would soon give birth to the Pony Express. They based their operations in Leavenworth, Kansas, a bigger and more prosperous town than Lexington, Missouri.

All went according to plan, and Russell, Majors & Waddell won the next several federal contracts in a row. But the large shipments did not always lead to large profits. On May 28, 1857, the company was required to provide supplies to soldiers on their way to Utah, where trouble was brewing between the government and Mormon authorities. Upon hearing of the approaching troops, Mormon president Brigham Young ordered his militia to bar the soldiers' entry and destroy the supply trains. In October, the Mormons attacked and burned three Russell, Majors & Waddell wagon trains and drove off the oxen.

Later that month, six more of the company's trains moved forward, but in November it turned bitterly cold, and a great number of the oxen froze to death. In all, the freight company incurred an enormous loss, including several thousand oxen and wagons, not to mention supplies, totaling nearly $500,000.

The partners' fortunes changed for the better in 1858, however. That year, the company made a profit of $300,000, a record for the three men. The profits and experience they gained would prove vital resources in establishing the unprecedented two-thousand-mile Pony Express system.

— 5 —

PREPARING THE WAY

ONCE COMMITTED TO the Pony Express, with a mere three months
to prepare, William Russell, Alexander Majors, and William
Waddell plunged in. They set up a separate corporation, the Central
Overland California & Pike's Peak Express Company, for liability pur-
poses. They bought up another, smaller passenger and freight business,
the Leavenworth & Pike's Peak Express Company, to gain additional
equipment, facilities, and experienced staff. They also purchased a number
of other companies and their routes, including the Hockaday Stage Line.
In February 1860 they bought some stations from the Chorpenning
Stage Company, along with some equipment and personnel.

Each of the three men contributed to the mighty undertaking in his
own way. William Russell went to Washington, D.C., to represent the
company in the highly complex world of national politics. Being very
personable, sophisticated, shrewd, and politically astute, he knew just
how to deal with congressmen, bankers, and high-level businessmen. If
anyone could convince the the federal government to award the Pony
Express system a large mail contract, it was William H. Russell. Meanwhile, he also approached his many contacts in business and banking to
try to persuade them to invest in or extend loans to support the Pony
Express project.

As it turned out, Russell, Majors & Waddell would never receive a
government contract for delivering the mail. The company made a commitment on its own to establish and finance the Pony Express in the
hope that it would eventually receive one. Throughout his time as president of Russell, Majors & Waddell, Russell would continue to seek funding for the Pony Express, unfortunately with limited success.

The actual running of the operation on the open range would be
left to Alexander Majors, and no one was better qualified. He was at
home on the prairie and knew how to handle horses and oxen, drive
heavy wagons through bad weather and over rough terrain, and most

important of all, manage unruly crews. William Waddell, for his part, would stay home and run the office, which was no easy task. There were thousands of items to be ordered, from lumber to grain, wagons, and horses. There were men to hire, land to purchase, stations to build, salaries to pay, books to keep, and a thousand little items to be recorded. Waddell's low-key, practical style made him well suited to attending to details behind the scenes.

The plan was to establish a route that basically followed the old Pioneer Trail. The service would start at St. Joseph, Missouri, and pass through Kansas, Nebraska, Colorado, Wyoming, Utah, and Nevada, ending in San Francisco, California—a distance of 1,840 miles.

The decision to establish St. Joseph, Missouri, as the eastern starting point for the Pony Express came as a surprise and a disappointment to the citizens of Leavenworth, Kansas, where Russell, Majors & Waddell had been headquartered since 1855. The firm's influence had converted the sleepy little town into a thriving business center. In fact the company, with its continual demand for oxen, supplies, and men, had an enormous influence on the economy of the entire upper Missouri area.

Before the decision to bypass Leavenworth was announced, a bold headline in the *Leavenworth Daily Times* jumped the gun and proclaimed:

GREAT EXPRESS ADVENTURE FROM LEAVENWORTH
TO SACRAMENTO IN TEN DAYS.
CLEAR THE TRACK AND LET THE PONY COME THROUGH.

A lot of misinformation preceded the Pony Express's debut. A Washington newspaper stated that the government was arranging for a "horse express" from St. Joseph, Missouri, to Placerville, California, delivering the mail in ten days. But the Pony Express was not a government project, being privately funded by Russell, Majors & Waddell.

Despite the town of Leavenworth's expectations, the partners chose to take their business to St. Joseph for practical reasons. The latter town had the Hannibal & St. Joseph Railroad as well as a telegraph line. In addition, St. Joseph had savvily agreed to provide the company at no charge twelve lots in town, office space on Second and Francis, an office building at Fifth and Francis, free railroad passage for Pony Express employees for one year, and free passage on the Missouri River ferry to Pony Express riders for two years.

Russell, Majors & Waddell planned to guarantee their customers that the Pony Express would deliver mail (letters and papers only) from St.

Lithograph, "View of St. Joe, Missouri, from the Kansas Side," from
Illustrated London News, *1861. St. Joseph was the eastern start-*
ing point of the Pony Express Trail. —Courtesy St. Joseph Museum

Joseph, Missouri, to San Francisco in an incredible ten days. To accomplish this, the riders would have to drive their horses at top speed. The animals, therefore, could not be expected to run a great distance; there would have to be a change of horses every ten to twenty miles, depending on the terrain. At each station the rider would quickly take the *mochila*—a specially designed saddlebag with mail pouches attached— from his saddle and throw it onto that of the fresh mount.

The company would need to set up nearly two hundred relay stations along the route. It also had to establish home stations with food and sleeping quarters for riders after they had ridden all day (or night). As soon as the worn-out rider stopped at the home station, a new rider would continue along the route.

Russell, Majors & Waddell already owned a couple of stage lines with a number of stagecoach stations that could be used as relay stations. In fact, the company's stage route between St. Joseph, Missouri, and Salt Lake City, Utah—the Eastern Division—was well supplied with stations. In addition, the Leavenworth & Pike's Peak Express Company had recently built fifteen stagecoach stations between St. Joseph and Julesburg, Colorado, twenty-five to thirty miles apart, which could also serve as Pony Express stations. On the western end between Roberts Creek and Carson City, there were about a dozen stage stations built by the Chorpenning Stage Company.

Even so, since the existing stage stations were often not close enough together for Pony Express use, additional stations would have to be built. Furthermore, most of the trail through Utah and Nevada crossed nothing but wasteland, so nearly all the relay stations required would have to be constructed from scratch. Most of these would be very rudimentary structures providing the barest essentials for survival.

In parts of the western route, the trail itself had to be surveyed to ensure that it was the fastest route. Much of the Pony trail followed the same route the pioneers used, but west of Salt Lake City it took a more southerly course. Several years before, the trail in the western portion of Utah, a rugged, barren desert area, had been mapped as a potential route for emigrant trains. One delightful human-interest story connected with these trail surveys concerned Captain James H. Simpson's survey of northern Utah in 1859.

Returning from Sacramento, Simpson and his men found themselves desperate for water in the Utah desert. Their animals were close to dying of dehydration and the entire mission was in jeopardy when an elderly Ute Indian named Quah-not directed them to a concealed spring. Simpson named the place Good Indian Spring. Quah-not then escorted the party to an even better supply of water at Death Canyon. Thus, a remote section of the future Pony Express Trail was explored, thanks to the compassion of an old Indian.

Preparing the trail and building the relay stations was difficult at best and downright agonizing at times. One of the original Pony Express riders, J. G. Kelly, left us a graphic description of some of his experiences helping with preparations, as recorded in Majors's *Seventy Years on the Frontier*:

> To begin with, we had to build willow roads across many places along the Carson River, carrying bundles of willows two and three hundred yards in our arms, while the mosquitoes were so thick it was difficult to discern whether the man was white or black, so thickly were they piled on his neck, face, and hands.
>
> Arriving at the Sink of the Carson River, we began the erection of a fort to protect us from the Indians. As there were no rocks or logs in that vicinity, the fort was built of adobes, made from the mud on the shores of the lake. To mix this mud and get it the proper consistency

to mold into adobes, we trampled around all day in it in our bare feet. This we did for a week or more, and the mud being strongly impregnated with alkali, you can imagine the condition of our feet. They were much swollen, and resembled hams. Before that time I wore No. 6 boots, but ever since then No. 9's fit me snugly.

In addition to preparing the trail and building stations and other structures, the company had to procure hundreds of top-quality horses. Obviously the horses were key to the success of the mail service. The horses the Pony Express used varied according to the terrain, but they were mostly half-breed California mustangs. Most of them were no more than fifteen hands high, weighed about nine hundred pounds, and were four to seven years old.

Some of the ponies came from Fort Leavenworth in Kansas, where an advertisement read, "Horses Wanted—well broke and warranted sound." A number were purchased from the quartermaster of the fort. Certainly army service was excellent training for the Pony Express. The company bought other horses in California, many of which had pulled stagecoaches for the Butterfield line and were known for their speed, stamina, and reliability.

Not all Pony Express horses were fully broken. As one rider explained, if a hostler could lead a mustang out of the stable without getting his head kicked off, the horse was ready to ride. One of the blacksmiths that worked for the service recalled that a pony often had to be thrown to the ground and staked down with each foot tied before he could be shod. To pare the hoofs and nail on the shoes, one man had to sit on the pony's head and another on its body. To shoe a single horse often required hours of backbreaking work.

Though sometimes feisty and untrained, the horses Russell, Majors & Waddell purchased were the best money could buy. One group of one hundred horses, mainly native California stock, cost an average of $175. Other ponies, especially ones used on the eastern end of the route, were high-quality stock from Kentucky and Utah Territory, priced as much as $200 each. The total bill for the initial five hundred horses was about $87,000.

In the end, the investment paid off. A rider's horse was often his best protection against attacking Indians. In addition to their good breeding, the Pony Express horses were well fed with the best grain, while the Indians' mounts were mostly inferior. Thus a Pony rider could always outdistance his attackers. These horses were also highly intelligent and had an uncanny sense of direction. In some cases they even saved the lives of their riders by finding their way on the trail, even under the most severe weather conditions.

Of course, the best horses were of no use without experienced riders, and so the partners assigned their division superintendents the task of hiring seventy to eighty riders each. They sought youngsters born to the saddle and with nerves of iron. A poster advertising the position read:

> WANTED—YOUNG SKINNY, WIRY FELLOWS NOT OVER
> EIGHTEEN. MUST BE EXPERT RIDERS, WILLING TO
> RISK DEATH DAILY. ORPHANS PREFERRED.

In addition to horsemanship and fearlessness, candidates needed knowledge of the portion of the Pony Express Trail to which they would be assigned. Anyone riding at top speed along a trail in rain, snow, or blackness of night had best be familiar with the terrain. For their efforts, the riders were paid from $100 to $150 per month according to their run, the highest wages in the service, except for the top executives. Wages for station keepers and general hands ranged down to

A Pony Express rider being pursued by Indian warriors. A rider's best defense in such cases was his horse's stamina and ability to outrun the Indians' horses. —Courtesy California State Library

$50 per month, plus room and board, which in most cases did not amount to much.

Once stations were built and staff hired, the partners and their staff had to finalize the routes, purchase supplies, and coordinate everyone's efforts so that the entire line could work together. They also had to set up collection points for mail. Mail collected in a number of major cities including New York, Washington, Chicago, and St. Louis would be channeled to St. Joseph. A similar arrangement was set up on the West Coast.

Finally, there was the matter of a schedule. Since this was a relay system, every rider would have to follow a very strict schedule, and it would have to be maintained day and night, in all weather, without exceptions. The mail must go through: this was the fundamental motivating force behind the heroic Pony Express riders.

The schedule of the westward run was published in the *St. Joseph Weekly West* as follows:

Marysville	12 hours
Fort Kearny	34 hours
Fort Laramie	80 hours
Fort Bridger	108 hours
Great Salt Lake	124 hours
Carson City	188 hours
Placerville	226 hours
Sacramento	234 hours
San Francisco	240 hours

All these preparations were made with little regard for accounting procedures or legal ramifications. There was no time for such niceties—the deadline was near.

As April 3, 1860, approached, everything fell into place. Now it remained to be seen whether the reality could match the expectations. If a late winter snowstorm did not blast its way across the barren plains or an Indian war did not ravage the countryside, these young, skinny, wiry fellows might just have a chance to amaze Congress as well as the citizens of the country and prove that the Pony Express was, indeed, the fastest way to deliver the U.S. mail.

— 6 —
OFF AND RUNNING

O N APRIL 3, 1860, both an Indian war and a civil war were brewing, one local and the other national. Both would significantly influence the Pony Express and seriously test its resolve. The upcoming civil war made the service's success crucial to western Americans, but it also created a volatile environment for its operation. The Paiute war on whites in Nevada posed a new and grave threat to Pony riders, and its escalation could challenge the very existence of the service.

But on that historic day in St. Joseph, Missouri, as well as in San Francisco, all thoughts of the people turned from conflict to anticipation, their hearts filled with admiration for the brave young men that would, they hoped, make this daring dream come true. This community spirit was rare in St. Joseph at that time, for a great deal of animosity divided the citizenry. The town was a hotbed of proslavery sympathy, yet many residents remained steadfastly abolitionist. Nevertheless, the mood on that spring day was joyous and festive. The incredible event that was about to originate from their town transcended all other concerns—for the time being, at least.

In St. Joseph, crowds had gathered early in the day to see the great event. And a great event it was: St. Joseph, Missouri, was about to be marked with the indelible stamp of history. This bustling community on the edge of civilization was the launch point for one of the most adventurous undertakings of the century. Its citizens were more than ready to take their place in history: red, white, and blue bunting decorated the buildings, flags flew from rooftops, and brass bands blared. On hand were the mayor, Jeff Thompson, and William Russell and Alexander Majors, along with other dignitaries. A big celebration was planned at Patee House, the town's elegant new hotel.

Jeff Thompson was a very popular politician and had a wonderful rapport with the citizens of St. Joe. His personality had so impressed Mark Twain that the famous author later based a character in *The Gilded*

*Jeff Thompson, mayor of
St. Joseph in 1860, was
present at the launching
of the Pony Express.*
—Courtesy St. Joseph Chamber
of Commerce

Age, Colonel Sellers, on Thompson. Thompson also dignified his position with his impeccable taste in clothes, usually a tall gray beaver hat,
tight trousers, a blue frock coat with polished brass buttons, and, around
his waist, a pair of ivory-handled pistols. On formal occasions, he added
a long curved sword to further enhance the picture.

In his younger years, Thompson, whose real name was not Jeff but
Meriwether, had lost all the teeth on one side of his face. He often used
this deformity to amuse a crowd by clamping his jaws to make his head
appear as flat as that of a snake. But the levity ended there, for Jeff
Thompson was a man of action. With undaunted determination he had
helped to build the first railroad line across Missouri, the Hannibal &
St. Joseph. When the first train rolled into St. Joseph, Thompson had
been at the throttle. A direct descendant of students of Kentucky and
Virginia oratorical schools, he could deliver his words with thunder,
moving a crowd to cheers.

On this most auspicious occasion, the well-loved mayor pulled out
all the stops, showering unbridled praise on the glorious effort of the
Pony Express. He extolled the great enterprise of Russell, Majors &
Waddell, hailing the partners as giants of progress in bringing the vast
lands of the United States closer together. In his own words:

This is a great day in the history of St. Joseph. . . . Now we are the connecting link between the extremes of the continent. . . . Hardly will the cloud of dust which envelops the galloping pony subside before the puff of the steam engine will be seen on the horizon. . . . Citizens of Saint Joseph! I bid you give three cheers for the Pony Express—three cheers for the first overland passage of the United States mail!

Next it was Alexander Majors's turn to speak. His speech alluded to greater things to come:

Another, a more important, and a greater enterprise, which must soon reach its culmination, viz: the construction of the road upon which the tireless iron horse will start on his long overland journey, opening up as he goes the rich meadows of nature, the fertile valleys, and crowning the eminences of the rocky range with evidences of civilization and man's irresistible mania of progression; diversifying the prairies with the lowing cattle herds, and making them yet lovelier by the dwellings of the pioneer, cheered in his western pilgrimage by the loved ones of his household, and aided by the fair hands and bright eyes of women. Of a truth, "the desert shall blossom as the rose."

The great event was no less heralded in the nation's newspapers, including the *New York Sun,* the *New York Herald and Tribune,* and the leading newspapers of San Francisco, Sacramento, Washington, D.C., and many other cities. Of course it was the front-page story in the April 3 edition of the *St. Joseph Daily West,* which wrote:

THE PONY EXPRESS
THROUGH IN TEN DAYS

Today inaugurates the greatest enterprise of modern times . . . and one that must benefit St. Joseph in a very marked and visible degree . . . that of running an express on the overland route between St. Joseph and San Francisco, in the extraordinary short space of ten days. This may seem an impossibility; but from the well known energy which has heretofore been displayed by the President and Directors of the company, we are confident they will accomplish the undertaking, however difficult it may seem. . . .

The first messenger on the route will leave the U.S. Express office at precisely five o'clock this afternoon. . . . Letters will be received from all points up to 4:30 and parties sending them may confidently rely upon ten days, quicker time than ever before made between the Atlantic and Pacific coasts. . . . A special train will arrive over the Hannibal and St. Joseph Railroad this afternoon, with the through messenger from New York and Washington. . . . The second Express will be dispatched from this point on Friday morning next, at nine o'clock precisely.

The magnitude of this enterprise can scarcely be conceived. By it we shall have intelligence from San Francisco in ten days, which, telegraphed from here, will make the time the same to New York. Pending the completion of the overland telegraph line, the transmission of messages over this route will be the most speedy known to modern times.

Through the courtesy of Mr. Hinckley, who is connected with the route, we are furnished with the time table by which the Express is run, and which we append as the fastest to be made by horseflesh.

Another St. Joseph newspaper, the *Daily Gazette*, was under the mistaken impression that they had been honored to be the first newspaper carried to San Francisco by the new mail service. With great pride they printed:

ST. JOSEPH DAILY GAZETTE
PONY EXPRESS EDITION
ST. JOSEPH, MO., APRIL 3ᴿᴰ, 6 O'CLOCK P.M.

Through the politeness of the Express Company, we are permitted to forward, by the first Pony Express, the first and only newspaper which goes out, and which will be the first paper ever transmitted from the Missouri to California in ten days. The nature of the conveyance necessarily precludes our making up an edition of any considerable weight. It, however, contains a summary of the latest news received here by telegraph for some days past, from all parts of the Union. We send its greeting to our brethren of the press of California.

Later the *Gazette* learned that the westbound Pony rider's mochila also carried, by invitation, a special edition, printed on fine tissue, of the *New York Herald and Tribune*. The first Pony Express west was also to deliver about seventy letters, including a letter of congratulations from President Buchanan to Governor Downey of California.

Five P.M. soon arrived—the time the first rider was to leave with the mail on the first leg of his long journey west. But the train carrying the mail from the East had not yet arrived in St. Joseph. Everyone waited patiently: 5:30 . . . 6:00 . . . 6:30, and no train.

Unbeknownst to the good citizens of St. Joseph, another drama was unfolding as the officials of the eastern railroads attempted to get the mail to the little western town on time. Special telegraph messages had been sent to all parts of the United States and Canada announcing where to send Pony Express mail for pickup. In the East, the plan was to collect the mail and take it all to Hannibal, Missouri, where the Hannibal & St. Joseph Railroad would carry it to St. Joe. On March 30, a special courier took mail from Washington, D.C., by train to New York City. On the morning of March 31, he picked up additional letters in New York and then headed west. So far, so good—he was on schedule. But in Detroit, the plan fell apart. The courier missed the train connection by a full two hours. What to do?

The courier's supervisors immediately sent a telegraph to J. T. K. Haywood, superintendent of the Hannibal & St. Joseph Railroad, about the delay. Haywood, a man of action, realized that nothing short of a superhuman effort was needed. He was determined that his railroad was not going to be the cause of the failure of the Pony Express. Haywood also stood to lose his own mail contract if this job failed. Up until that time, the government had been delivering mail to St. Joseph by boat, via St. Louis, and had not as yet agreed to contract the railroad to take over this service. This first Pony Express job was Haywood's opportunity to demonstrate that the Hannibal & St. Joseph could indeed provide a fast and efficient mail-delivery service across Missouri.

Haywood immediately gave road master George H. Davis orders to clear the entire line and put together a special high-speed train with just

The steam engine Missouri *carried the first load of Pony Express mail to St. Joseph, Missouri, in a treacherous high-speed run.* —Courtesy St. Joseph Museum

an engine and one car. Every man on the line considered himself an important part of the effort and went to work. To avoid mishaps, Davis ordered that every switch along the two-hundred-mile route to St. Joseph be spiked closed. He himself would make the run from Hannibal, with an engineer named Addison "Ad" Clark, a man who knew no fear, at the throttle.

All was ready for the courier when he arrived in Hannibal. He showed up two and a half hours late. It was a lot of time to have to make up, but old Ad would give it a try. Davis told Clark to pull the throttle all the way back, to set a record that would last fifty years. The locomotive, the *Missouri*, fired up to full steam and headed down the track, the first train in the United States to run for the express purpose of carrying mail. As though the mighty engine understood the importance of its mission, the *Missouri* picked up speed and began to burn up the miles.

Word had gone out by telegraph about the *Missouri*'s record-attempting run. All along the line, in every small town, people were waiting by the tracks to cheer the train on. The first seventy miles went along mostly level terrain, so the train averaged about sixty miles per hour through Monroe and Shelby Counties. As they approached Macon, Missouri, the land became hilly, filled with treacherous curves and steep grades—no place for high speeds. But the *Missouri* was riding on the cutting edge of peril, at the confident hand of Ad Clark, and he barely eased up the pace.

The train could not make the full run without stopping for fuel and water along the way. Even these relatively brief stops had been planned with great detail to minimize the delays. Their first refueling was in Macon, where they stopped at L. S. Coleman's wood yard. Coleman had hastily built a platform that was level to the train's tender. A group of men waited, each with an armful of wood. The instant the train halted, they stepped forward and emptied their loads. In the incredible time of fifteen seconds, the tender was filled and the *Missouri* ready to resume its run. The remainder of the hazardous journey to St. Joseph was well described years later in a story in the *New York Sun*:

> Out of Macon at that time was a steep grade running down to the Chariton River. If Clark shut off his steam ever so little on that stretch, none of those on board recollect anything about it. If the man at the throttle were alive today he could look with grim satisfaction at the record he made down that hill. That part of the run, at least, had never been beaten by any engineer who has been in the company's employ.

It was like an avalanche. If there had been a tenderfoot on board, a more than reasonable doubt would have arisen in his mind as to whether all the wheels of the train were on the track or not. The furnace was drawing magnificently. A streak of fire shot out of the stack, and the wood sparks flew through the air like snowflakes.

Across the Chariton River there came the New Cambria Hill, a still greater grade than that down from Macon. The momentum attained served to drive the train halfway up with scarcely any perceptible reduction in speed, but the exhausts became slower before the peak of the grade was approached. The fireman piled his dry cottonwood, and the safety valve sent a column of steam heavenward. The white-faced passengers breathed easier, but the relief did not last long. The summit of the hill was reached and the little engine snorted as something alive, took the bit in its teeth, and was soon rushing along at top speed.

At about 7:00 P.M. the distant sound of a train whistle alerted the eager crowd in St. Joseph that the historic moment was approaching. The *New York Sun* described the dramatic scene:

> When the train pulled in and stopped, Engineer Clark stepped majestically from his iron horse, looking mussed up, grimy and grand. For the present, he was the hero of the hour. He had made the run from Hannibal to St. Joseph, 206 miles, in four hours and 51 minutes—a feat hitherto regarded as impossible. Everybody wanted to shake hands with the keen-eyed man who had done this great thing. It was up to blood and muscle to take up the burden where fire, steam and mechanical skill had left off.

After the mail train arrived, the people gathered around the Pike's Peak Livery Stables, where the great ride would begin. Over the noise of the crowd a shout of "Time to go!" rang out. It was 7:15 P.M. Historical records are unclear whether the first horse led out of the stables was a bay mare or another color. More important, it is not certain who the first rider was from St. Joseph. Nor is it certain who the first rider was going east from Sacramento. Because so many records in St. Joseph and elsewhere were destroyed during the Civil War, information on this subject is inconclusive.

As many as seven names are listed as the first westbound rider in various surviving documents. Historians have narrowed the possibilities to two riders: John Frye and William Richardson. There is strong evidence that Johnny Frye, who was an expert rider and had won local fame riding racehorses, was the one. He was born and raised in St. Joseph and was said to be an expert gunfighter. But Bill Richardson, who

*Pike's Peak Livery Stables, the eastern starting point of the
Pony Express Trail.* —Courtesy Nebraska State Historical Society

had been a sailor, was mentioned in a later newspaper story as having
been the rider.

In 1923, Louise Platt Hauck of St. Joseph conducted an in-depth
study of the subject. She read personal diaries, searched municipal records,
investigated the statements of eyewitnesses, and studied stories from
various local newspapers published in St. Joseph and nearby Elwood,
Kansas. Although popular tradition insisted that John Frye was the first
rider, none of the newspaper accounts named him as such. Although
evidence suggests that Frye was in town that day, a story in the *Weekly
West*, printed April 7, 1860, described the event in detail and named
J. W. (William) Richardson as the first Pony Express rider to leave the
stables. Years later, in October 1931, Richardson revealed that he, having been a mere youngster at the time, had not made the first ride out of
St. Joseph—at least not the complete run.

Bill Richardson's brother was the livery stable manager. Perhaps wanting to give his little brother a moment of glory, he may have let him

have the first portion of the ride. According to the *Weekly West*, on that historic evening, at 7:15 P.M., a cannon boomed the signal and young Richardson, dressed in a red shirt, blue trousers, fancy boots, and buckskin jacket, leaped onto his horse, and with wild cheers and brass bands ringing in his ears, raced down the street a short distance to the *Ebenezer*, a paddle-wheel steamboat, which was waiting for him at the wharf at Levee and Francis Streets.

But, according to other historical sources, the *Ebenezer* would not carry Richardson across Old Muddy to Elwood. Waiting on the boat was Johnny Frye, ready to take the reins for the first leg of the first Pony Express run—without the glory. As the ferry touched shore, Frye was off and running through the desolate night toward Cottonwood Springs Station, the first relay station in Kansas. Arriving there about one hour after he had left the ferry, Frye quickly threw the mochila onto a fresh horse, leaped into the saddle, and was off at top speed heading west.

Not much is known of the first westbound ride, nor of the eastbound. Some sources state that the first home station on the route west was Seneca, and Don Rising was the next rider. Because the easternmost part of the Pony trail, through Kansas, followed the emigrant trail, the well-worn path was easy to follow, even at night. In the end, the mail arrived in Sacramento within an hour of its schedule.

Eighty riders escorted the first Pony Express rider into Sacramento, where a wild celebration awaited him. —Courtesy California State Library

The first Pony Express rider into Sacramento at 5:45 P.M. on April 13, 1860, received an unforgettable reception. —Courtesy California State Library

For William Hamilton, the final rider on the first Pony Express trip west, the approach to Sacramento must have been most exhilarating— he was culminating a nearly two-thousand-mile run by forty tough and dedicated young men. The journey had continued relentlessly, day and night, through danger, pain, and privation, with a single purpose: the mail must be delivered.

The welcome at Sacramento was unforgettable. A group of eighty riders had assembled outside of town at Sutter's Fort and formed an escort of two lines to accompany Hamilton right and left. When Hamilton came into sight, the cheering started. His escort into town kicked up so much dust that poor Hamilton nearly choked. At 5:45 P.M. on April 13, exactly ten days after the first rider left St. Joseph, Hamilton and his entourage entered downtown Sacramento, which was wild with joy and excitement. A holiday had been declared—bands played, bells rang, and people stood on balconies and rooftops waving flags, singing, and shouting as young Hamilton rode to the Alta Telegraph office, where he would deliver the historic first mochila of mail.

Though the Pony ride was over, some of the mail still had to be delivered to San Francisco. The large side-wheeler steamboat *Antelope* was waiting at the dock to carry Hamilton downriver. He was undoubtedly grateful for the break from the saddle. As the *Antelope* approached the San Francisco Bay, all the steamboats began to sound their whistles in a wild welcome.

It was close to midnight when the *Antelope* docked, but the city was wide awake. It seemed as though all of San Francisco was there to greet him. Cannons fired, bonfires blazed, rockets streaked through the sky, crowds cheered, and a vast procession formed at the slip to escort the conquering hero into town. Crowds of people, holding torches, lined the streets. Even Jessie Benton, daughter of the famous pathfinder John C. Frémont, was there to welcome the Pony Express rider. There was a wonderful sense of joy in the air. No longer was San Francisco an isolated town.

For its part, the first eastbound Pony Express ride, from San Francisco to St. Joseph, was equally exciting—and equally successful. Like the westbound run, the eastbound delivery began on April 3, when the mail was placed on a steamer to Sacramento. The first rider out of Sacramento was William Hamilton, the same man would deliver the first westbound mail. Ten days later, the first eastbound rider into St. Joseph, who likely was Johnny Fry, the first westbound rider, received an equally warm and noisy reception. His delivery arrived a few hours ahead of the westbound.

With the historic first ride, the Pony Express fulfilled its promise to get the mail from St. Joseph to San Francisco in ten days. Never before in history had letters been delivered over such a distance so quickly. However, one successful trip merely proved it was possible. The big question remained: Could it be done on a regular basis? Next time things might not go so well. Ultimately, over time, there would be a great price to pay in human lives, and the courage of the riders and station keepers would be severely tested. Breathtaking adventures awaited the young riders, and these would be recounted for generations to come.

— 7 —

THE RAMRODS

R UNNING THE DAY-TO-DAY operations of a two-thousand-mile route was a task far too demanding even for Alexander Majors. To keep the Pony Express running, on time, at all times, and under all conditions—with no exceptions—he needed hard-driving, dedicated men who would stand firm in the face of danger and adversity. He hired seven iron-willed men: division superintendents A. E. Lewis, Jack Slade, James Bromley, Major Howard Egan, and Bolivar Roberts; western superintendent William W. Finney; and general superintendent Benjamin F. Ficklin, who oversaw the entire route. These were the ramrods of the Pony Express. All problems on the trail fell upon their strong shoulders.

The organization of the Pony Express was surprisingly simple. Russell, Majors & Waddell continued to operate out of the St. Joseph office, although Russell's activities often took him east and Majors spent a great deal of time in the saddle. The route was divided into five sections, or divisions, each with its own superintendent. In a crisis, the division superintendents had to be ready to replace a Pony Express rider, day or night, winter or summer, and still manage the division. The superintendents were supervised by the general superintendent (Ficklin), based in St. Joseph. The company also hired a western manager (Finney) to establish and maintain the especially isolated and rugged western portion of the route, between Roberts Creek, Nevada, and the end of the horse trail in Sacramento.

The easternmost division, Division One, extended from St. Joseph to Fort Kearny, Nebraska; it was under the supervision of A. E. Lewis, who was headquartered in St. Joseph. Although his division was operated with great efficiency and effectiveness, Superintendent Lewis remains a total mystery. Perhaps records of his background and his performance with the Pony Express were lost when proslavery elements burned a number of buildings in St. Joseph at the start of the Civil War.

We know little of the man except that the mail was delivered on time in his division. Where he came from and where he went after he left Russell, Majors & Waddell may never be known.

Division Two encompassed the Platte Valley between Fort Kearny and Horseshoe Station, high in the Wyoming Rockies. The superintendent for this stretch of trail was the famous gunslinger Jack Slade, who maintained his headquarters at Horseshoe Station, about thirty miles west of Fort Laramie, Wyoming. Slade was one of the few men employed by the Pony Express that apparently missed Alexander Majors's careful scrutiny. Slade was a holdover from the Hokaday Stage Line, one of the companies Russell, Majors & Waddell had purchased. Slade was not the kind of man Majors would have hired knowingly.

Joseph A. "Jack" Slade's life story was a string of troubling events. He was born in Carlyle, Illinois, in 1828, the son of Congressman Charles Slade. As a youngster, he started off on the wrong foot. At thirteen, Slade killed a man with a stone and was sent to Texas to hide. By the time he fought for the U.S. Army in the war with Mexico, he had already killed ten men. He had a reputation for shooting fast and straight and having nerves of steel. The stories of his escapades were plentiful,

Jack Slade, Division Two superintendent, was said to have been in twenty-six gunfights and to have killed twenty-six men.
—Courtesy American Heritage Center, University of Wyoming

some of them connected with his service as a Pony Express division superintendent.

One of these episodes took place at a relay station along the South Platte River, in southeastern Colorado, called Julesburg. The post was named after its keeper, Jules Reni, an old French fur trapper. It soon became apparent that Reni had been a bad choice of employee. Soon after his assignment, horses and other valuable property began to disappear on a regular basis. The company directed Slade to go to the station and fire old Jules. In this they had chosen the right man for the job. But when Slade discharged him, Reni became so angry he later ambushed Slade and shot him. Ben Ficklin, the Pony's no-nonsense general superintendent, heard about the shooting and had Reni captured and strung up. But as soon as Ficklin left the scene, some of the old trapper's friends cut him down, saving his life.

Meanwhile Slade had found help to treat the gunshot wound, escaping death by a hair's breadth. Soon he was out looking for the man who had shot him and had cheated the rope. He tracked Reni for a long time. When he finally found him, he shot him off his horse, tied him to a post, and used him for target practice. After the incident, Slade's division was kept very honest.

In another incident, Slade, who also doubled as the stage line manager, went in search of four men accused of robbing a stagecoach. He found the cabin where the bandits were hiding, kicked in the door, and entered with guns blazing. With lightning speed, he killed three of the robbers. The fourth had leaped out a back window and was running at top speed, but a quick shot from Slade's gun dropped him before he had gotten a hundred yards.

Tom Riverton, a former resident of Gering, Nebraska, told of an event at Weber Station in Utah, in which Slade was called in to rid the station of the "Racket Gang," who had been perpetrating a con on the Pony Express company:

> Horses would disappear from the company's corrals, a sizeable reward would be posted and a few hours later the horses would be returned and the reward collected. There are a number of unmarked graves in Echo Canyon. No doubt, some of them hold the bodies of the "Racket Gang" who found the Pony Express and stage horses a good source of income and walked into Slade's trap.

Riverton was one of many people who experienced another side of Slade, a charming, fun-loving man who liked parties and loved to tell stories of his exploits. He describes another, lighter incident at Weber Station:

> One summer, Lottia Crabtree and her show troupe were detained at the station until a wheelwright could repair the stage which had been wrecked while rounding a curve in the canyon. . . .
>
> Captain Jack Slade, then superintendent of the Butterfield Overland stage line, sat at the head of the table smiling and telling of past experiences while an agent for the Butterfield company. Mark Twain sat at his left in stunned silence, as if unable to believe the good-natured and entertaining young man was the reputed killer whose name struck fear in the hearts of outlaws. . . .
>
> Jack Slade, always a good entertainer, gave a humorous talk on the different people traveling over the Butterfield Overland stage route during his term as superintendent. He told of the "Play Killings"which caused the green travelers to tremble with fear, often pulled off by stage drivers and wranglers for the traveler's benefit. [He explained] that these "Play Killings" were often written up afterwards as real, which caused eastern people to suppose that eight men out of ten were shot in the West each year.
>
> Mark Twain rose to the occasion, giving a reply to Slade's talk, telling how passengers were carried over the Overland route in the old leather spring rocking coaches. With his long hair waving, he gave so humorous an imitation of the lurching and bouncing accorded the passengers enroute, his listeners were thrown into a fit of laughter. Slade laughed the heartiest of all.

Although Slade was normally courteous and kind when sober, he was a terror when he got drunk. Several times he had gotten into fights in saloons and caused great damage. In one incident, while shooting up a saloon in Denver, he shot a stranger who was trying to calm him down. The stranger turned out to be a Pony Express company executive named David Street. The wound was superficial, and after Slade sobered up he apologized profusely. Street did not fire him, but Slade never mended his ways and eventually he was discharged from the Pony Express.

Jack Slade was said to have been in twenty-six gunfights and to have killed twenty-six men. According to James Bromley:

> The large number of killings blamed on Slade are, no doubt, fictional. Slade was not a killer at heart. However, he was dangerous in a gun fight, as he was a dead shot and had a steel nerve. I believe the large number of killings charged to him were, no doubt, victims of agents hired to guard property of the Overland Stage Company, hired by Slade and working under his orders.

Some time after leaving the Pony Express, after a very serious fight in which a saloon was wrecked and some men hurt, Slade was arrested. When he threatened the judge with a gun, he was taken out and hanged. His name is still remembered in Julesburg as one of the more colorful characters of the Pony Express. Tom Riverton wrote, "Slade, although a walking arsenal, was always a gentleman and a good entertainer."

Not nearly as colorful, but extremely knowledgeable, was James Erwen Bromley, superintendent of Division Three, between Horseshoe Station and Salt Lake City. Bromley was born in Sturgis Prairie, Michigan, in 1832, where at an early age he developed a great love for horses and a desire to become a stagecoach driver. At twenty-two he migrated to the wilds of Utah as a seasoned stage driver, having picked up extensive experience in Toledo, Chicago, and Springfield, Illinois. Bromley operated a monthly mail service for the Butterfield Overland Mail Company, driving a six-mule team from Independence, Missouri, to Salt Lake City, a difficult and at times dangerous route.

In May 1857, after his mail service had ceased operation, he joined the Pacific Wagon Road Expedition, an outfit traveling from Independence, Missouri, to settle the far West. Just about the time they reached the Sweetwater River in Wyoming, they received news that General Albert Sidney Johnston's army was approaching Utah Territory to confront Mormon authorities. Because of his expert knowledge of the trail, Bromley was made a scout for Johnston's army. Unfortunately for him, the Mormons ravaged army supply trains and forced Johnston's troops to turn back.

In 1858, Bromley went to work for J. M. Hockaday as general superintendent of the stage line. As he explained:

> I was put in charge of the road; I bought mules, built stations, fought Indians and did everything that came in the line of my duty. I started from Atchison [Kansas] and as I got one division in order, I was sent to the next, until, finally, I was permanently located on the Salt Lake City division, having charge of the road from Pacific Springs to Salt Lake City.

In 1860, Russell, Majors & Waddell bought the Hockaday line and made Bromley superintendent of the area. Bromley lived at Weber Station, which he had built shortly after settling in Utah. With his knowledge of and experience in mail service, horse handling, and the region, he served the Pony Express well.

A few months after the Pony's demise, in August 1861, Bromley married Elizabeth Major Stevenson, with whom he had four children.

After a few more years in the stagecoach business, Bromley had brief stints in merchandising, innkeeping, and city planning. He finally settled into ranching and raising racehorses. He died in 1888.

Howard Egan, superintendent of Division Four, Salt Lake City to Roberts Creek Station in Nevada, stands out as one of the great names in pioneer history. In fact, a 658-mile section of the Pony Express route is known as the Egan Trail. Egan was born on June 15, 1815, in Tullamor, Kings County, Ireland. When he was eight, his mother died, and shortly thereafter the family migrated to Montreal, Canada. Tragedy struck again with the death of his father when Egan was only thirteen.

Howard Egan, division superintendent of the Pony Express Trail from Salt Lake City to Roberts Creek Station —Courtesy Historical Department of the Church of Jesus Christ of Latter-day Saints

Several years later, Egan became a sailor, but at twenty-three, tired of shipboard life, he went to Salem, Massachusetts, where he met and married Tamson Parshley. The couple joined the Mormon Church and soon afterward moved to Nauvoo, Illinois, where their two sons were born. Young, energetic, and very industrious, Egan built a rope factory in Nauvoo and helped build the town as well. In addition, he became a member of the police department and the Nauvoo Legion, attaining the rank of major, thus his lifelong title, Major Howard Egan.

After Mormon leader Joseph Smith's murder in Nauvoo in 1844, the Egan family moved to Missouri. But soon trouble developed there, too, and in 1847 Egan, leaving his family behind to wait, accompanied Brigham Young to the frontier settlement at the Great Salt Lake, where he helped haul logs to build the town's first fort. The following year, he returned to the states for his family and brought them back to Salt Lake. There he built an adobe house at what would become First North and Main Streets.

Egan became so familiar with the frontier that he hired himself out as a scout. In 1849 he guided a large group of gold prospectors to California. There were three routes across Utah to California: the northern, the central, and the southern. Egan had pioneered the central route, which was the quickest and therefore popular with gold seekers. The northern route led around the northern rim of the Great Salt Lake, then crossed the western desert and followed the Humboldt Valley west. Early emigrants preferred this route because it had a good supply of grass and water. The southern route was more circuitous, passing through a number of small mountain ranges. It was mainly used for military and exploratory expeditions.

Egan's central route skirted the southern edge of the Great Salt Lake and headed southwest to the Humboldt Mountains in Nevada, through Carson City, then south to Genoa and on to California. Emigrants called this route the Egan Trail. It was also known as Simpson's Trail because Captain James H. Simpson had also explored the route. Egan mapped about fifty-six potential sites for Mormon settlements along the Egan Trail. In the mid-1850s Egan went into business with George Chorpenning to deliver mail between Salt Lake City and California.

When the Pony Express was established in 1860, a three-hundred-mile portion of the Egan Trail was incorporated into the Pony route, and Egan became superintendent for that portion, Division Four. Not only was Egan a great division superintendent, he was also an expert rider, capable of competing with any of his young couriers.

According to his son, the famous trailblazer Howard Egan, a Pony Express division superintendent, rode on the first mail run from Rush Valley Station to Salt Lake City. It was not an easy ride, as Howard Ranson Egan recorded in his memoirs:

> It was a stormy afternoon but all went well till the home stretch. The pony on this run was a very swift, fiery and fractious animal. The night was so dark that it was impossible to see the road, and there was a strong wind blowing from the north, carrying a sleet that cut his face while trying to look ahead. But as long as he could hear the pony's feet pounding the road, he sent him ahead at full speed. When he got to Mill Creek, which was covered by a plank bridge, he heard the pony's feet strike the bridge and the next instant pony and rider landed in the creek, which wet father above the knees; but the next instant, with one spring, the little brute was out and pounding the road again.

Egan remained a division superintendent for the entire eighteen months of the Pony Express. Afterward, he managed the line for the stagecoach service. In 1874–75, Egan worked as a missionary to the Goshute Indians, after which he returned to his modest home in Salt Lake City and lived a quiet life until his death in 1878.

Bolivar Roberts, superintendent of Division Five, between Roberts Creek, Nevada, and Sacramento (he made his home at the Carson City Station), was by far the most outstanding of the division managers in terms of versatility and diversity of interests. He was born on July 4, 1831, in Winchester, Scott County, Illinois. Throughout Bolivar's young life his father, Daniel Roberts, a physician, moved his family from one town to another throughout the Midwest, eventually settling in Lancaster, Missouri.

At the age of nineteen, Bolivar, demonstrating his inherited wanderlust, decided to cross the Great Plains. His entire outfit consisted of a horse, a saddle, a bridle, and a rifle, along with some meager basic supplies. Accompanied by another man, Bolivar acted as the hunter for the pair, oftentimes risking his life while riding among the huge herds of unpredictable buffalo. After an adventurous journey, he arrived in Utah and, though not a Mormon, settled in the community of Provo. His parents and siblings joined him a year later, in 1851.

The following year Bolivar, his father, and his brother William traveled to California. They settled for a while in Placerville, then San Jose, then San Bernardino. Dr. Roberts practiced medicine while his two sons worked at mining. In 1853 Dr. Roberts and William returned home. A year later Bolivar gave up mining and got a job with the Mail & Express Company, which operated between Salt Lake City and Carson City.

Exhibiting dedication and responsibility on the job, Roberts soon rose in the ranks. But he was a restless soul and could not seem to stay put. In 1859 he went to Dayton, Nevada, where he built a bridge across the Carson River, which absorbed his attention for about a year. In the spring of 1860, Roberts answered the call for experienced men to establish and operate the Pony Express, and he stayed with the service for its entire run.

After the Pony Express shut down, Roberts returned to Salt Lake City, and in 1863 he married Pamela Banson, with whom he had five children. Even after he settled down, his career path continued to twist and turn. For a while he worked as a scout, then he joined the mercantile firm of Bassett & Roberts as a partner. Shortly after that, he became a contractor for the Central Pacific Railroad. In 1864 he served as a city councilman in Salt Lake City and as director of the Utah Commercial & Savings Bank. As though that were not enough, Roberts also served as president of a local building and loan trust company. Two years later, the governor appointed him Treasurer of the Territory of Utah. Bolivar Roberts died on August 10, 1893, in his home in Salt Lake City.

Western superintendent William W. Finney's background is largely a mystery, though a slightly lesser one than that of A. E. Lewis. We know Finney came from New York, traveling by sea to California, to establish the western end of the Pony Express route. His responsibility was to build and supply the relay stations from Roberts Creek to Sacramento. He and his crew had to work in some of the most remote desert wilderness of the entire trail. In addition to the physical hardships, there was also the constant danger of an Indian attack, especially from the Paiute, who were at war with white settlers at the time.

Soon after Finney arrived in Sacramento, he began buying stock and supplies and hiring a crew. When he set off for the Ruby Valley in Nevada, he had hired 21 men and had bought 129 mules, approximately 100 horses, and an assortment of equipment including saddles, bridles, blankets, tents, tools, and provisions. Everything was loaded into wagons, and the party headed east to accomplish the nearly impossible task of building a series of relay stations along four hundred miles of pure desolation.

Since he was working westward from Roberts Creek, in central Nevada, Finney obviously had to coordinate his efforts with Division Five superintendent Bolivar Roberts, who was extremely familiar with the land. Once the service was established, it was expected to run at peak efficiency, even under the most challenging conditions. As Roberts explained, "The big bosses [presumably Ben Ficklin and Alexander

Majors] would be checking on the initial run. Ficklin would be having his eyes peeled for any lapses in time not satisfactorily explained."

Finney, a natural leader, took it upon himself to take out loans for additional operating funds when the company's money ran out. He was also stubborn, which—although the details are murky—may have ultimately caused his dismissal from the Pony Express. Finney had a running dispute with the San Francisco newspapers and business community. As a service to local businesses, some of the newspapers were publishing a list of the recipients of the incoming Pony Express mail from the local mail collection office. This list helped business owners anticipate orders, rates of money exchange, and the like by informing them of whom to contact for the latest information. Upon learning of this practice, Finney ordered the newspapers to desist giving out what he likely felt was privileged information. Angry business leaders sent Finney a stiff protest letter via a newspaper in Carson City. When Finney offhandedly dismissed the letter, the paper published it for all to see.

Several weeks later, Finney, having worked for Central Overland California & Pike's Peak Express Company for only six months, was gone. With no written farewell or indication of his next destination, he simply vanished. The man who took Finney's place was W. C. Marley, who had been in charge of the Buckland's relay station. He remained in that position to the end of the Pony Express service, after which he became sheriff of Nevada Territory.

The chief ramrod of the entire Pony Express route was the no-nonsense, tough-as-nails, hot-tempered Ben Ficklin. Ficklin was born in Charlottesville, Virginia, in December 1827, the son of a Baptist preacher and tobacco farmer. Young Ben was a feisty boy, full of energy and a bit mischievous. Even the Virginia Military Institute did not succeed in inculcating in him much discipline—he was eventually dismissed for repeated pranks. His desire for adventure led him into service with the U.S. Army during the Mexican War, after which he returned to the Virginia Military Institute more inclined to study, and he graduated in 1849.

Sometime in the 1850s, Ficklin followed his wild spirit to the western frontier. He became a route superintendent for the Leavenworth & Pike's Peak Express Company, which operated a huge freighting network. During this time he helped in the enormous operation to supply General Johnston's army, which had been directed to confront the Mormon leaders in Utah. In his position with the freight company Ficklin had gained extensive knowledge of the central overland route, and the government asked him to join a survey party to map the first overland wagon trail for general use from South Pass, in the Wyoming Rockies, to Salt Lake City.

When William Russell told Ficklin the idea for the Pony Express, Ficklin was extremely enthusiastic and ready to serve a major role. He became one of the key men in organizing the route and became the company's general superintendent. Strong-willed and tough, Ficklin had marvelous credentials for the job. He knew the difficulties of frontier life and was a natural leader.

Unfortunately he was also hot-tempered, which eventually got him into serious trouble with William Russell and led to his resignation. Ficklin, overjoyed with the success of the first Pony Express ride, had contacted Russell to suggest that the mail service be increased to semi-weekly. Russell, well aware of the company's financial distress, promptly rejected the idea. This led to a violent disagreement between the two men, which culminated in Russell demanding and getting Ficklin's resignation a few weeks later.

When the Civil War broke out, Ficklin, maintaining his allegiance to his home state of Virginia, served in the Confederate Army as a purchasing agent, operating in Europe. With the end of the war, Ficklin came out west again, working in mail delivery and stagecoach operations in Texas. In the late 1860s this courageous man of the plains died at the Willard Hotel in Washington, D.C., from choking on a fish bone.

— 8 —

THE CHALLENGE AND
BEAUTY OF THE LAND

THE ASTOUNDING 1,840-MILE distance of the Pony Express route was itself enough to tax the endurance of the sturdiest team of riders. But distance was only part of the challenge. Covering eight states—Missouri, Kansas, Nebraska, Colorado, Wyoming, Utah, Nevada, and California—Pony Express riders encountered nearly every type of natural surrounding imaginable, from roaring rivers that could sweep away man and horse to bone-dry deserts that could burn the last drop of life-sustaining moisture from rider and beast. They also experienced an equally varied array of extreme weather conditions, from severe blizzards to ferocious lightning storms.

East to west, the starting point of the Pony Express route was the young yet bustling town of St. Joseph, Missouri, in northwestern Missouri. Before 1826 it was no more than a desolate tract of forest and meadow along the Missouri River, at the foot of the Black Snake Hills. In 1826 a rugged fur trader named Joseph Robidoux decided that it would be an excellent site for a trading post. It was an accessible spot, and soon trappers came from as far away as Wyoming, South Dakota, Colorado, and Utah to sell their furs. By the end of 1843 it had grown into a settlement of about five hundred people.

Among St. Joseph's early merchants was Israel Landis, who came from St. Louis to open a saddle and harness shop. Landis may have been the man who designed and constructed the mochila and saddles for the Pony Express riders. St. Joseph's first newspaper, the *Gazette*, came out on April 25, 1845. By then the town's population was large enough to support two boardinghouses and several saloons.

By the 1850s St. Joseph had become an important meeting place not only for fur traders and local Indians, but also for huge numbers of emigrants, who chose the town as the jumping-off point for their journey west. The streets were filled with Kickapoo, Pottawatomi, Musquakee

(Fox), Iowa, and Oto Indians, who came to shop and use the ferry to the Kansas Territory; fur company employees unloading furs from pack mules; businessmen congregating; and hordes of emigrants stocking up on supplies. With regard to this last group, the town was so overrun with their tents that it made St. Joseph look as if it were besieged by an army. It is estimated that in 1849, about thirty thousand emigrants passed through the town.

By the 1850s, with a population of about five thousand, St. Joe had a train line and a telegraph, making the town truly a center of commerce and communications. Also by that time, about nine thousand miles of railroad track had been laid east of the Mississippi River. The two-hundred-mile Hannibal & St. Joseph Railroad—the line that played a critical role in the first mail delivery of the Pony Express—was completed on February 13, 1859. Along with the trains came railroad yards, pawnshops, stores, saloons, and hotels. The pride of St. Joseph was a splendid four-story hotel called Patee House, named after its builder, John Patee. This grand establishment became renown not only for its luxurious accomodations but, after 1860, for the fact that it served as the headquarters for the Pony Express.

Riding west from St. Joseph, the Pony rider crossed the Missouri River on a paddle-wheel ferry to Elwood, Kansas, where his long, lonely ride really began. The great territory of Kansas was a vast, desolate area that included coal mines, high plateaus, forests, and prairies. Northeastern Kansas is a continuous series of rolling hills, ridges, and valleys, not very difficult for a horse and rider to gallop along at a good clip. Yet even on this relatively easy part of the trail, riding at high speed could be treacherous, especially after a heavy rain. Historian Sir Richard Burton provided a description of the first five miles of the Pony trail:

> A deep tangle wood, rather a thicket or jungle than a forest—of oaks and elms, hickory, bass-wood, and black walnut, poplar and hack-berry, boxelder, and the common willow, clad and festooned, bound and anchored by wild vines, creepers, and huge Ilianas, and sheltering an undergrowth of wild alder and red sumac, whose black mire [is] strongly suggestive of chills-fever and ague.

Though sometimes dry, northeastern Kansas has some of the richest farm soil in the nation. Nevertheless, the Kansas prairie remained sparsely inhabited until the late nineteenth century. In fact, the Pony station at Hollenberg was believed to be the first pioneer house built in the area.

A pioneer woman named Emma Mitchell New described the desolation of this area most vividly in 1877: "Many a homesick day I saw;

many a tear was shed. I couldn't bear to go to the window and look out. All I could see everywhere was prairie and not a house to be seen."

Continuing west through northeastern Kansas, the Pony Express route led through an area north of the Flint Hills, one of the most beautiful segments of the western prairie. Here the land curved in gently sloping hills, the prairie alive with bright flowers and an array of animals. Hardy grass grew waist high in most parts and as tall as eight feet in some areas. As it bent to the passing breeze, the grass flashed shades of bronze, wine, and gold in a delightful kaleidoscope of nature's art.

Kansas is part of the Great Plains, a vast region that covers one-third of the contiguous United States, from Indiana to the Rocky Mountains and from northern Minnesota to east Texas. In 1860 the Great Plains were a golden sea of waving grass, home to elk, mule deer, white-tailed deer, black bear, prairie chicken, ferret, sharp-tailed grouse, wild turkey, ground squirrel, pocket gopher, and a plethora of other fauna. Pioneers traveling with their lumbering covered wagons could travel for several weeks and still find themselves in this "tall grass country." As one goes farther west, the land becomes drier, the grass grows shorter, trees become sparcer, and the soil becomes increasingly porous, sandy, and alkaline.

Summer on the plains brought blistering heat that could hover at more than 115 degrees, alternating with vicious lightning storms that could put fear into the stoutest hearts. In the driest part of summer, smaller streams dried up, and there was little water to be found. In winter, bitter cold temperatures plunged far below zero, and furious blizzards submerged the land and its bare foliage beneath a blanket of blinding white, swirling powder, creating a frigid desert. The springtime was a mixed blessing, as riders had to ford furiously rushing, swollen streams that could easily carry away a careless rider and dash him against a boulder. On the other hand, the countryside was ablaze with delicately scented wildflowers, which dotted the prairie in small bouquets waving in the gentle breeze.

All across the western plains, millions upon millions of wooly bison (buffalo) thundered across the land in a show of living force second to none on earth. This tremendous beast, which could weigh up to twenty-five hundred pounds, was the largest mammal in North America, and the stories of the unimaginably large herds are legendary. In 1541, one of Coronado's men expressed his amazement of the size of buffalo herds in his diary: "There is such a quantity of them that I do not know what to compare them with, except with the fish in the sea. . . . Many times

*Black bears, mule deer, and hundreds of other creatures made their homes
on the Great Plains.* —Courtesy Wyoming Division of Cultural Resources

when we started to pass through the midst of them . . . and go to the other side, we were not able to because the country was covered with them." Nathaniel Langford, who later became the first head of the Yellowstone National Park, heard the ground-shaking rumble of a colossal herd half an hour before he spotted them on the horizon. "They were running as rapidly as a horse can go at a keen gallop, about twelve miles an hour. . . . The whole space, say five miles by twelve miles, . . . was a seemingly solid mass of buffaloes." This condition would not last of course. By the turn of the twentieth century, the mighty bison was nearly extinct.

Even more numerous than the bison were pronghorns, an antelope-like mammal that is native to North America. At the time of the Pony Express, there were fifty million to one hundred million pronghorns roaming the wilderness, and probably thirty million buffalo. Still more spectacular in numbers was the prairie dog, a small brown mammal that lives in underground colonies, some of which cover hundreds of square

During the time of the Pony Express, there were perhaps thirty million bison, or American buffalo, roaming the great prairies of the West. Because of overhunting by whites, by 1905 the buffalo population was down to a mere seven hundred. (Painting by W. H. Jackson) —Courtesy Scotts Bluff National Monument

miles. There were upwards of a billion such animals in the Great Plains. Unfortunately for the Pony Express rider, there was always the possibility of a horse at full gallop catching its hoof in a prairie-dog hole and breaking a leg.

About one hundred miles west of the Missouri, the Pony Express rider arrived at the banks of the Big Blue River. Here he would be entering a more barren and rugged land, encountering sharp rocks, large boulders, and spiny yucca plants. In springtime, the crossing of the Big Blue was life-threatening, as its fierce waters surged forward, crashing against rocks, swirling into whirlpools, and foaming and billowing in its mad dash to the Kansas River. If the rushing current did not get the rider, there was still the danger of the unpredictable river bottom, which could change with any step from a firm sandy surface to a treacherous mud that could suck its struggling victim down deeper and deeper until he drowned.

Some sources believe that Pony Express riders took a ferry across the Big Blue; there is evidence that a ferry was in operation in the 1850s,

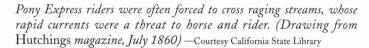

Pony Express riders were often forced to cross raging streams, whose rapid currents were a threat to horse and rider. (Drawing from Hutchings *magazine, July 1860)* —Courtesy California State Library

but whether it was operating in 1860 and if so, whether Pony riders used it cannot be substantiated. In 1849 Frank J. Marshall established a ferry and a trading post on the east shore of the Big Blue, where thousands of wagon trains forded the river. Eventually Marshall built a second ferry and handled a great deal of traffic. Soon emigrants began to settle around the post, and a town, which Marshall named Marysville (after his wife), developed. In 1860 the Pony Express built a relay station at Marysville. Though records do not indicate whether the ferries were still operating at the time, it is reasonable to conclude that with such heavy traffic the ferry operation would have been maintained.

Once past the Big Blue River, the Pony rider continued west until he entered the shallow valley of the Little Blue, which directed his progress to the north. He followed the river along the eastern bank out of Kansas Territory and into Nebraska. Captain John C. Frémont made the following observation concerning this part of the trail:

> [T]he valley, which, bordered by hills with graceful slopes, looked uncommonly green and beautiful. The stream was about fifty feet wide, and three or four deep, fringed by cotton-wood and willow, with frequent groves of oak tenanted by flocks of turkeys. Game here, too, made its appearance in greater plenty. Elk were frequently seen on the hills and now and then an antelope bounded across our path, or a deer broke from the groves. . . . [T]he valley . . . is sometimes rich and well timbered, though the country is generally sandy.

Here, to the rider's relief, the land was extremely flat, in contrast to the rugged area around the Big Blue. When the route left the Little Blue, it crossed Thirty-Two Mile Creek and entered the Platte Valley, the long corridor that led west across Nebraska to the base of the Rockies. From here, the riders would follow the south bank of the Platte for several hundred miles of endless dunes, riding over one hill after another through an area that could whip up a blinding sandstorm or a paralyzing snowstorm at almost any moment.

The Platte River has been described as being "a thousand miles long and six inches deep." Its name, in fact, is from the French word for "flat" or "shallow." But after a serious rainstorm the water rushes at breakneck speed through its wide channels as it hurries to discharge its mountain waters into the Missouri. Along the Platte and along much of the trail, travelers were plagued by millions of gnats, which bit the tender parts such as the eyelids and ears, causing unbearable discomfort. At night the mosquitoes took over, thick clouds of them, making sleep nearly impossible.

A dugout home in Red Willow County, Nebraska, just north of the Kansas border. Life on the open prairie in the 1860s was a constant fight against the elements. —Courtesy Nebraska State Historical Society

The two branches of the Platte—the North Platte, originating in the Wyoming Rockies, and the South Platte, originating in the Colorado Rockies—join in Nebraska, just west of Fort McPherson, to form the main body of the Platte. The gradient of the river varies greatly over its 442-mile course. The main body of the Platte is a meandering, sandy, island-studded stream, receiving much of its waters from hundreds of underground and surface tributaries, the largest of which is the Loup River, flowing out of the sand hills of Nebraska.

Because of the availability of grass and water along the river, and because it was a fairly level avenue leading to South Pass through the Rocky Mountains, by the mid-nineteenth century the Platte had become the "highway to the West." Thousands of pioneers traveling to Oregon and later to California and Utah left their wagon ruts along the Platte.

In his well-researched book *Kansas and Nebraska*, published in 1854, Edward Everett Hale provides some descriptions of the Platte (then called the Nebraska) River and the Platte Valley:

> The lower part of the valley of the Nebraska, with the uplands on either side, offers an attractive soil and climate. . . . It often seems almost lost in the broad bed of sand through which its various currents

pass. It does not make any considerable falls in its long eastward course. ... [M]ore than five hundred miles west from the Missouri ... a more inhospitable country then begins, on both sides of the Nebraska, which affords pasturage for buffalo and for cattle, but little more which tempts the farmer. It is for a great distance unbroken by hills. For eighty-five miles west of Fort Kearney the road to Fort Laramie is wholly level. A gently rolling country then begins. It is upon these sandy plains that the buffalo are now first found by westward emigrants.

The great Platte Valley was the main thoroughfare of the pioneers and the forty-niners on their long trek to California and Oregon. The discovery of the Platte River overland route through the Rocky Mountains is a story of amazing courage and fortitude.

In late spring 1812, fur trader Robert Stuart led a small group of traders overland from Fort Astoria in Oregon to St. Louis to deliver some reports to John Jacob Astor. Rather than follow Lewis and Clark's route, they struck out on a new route through the lower Rockies, crossing over the mighty Tetons. Before long they began to run short of food. They also endured sweltering heat, rough terrrain, mosquitoes, rattlesnakes, and threats from Indian war parties. Yet they survived.

Reaching the Tetons in October, rather than take one of the known passes through the mountains, Stuart decided to take one he had heard about from the Indians. This pass was farther south and led to the Platte River. Thus did Stuart discover South Pass, the easiest way through the Rockies, over which thousands of wagons would one day travel.

When winter came, the party had to trudge through knee-deep snow and bitter winds to escape hostile Indians. In April Stuart paid some Indians to construct a large raft on which they sailed down the Platte River and into the Missouri. Thus Stuart and his small band of mountain men had crossed the continent by way of the Platte River route. The agonizing trip had taken ten months, but they had not lost a single man. This amazing feat opened the overland route that would later become part of the pioneer trail and the Pony Express Trail.

Following the Platte, the Pony rider passed Fort Kearny and Midway Station, riding on to Cold Spring Station, where the Platte divided into north and south branches. The trail followed the South Platte for about one hundred miles, into the northeast corner of Colorado. Here horse and rider found themselves in a land where the deep blue sky rarely blessed the earth with rain and the horizon was a nearly perfect straight line.

*Early settlers in Custer County, Nebraska, late 1870s. There were
precious few settlements along the Pony Express Trail in Nebraska.*
—Courtesy Nebraska State Historical Society

Leaving the South Platte after fording its rapid waters at Julesburg,
the rider headed northwest again and back into Nebraska, where the
trail again joined the main path of the Oregon-California Trail. Here
the land began to rise, giving way to buttes, spires, mesas, and some of
nature's most startling monuments of the journey west. The first of these,
visible against the horizon for miles, were Courthouse Rock and Jail
House Rock in hilly western Nebraska. Courthouse Rock, its shape
evocative of an old-time courthouse, rises about four hundred feet from
the ground. Next to it is the smaller Jail House Rock, thought to resemble a jail. These huge sandstone and clay formations were about
four miles off the trail, but they were so massive that travelers often
mistakenly thought they were just a brief walk away. For Pony Express
riders and emigrants alike, these landmarks were a welcome sight. But
travelers also had to be mindful of the deadly rattlesnakes, which could
bite a leg or spook a horse at any moment.

The next milestone on the Pony Express Trail, which could also be
seen from many miles away, was Chimney Rock. This inverted funnel
against the far horizon signaled that a traveler would soon be leaving
Nebraska Territory and entering the wild and magnificent realm of the

A Pony rider could easily see Chimney Rock as he raced along the Pony Express Trail in Nebraska. —Courtesy Nebraska State Historical Society

Wyoming Rockies. Made of a mixture of clay and volcanic ash, Chimney Rock projects its spire 325 feet into the sky; the base of the cone measures 205 feet.

At this point, the rider was eighty miles from Fort Laramie, mostly uphill. Not too long after passing Chimney Rock, the rider viewed what looked like a giant wall on the horizon, a steep cliff barring the way west. This was Scotts Bluff, a huge rock formation nearly a mile wide and rising 760 feet above the Platte River. Luckily for the rider, cutting through the center of this massive clay and soft limestone obstruction was a great gash known as Mitchell Pass. During the great pioneer migration in the 1840s and 1850s, the route through Mitchell Pass was used almost exclusively. In 1860 and 1861 many a lonely Pony Express rider was thankful for this shortcut through Scotts Bluff.

Shortly after leaving Mitchell Pass, the Pony Express Trail climbed into the higher elevation of a new territory—Wyoming, an area of nearly one hundred thousand square miles. This land of cloud-piercing peaks, thousands of ice blue lakes, rushing streams, and magnificent forests was home to a dazzling array of wildlife. Here elk, moose, and grizzlies reigned supreme, while fleet-footed pronghorn antelope and wild horses

A freight wagon train making its toilsome way through Mitchell Pass through Scotts Bluff in Nebraska. This was also the trail Pony Express riders used. (Painting by W. H. Jackson) —Courtesy Scotts Bluff National Monument

raced across the landscape. It was a world where a sudden blizzard could change mountain forests and streams into a sparkling white wonderland in minutes.

Entering Wyoming Territory, the Pony rider had to ford several numbingly cold rapids as the trail gradually climbed more than seven thousand feet in elevation. Past Fort Laramie, the trail continued up one hill and down another for more than 150 miles until another strange formation appeared in the distance. To the south ran the Sweetwater River, and to the north lay what appeared to be a tremendous gray turtle shell. Measuring more than five thousand feet around and 193 feet high, Independence Rock became known as the "Great Register of the Desert" after thousands of emigrants climbed its sloped walls to engrave their names into the granite. But Pony Express riders had no time to stop or even slow down as they raced across the plateau toward the Green River in southwestern Wyoming. A few miles past Independence Rock was another landmark, Devil's Gate, a narrow gash in the walls of a three-hundred-foot-high cliff. After Devil's Gate, following the Sweetwater River for about a hundred miles, the rider ascended gradually into the

Rockies until he arrived at South Pass, on the Continental Divide. Thousands of covered wagons passed over its saddlelike terrain on their way to Oregon and California.

Contrary to those who envision South Pass as a deep canyon cut out of steep-walled mountains, it is actually a twenty-mile-wide, gently sloping valley, best envisioned by reading the words of this emigrant:

> I am disappointed in the appearance of the South Pass—I had expected to see rough precipitous mountains on each side the road & in fact to climb such & that the real pass would run through a narrow gorge & plunge quite suddenly down on the Western side. Instead I find we are travelling over a quite level but somewhat rolling terrain varying in width from 10 to probably 25 miles—a fine hard gravel road—The snow caps are only visible on the right & probably 15 or 20 miles distant.
>
> —Henry M. Judson, July 18, 1862

Not all emigrants were disappointed, however:

> The South Pass has some of the appearance of the broken prairies in the western states. At the right of the pass the snow peaks commence to rise one above the other, until they get to a very considerable height and run to a sharp point at the top and white with snow, which presents a scene almost unsurpassed by nature.
>
> —Orange Gaylord, June 20, 1850

With the Sweetwater Mountains and Antelope Hills on the south side and the Rattlesnake Mountains and Wind River Range on the north side, South Pass was the highest point of the Pony Express Trail, at an elevation of 7,550 feet. From here the trail headed southwest along Sandy Creek, down along the butter-colored banks of the swiftly running Green River, into Utah Territory.

As treacherous as the Pony Express Trail was through the Rockies— with its steep, winding grades, often blanketed with several feet of snow or glazed with ice—the worst part was yet to come. For it now crossed hundreds of miles of desert, much of it salt flats, where few living creatures could survive very long. The alkali dust and incredible heat were suffocating. This vast area, known as the Great Basin because no drainage occurs from it, covers most of Utah, a small southwest section of Wyoming, and most of Nevada. In 1843 Captain John Charles Frémont headed a group of explorers across the Great Basin. His findings helped the Pony Express establish portions of the trail across Utah and Nevada.

The Great Basin receives less than five inches of rain per year, and much of the little water that does fall either evaporates into the hot

The Wind River Range of the Rocky Mountains. Its peaks can be seen looking north from South Pass. —Courtesy Wyoming Division of Cultural Resources

atmosphere or quickly sinks into the sandy soil. Whatever water remains on the surface is extremely saline or alkaline—totally undrinkable. Running rivers and streams are rare: they include the Humboldt, the Colorado, the Gila, and the Rio Grande. In places where pools of stagnant water collect, insects abound in swarms. Gnats and mosquitoes torture every living creature in sight.

Many sections of the Great Basin, including the spectacular canyon system of Utah, are characterized by rugged plant life such as creosote bush, sagebrush, piñon, and juniper. In the far south, giant cacti and the unique multibranched Joshua tree survive. Weather conditions vary from deadly hot temperatures in the summer to paralyzingly cold weather in the winter.

But as barren as it may appear, there are areas of the Great Basin that abound with wildlife. A sharp-eyed Pony rider might spot a pronghorn running fleetly across the desert or a mountain goat, a mule deer, or a bighorn sheep bounding across a crevice along the canyon trail. The sound of his horse's hooves might scare up a sharp-tailed grouse,

John C. Frémont's exploration of the Great Basin laid the groundwork for later developments, including the Pony Express Trail.
—Courtesy California Historical Society

a ring-necked pheasant, a mourning dove, or a wild turkey. More often, a white-tailed or black-tailed jackrabbit, a cottontail rabbit, or a snowshoe hare might scamper across the trail. Near the Great Salt Lake, a rider might marvel at the great flocks of ducks, geese, and swans that migrate to their favorite nesting grounds in the area.

During the driest stretches of his ride, a Pony rider might see extraordinary mirages on all sides, lakes dotted with islands and bordered by groves of green trees. A sudden salt storm could nearly blind him and the bitter air choke him. A graphic description of the terrible Great Salt Lake Desert appears in the diaries of Mark Twain in a story, "Mark Twain Follows the Trail":

> The dawn wind was chilly, but an hour later the August sun beat down mercilessly. On all sides the endless desert lay parched and

forlorn, an ocean dead and turned to ashes. The Clemens boys suffered with thirst and drank copiously from their canteens. By noon
their water was gone.

Outside [the stagecoach], the lifeless solitude showed no bird, no
insect, no reptile—space devoid of matter, a vacuum. Even the air
seemed dead. . . . Great clouds of dust rose around them and settled
on the coach. The men's faces, eyebrows and mustaches became col-
orless with the gray powder, their clothes became dusty as a miller's.
The . . . alkali began to burn their faces, chap their lips, redden their
eyes. The sight of the next station late in the afternoon looked like
paradise. For the first time, Sam said, he was glad that they had brought
along the six-pound dictionary, but even it, unabridged as it was, failed
to have suitable words to describe the desert journey.

Luckily the Pony Express Trail did not cross the main body of the
salt flats. It entered Utah just east of the Great Salt Lake, passed
through Salt Lake City (where there was a home station), headed south
toward Utah Lake and then west again, passing through a maddening
array of hills and mountain passes. Once past the Topaz Mountains, it
skirted along the southern edge of the dreaded flats, a deposit of a
billion tons of salt left by a prehistoric twenty-thousand-square-mile
lake. Even through this harsh landscape, the Pony Express had to establish relay stations, and the men and horses had to keep up their
demanding schedule.

Eventually the trail headed northwest, across the Deer Creek Mountains and into Nevada Territory, remaining south of the Humboldt River,
twisting and turning through endless hills, ravines, and crevices. Nevada was an unimaginably hostile land, sparsely vegetated, dry, tangled,
rocky, dusty, alkaline, and desperately lonely. John C. Frémont led the
first official government explorations of the Nevada Territory in 1843.

A number of attempts to develop a trail through this area were made
with little success until 1858, when Captain James H. Simpson conquered the country south of the Humboldt. Taking along with him the
highly knowledgeable Howard Egan, who had discovered a number of
passes through the Ruby Mountains, Simpson blazed a trail all the way
from Salt Lake to the Carson Sink. The Simpson route was 565 miles
as compared to the 853-mile emigrant trail along the Humboldt River.
The route was dry and lacked good grazing grass, but it was a shortcut,
and that is what was needed for the Pony Express Trail.

At Carson Sink, dust storms could blot out the sun and tear at a
rider's skin like sandpaper. Or, just as suddenly, a rider could encounter
a pogonip—an unusually dense fog that sometimes appears in winter,

covering the landscape with a mantle of ice crystals. At other times the rider faced blinding sunlight and sticky clutches of alkali mud pulling at his pony's hooves. It was a landscape of a hundred shades of brown against a vivid blue sky, a challenge to the very idea of life. Certainly it was one of the most unpleasant sections of the Pony Express route.

At this point the trail headed southwest toward the Sierra Nevada. The trail through this range was a thing of great beauty but could also be pure agony. The Sierra Nevada is the largest unbroken mountain range in the Pacific states, running about four hundred miles north and south. Along with the Cascade Range it forms a high barrier extending

A Pony Express rider crossing the Sierra Nevada in a raging snowstorm. The rugged and steep terrain coupled with snowdrifts up to thirty feet high made this one of the worst stretches of the trail. (Drawing from Hutchings *magazine, July 1860)* —Courtesy California State Library

from southern California to Canada, nearly isolating the Pacific Coast from the rest of the country.

It was through these giants of nature that the Pony Express Trail had to pass. Leaving the sagebrush of the Great Basin, the land quickly changed as the piñon and juniper became more plentiful and the air became cooler and clearer. Later the stately ponderosa pine dominated the scenery, providing much shade and purifying the high mountain air. But along with the beauty came steep grades, narrow canyons, howling winds, and frightening blizzards that created incredibly deep drifts. Many a rider must have looked up and seen the giant California condor gliding through the canyons, wishing that he too could cross these mountains so easily.

Finally the trail reached its high point over the Carson Pass, overlooking glorious Lake Tahoe. From here the trail descended the California side of the mountains and went once again into the desert, where during the day it was hot enough to fry an egg on a rock and at night it got cold enough to make you shiver under several woolen blankets. Once in California, the rider headed west through Placerville and Folsom and followed along the American River to Sacramento.

The Sacramento Valley was known for its mild, wet winters and hot, dry summers, and for its heavy fogs, which could cover the valley for weeks on end, making travel very difficult, especially on a speeding horse. As one descended from the mountains and crossed the desert, the vegetation became richer and greener. Lodgepole pines gave way to fir, spruce, and pine forests, then to the grand oak forests of Sacramento. There the Pony rider boarded a paddle-wheel ship, which would carry him down the swift and powerful Sacramento River to the open waters of San Francisco Bay, and to San Francisco, the trail's end.

— 9 —
DANGEROUS TRESPASSING

THE PONY EXPRESS rider faced a host of perils, many deriving more from human nature than from Mother Nature. In addition to the discomfort and danger of the rough terrain, harsh weather, insects, and scarce water on the trail, hostile Indians threatened riders and station keepers alike.

Various Indian tribes had inhabited the land along the Pony Express Trail for hundreds, if not thousands, of years before the mail service came through. By 1860 they had already watched white settlers swarm in droves across their hunting lands, recklessly chopping down trees, allowing their livestock to gnaw good grazing land down to bare ground, and killing buffalo far beyond their needs. The white men built farms and towns on choice tracts of land in tribal hunting ranges. At this incursion into their home many Indians became resentful, and in some cases their war parties threatened the pioneers and other adventurous souls who braved the great wilderness, including Pony Express workers.

On the eastern section of the Pony Express Trail (Kansas and Nebraska) were a great variety of tribes, including Osage, Iowa, Kickapoo, Pottawatomi, Fox, Sac, Kansa, Pawnee, Oto, Winnebago, Omaha, and Ponca. Many of these tribes were members of the great Dakota, or Sioux, family. In Wyoming lived mostly Cheyenne, Shoshone, and Arapaho. On the western portion of the trail, Utah was the home of the Ute as well as the Paiute and Goshute, and Nevada was dominated by the various bands of the Paiute tribe. Most tribes living around the eastern part of the trail were essentially friendly toward whites. West of the Rockies, however, the Paiute and other tribes were at war with the intruders.

The rebellion that finally broke out against the whites was the result of many past events that had fueled the fires of hatred. As far back as 1832, trappers had begun to create tension between the Indians and the Europeans. For example, in 1832 trapper Joe Meek casually shot and

Meeting of Shoshone and Arapaho Indians on the Little Wind River in Wyoming (c. late 1800s). These two tribes were peaceable with whites, but during the 1860 Paiute War, Pony Express workers in western Utah and Nevada were under a constant threat of violence. —Courtesy Wyoming Division of Cultural Resources

killed a Shoshone man along the Humboldt River "as a hint to the other Indians to keep them from stealing our traps." The following year a party of trappers along the Humboldt spotted a number of Shoshone on the opposite bank and without a thought fired at them, killing twenty-five. During the gold rush of 1849, hoards of miners began passing through the lands along the future Pony Express Trail, and a number of them also committed terrible atrocities against the Indians.

During the 1850s, the cauldron of hatred began to boil over. In the mid-1850s a band of Shoshone attacked a number of wagon trains traveling along the Humboldt River and stole their cattle. In turn, the settlers went after the Indians, killing thirty of them. And so it went, back and forth, violence bringing on more violence.

The U.S. government negotiated many peace agreements with the Indians, only to break them afterward. One of the largest treaty gatherings took place on September 11, 1851, near Horse Creek in Wyoming. More than ten thousand natives from Arapaho, Cheyenne, Sioux, and many other nations met with government representatives to discuss an accord. The chiefs agreed to stop attacking settlers, miners, and trappers, and the United States agreed to recognize the tribal boundaries and pay a fee for crossing Indian lands. It was not long before the government broke the treaty and the violence returned.

In May 1860, during an Indian war council at Pyramid Lake in Nevada, a serious episode occurred at a Pony Express station that incited the infamous Pyramid Lake massacre by the Paiute. What happened is not entirely clear, but it is believed that some of the men at Williams Station, on the Carson River about ten miles east of Buckland's, kidnapped and sexually assaulted two Paiute women. On May 7 some men from the tribe rode to the station intent on revenge.

The station was operated by J. O. Williams and his two brothers, David and Oscar. It so happened that on this fateful day some friends, Samuel Sullivan, James Fleming, and a man known as Dutch Phil, had stopped in to visit. David and Oscar Williams stood talking just outside the station when the Indians attacked, killing both brothers. Sullivan made an attempt to flee, but he did not get very far before they slayed him. Then they entered the station and dispatched Fleming and Dutch Phil. After burning down the station, the small war party headed west

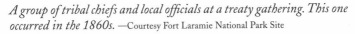

A group of tribal chiefs and local officials at a treaty gathering. This one occurred in the 1860s. —Courtesy Fort Laramie National Park Site

for Buckland's Station, driving off the cattle of a nearby rancher, W. H. Bloomfield, on the way. But as daylight approached, they decided to return to Pyramid Lake, where the war council was in session.

At the council, some Indians had been arguing for peace and others for war on the whites in response to various recent conflicts. Meanwhile, hotheaded warriors had murdered several more settlers in the area. When the news of the Williams Station massacre and other killings reached residents of nearby settlements, their reaction was instant and strong. Armed men from Genoa, Carson City, Silver City, and Virginia City gathered in Virginia City to form a hasty militia. One man, Major William Ormsby, tried to persuade the mob to elect a leader, but they refused. On May 12, about 105 unorganized and undisciplined volunteers headed for the Indian village at Pyramid Lake, believing the Indians would offer little resistance.

Upon reaching Pyramid Lake the ragged little army saw a group of Indians on a hill and immediately charged. But instead of running, the Indians began to fire arrows. The white men retreated toward a grove of cottonwood trees, where they hoped to reorganize. But the Paiute had already seen them coming and lay in ambush in the grove. When the warriors jumped out, shooting arrows from all directions, the militiamen panicked. Almost immediately twenty of them were killed as they tried to run, and twenty more were killed before they were able to ride clear of their attackers.

One of the militiamen was Bartholomew Riley, who soon after the battle made a ride for the Pony Express. Upon learning that the rider due to leave Smith's Creek Station refused to go for fear of the Indians, Riley volunteered to take his place and successfully made the mail run in good time. In a sad twist, the very next day, a friend of Riley accidentally shot him, and he died a few days later.

In late May, a force of about eight hundred men rode against the Paiute, killing about twenty-five and chasing the rest into the endless hills of Nevada. But the violence was far from over. The plight of the Indians would worsen and more whites, including Pony Express workers, would be killed.

One might think that the station keepers were safer than riders, that they could hide safely behind the cabin walls during an Indian attack. Not so. More Pony Express station workers were killed than were riders. Unlike riders, who could usually outrun Indians and other threats, station workers were sitting ducks. The stations were flimsy shelters, far from fortresslike, and most were in remote areas.

There is no scarcity of examples of station workers' vulnerability, such as the case of Albert Armstrong and Henry Woodville "Wood" Wilson. Along with Mike Holton, Armstrong and Wilson worked at the Egan relay station, a one-room log structure in a desolate, foreboding area on a winding trail with large boulders that presented a formidable hiding place for attackers.

On the day of this incident, Holton was not at the station. Armstrong and Wilson had just finished breakfast when Armstrong heard a low moaning sound outside. Pulling aside the calico curtains, he peeped out the window. What he saw made his blood run cold. "My God," he gasped, sounding an alarm to his partner. It was a large war party of Paiute Indians, dressed in loincloths and feathers, bodies oiled and painted for battle. There had been recent uprisings of the Paiute nation, with blood flowing on both sides. The fierce-looking warriors were not here on a social call. The only bit of luck going for the white men was the fact that the Indians did not seem to have any firearms, only bows and arrows.

Instantly, Armstrong and Wilson grabbed their rifles, threw themselves on the floor, and began firing through the cracks in the cabin wall. As long as they kept shooting, the Indians did not advance. Unfortunately, they were soon out of ammunition. In no time the Indians charged the cabin, crashed in the door, and held the two men at bay. The chief stepped into the cabin and demanded food for all his men. The station keepers obliged immediately, distributing whatever food they had. They even baked extra bread from the supply of flour they had in store, all the while aware of what awaited them: they were dead men; it was just a matter of time.

The Indians gorged themselves and made merry. Shortly the two white men learned their fate: they were to be burned at the stake. The warriors drove a stake into the ground and gathered dry sagebrush. They tied Armstrong and Wilson to the pole and lay the brush piles around their feet. The last vestige of hope was now all but gone. In a few moments they would experience a hideous death.

Suddenly they heard a sound that must have seemed to come straight from heaven: dozens of hoofbeats—a company of soldiers at full charge. Next came the crack of rifle shots and the howls of the Indians fleeing the scene. The soldiers raced by in hot pursuit of the Paiute, and they killed a good number of them. It was an unbelievable turn of events—Armstrong and Wilson were saved.

Tragically, as though this episode had been but a prologue of what was to come, some of the Paiute returned that same night to the Schell

Creek Station, killed the three station keepers, and stole the horses. Several months later they again attacked Egan Station, burned it to the ground, and killed all the men. (It is not known whether Armstrong, Wilson, and Holton were still working there.)

If the Pony Express station keepers were exposed to as much danger as—if not more than—the riders were, they also proved themselves to be every bit as courageous. One morning at Dry Creek Station in Nevada, two of the station workers, Ralph Rosier and John Applegate, had gotten up early to start the day's work. Applegate started a fire to make breakfast as Rosier went out to the spring to fetch a bucket of water. The third man, "Bolly" Bolwinkle, remained in bed for a few more minutes. Suddenly a rifle shot rang out, and Applegate heard Rosier cry out in mortal agony. He raced to the door and looked out to see his friend lying on the ground dying.

At that instant a man named McCandless, who operated a small trading post across the road, came dashing in. Another shot rang out, and Applegate fell to the floor in excruciating pain, with a horrible wound to the hip. Meanwhile, Bolwinkle leaped out of bed in his stocking feet and grabbed his gun. McCandless and Bolwinkle quickly stacked grain bags in the doorway to protect themselves from the Paiute attackers. Then they started shooting back.

Applegate implored them to escape while they had a chance and not worry about him. They refused. A few minutes later the wounded man asked for a gun. Thinking that he wanted to join in the fight, they gave him a six-shooter. A moment later, Applegate, afraid he would be the cause of his friends' death, put the gun to his temple and fired.

Suddenly the Indians stopped firing, and McCandless told Bolwinkle that their only chance was to make a run for it. Bolwinkle objected, but McCandless claimed that the Indians knew and trusted him and wouldn't shoot at him. Bolwinkle nervously agreed, and the two men dashed from the cabin. With McCandless keeping himself between Bolwinkle and the Indians, the two men ran up the road to safety. In spite of their harrowing experience, Bolwinkle continued working for the Pony Express.

Stories of both narrow escapes and tragic endings abound in the Pony Express annals. One day, young Pony rider Nick Wilson came dashing into Deep Creek Station after an exhaustive ride through the desert, ready to hand the mochila over to a fresh rider. But there was no replacement rider. The station keeper did not know what happened to the rider, but now there was no choice—Nick had to take the next run. So, exhausted as he was, off he rode. About two hours later, Nick arrived at Willow Creek, ten miles east of Burnt Canyon, where he learned that the replacement rider had been killed by an Indian war party. Nick decided to rest before starting out again.

About 4:00 P.M., seven Indians rode up to the station and asked for food. Peter Neece, the station keeper, offered the Indians a twenty-pound sack of flour. They rejected it and insisted that he give each of them a sack. Neece, a powerful and short-tempered man and a crack shot, ordered the Indians out of the station. This enraged the Indians, but since there were several men with guns ready, they rode off. On their way out, they shot some arrows into an old lame cow that was standing peacefully under a shed. This callous act infuriated Neece, who drew his two pistols and fired after the Indians, knocking two of them clean off their horses. The others ran away.

Neece turned to Nick and the other two men and told them grimly that they were in for trouble. There were about thirty Indians camped in the canyon, and Neece anticipated that as soon as it got dark, the warriors would attack. But the daring station keeper had a plan: instead of waiting in the cabin, they would gather up all the guns and ammo they had in the station and hide about a hundred yards away, taking the Indians by surprise. Spacing themselves about five feet apart, the four men took their positions and waited. Neece had instructed them to fire and immediately jump aside, in case an Indian fired at the flash from their gun. What happened next is best described in Nick Wilson's own words:

> We all took our places, and you bet, I lay close to the ground. Pretty soon we could hear their horses' feet striking the ground, and it seemed to me as if there were thousands of them; and such yells as they let out, I never heard before. The sounds were coming straight towards us, and I thought they were going to run right over us. It was sandy where we lay, with little humps. Finally the Indians got close enough for us to shoot. Pete shot and jumped to one side. I had two pistols, one in each hand, cocked all ready to pull the trigger, and was crawling on my elbows and knees. Each time he would shoot, I would jump. I never shot at all. After I had jumped a good many times, I happened to land in a little wash or ravine. I guess my back came pretty nearly level with the top of it. Anyhow, I pressed myself down so I could get in. I don't know how I felt, I was so scared. I lay there and listened until I could hear no more shooting, but I thought I could hear the horses' hoofs beating on the hard ground near me until I found out it was only my heart beating. After a while, I raised my head a little and looked off towards the desert, and I could see those

humps of sand covered with greese-woods. They looked exactly like Indians on horses, and I could see several of them near the wash.

I crouched down again and lay there for a long time, maybe two hours. Finally everything was very still, so I thought I would go around and see if my horse was where I had staked him, and if he was, I would go back to my station in Deep Creek and tell them that the boys were all killed and I was the only one that had got away. Well, as I went crawling around the house on my elbows and knees, just as easily as I could, with both pistols ready, I saw a light shining between the logs in the back part of the house. I thought the house must be full of Indians, so I decided to lie there awhile and see what they were doing. I lay there for some time listening and watching and then I heard one of the men speak. "Did you find anything of him?" Another answered, "No, I guess he is gone." Then I knew it was the boys, but I lay there until I heard the door shut, then I slipped up and peeped through the crack and saw that all three of them were there all right. I was too much ashamed to go in but finally I went around and opened the door. When I stepped in Pete called out, "Hello! Here he is. How far did you chase them? I knew you would stay with them. I told the fellows here that you would bring back at least half a dozen of them." I think they killed five Indians that night.

Division superintendent Howard Egan left a description of a tragic incident at a remote station in western Utah. Dugway Station was merely a hole dug in a hill, covered with sod, with a wooden door. Though the hardy men of this station survived the primitive conditions, they did not stand a chance in a sneak Indian attack. Egan wrote of the massacre:

> The Indians waited till the men had been called to breakfast in the dugout, and were down in the hole without guns, all except the hostler, William Riley, who was currying a horse just outside the south door of the stable at the time of the first alarm, and he was shot through the ankle and the bone broken short off. He started down the canyon on the run, but did not get very far before he was caught and killed.
>
> The men at breakfast were mostly all killed as they came out of the dugout to reach their arms that were stacked in the south end of the barn. Not one of them ever reached his gun. One man, though wounded, tried to escape by running down the canyon as Riley did. He got further away, but was caught and killed, and, as he was some bald on top of his head, and a good growth of whiskers on his chin, they ["scalped" his face] and left him where he fell. . . . They took the clothes off every man and left them just where they fell. All this had been done without a shot being fired by the white men. A most complete surprise and massacre.

The scattered remains of Dugway (Shortcut Pass) relay station. At one of the most remote and desolate locations along the entire trail, it was the site of a brutal massacre of all the station workers. —Courtesy David C. Bagley

Stories of these incidents reached the Pony Express riders and station workers, of course, but they did not deter these intrepid men from fulfilling their duties. In Nevada especially, a station keeper always kept his gun within arm's reach, and a rider scanned the horizon continually for signs of trouble.

— 10 —
STATION TO STATION:
KANSAS, NEBRASKA, AND WYOMING

EVEN IF THEY were not altogether safe and comfortable harbors, the stations along the route were welcome stops for both man and horse after a long, lonely, and often perilous run. These often remote outposts were also homes to the unsung station workers of the Pony Express. Not much is known about the stations themselves, but in most cases, it is fairly certain, they were not built for comfort.

The relay posts, as opposed to the home stations, were mostly rough, simple cabins, with a few stalls and a corral for the horses. Each station was staffed by a station keeper and one or two helpers who took care of the livestock and did daily chores. A rider rarely spent more than two minutes at these stations, just enough time to leap off his horse, throw the mochila over the saddle of a fresh mount, hop on, and wave goodbye as he sped off on his appointed run. Observer Tom Riverton gave a description of the change:

> A . . . mounted man leading a saddled pony raced east from the station to meet the incoming westbound express rider. As they met, the rider with the fresh mount turned and raced alongside of the incoming pony and rider. The express rider was seen to reach over, snap two saddle bags behind the light saddle of the fresh mount, hand the wrangler a small package and giving a slight twist he was in the saddle of the fresh mount. With a wave of the hand he disappeared around the point, into the west, over a cut-off which was considered too narrow for the cumbersome stages, which must go miles around to reach Salt Lake City.

The mochila was held in place by the rider sitting on it. It had four pockets called cantinas, one in each corner, so that two pockets were in the front of the rider's legs and two in the back. The cantinas were locked; three of them could be opened only at the military forts and the fourth

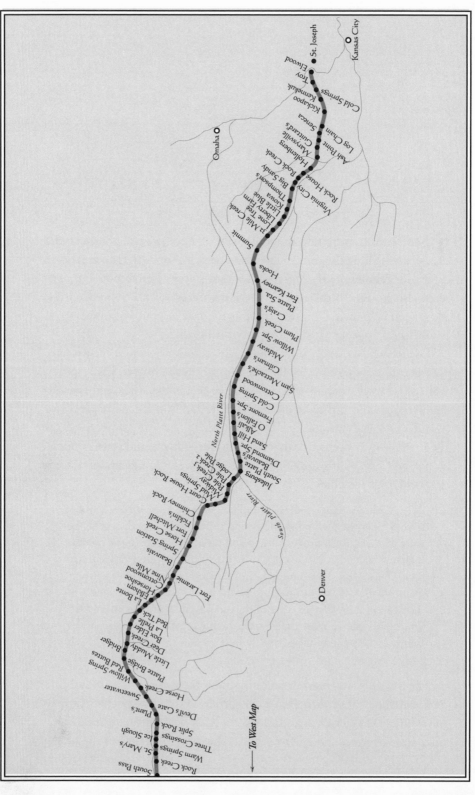

Pony Express stations (eastern half)

To East Map →

Big Sandy
Little Sandy
Dry Sandy
Pacific Spr.
Big Bend
Green River
Michael Martin's
Hams Fork
Church Buttes
Millersville
Fort Bridger
Muddy Creek
Quaking Asp
Bear River
Needle Rock
Echo
Halfway
Hanging Rock
Weber
Heneferville
Dixie
Weaton Spr.
Salt Lake City
Mtn. Dell
Travelers Rest
Rockwell's
Joe's Dugout
Fort Critenden
Faust's
Pt. Lookout
Pass
Simpson's Spr.
River Bed
Dug Way
Black Rock
Fish Spr.
Boyd's
Willow Spr.
Willow Creek
Canyon
Deep Creek
Prairie Gate
Antelope Spr.
Spring Valley
Schell Creek
Egan
Butte
Mountain Spr.
Ruby Valley
Jacob's Well
Diamond Spr.
Sulphur Spr.
Roberts Creek
Camp Station
Dry Creek
Cape Horn
Simpson's Park
Reese River
Mt. Airy
Smith's Creek
Castle Rock
Edward's Cr.
Cold Spr.
Middle Cr.
Fairview
Mountain Well
Stillwater
Old River
Busby's
Nevada
Ragtown
Desert Well
Miller's
Dayton
Carson
Genoa
Friday's
Fountain Place
Yank's
Lake Tahoe
Strawberry
Webster's
Moss
Sportsman's Hall
Placerville
Pleasant Grove House
Folsom
Mills
Sacramento
San Francisco

Green River
Great Salt Lake
Humboldt River

N E S W

Pony Express stations (western half)

Pony Express rider switching horses and mochila at a relay station. The time allowed at each station was about three minutes. —Courtesy Wyoming Division of Cultural Resources

by the station keepers. The fourth pocket held a time card on which the station keepers would record the time a rider arrived to change horses.

For the first few weeks of the service, riders carried a rifle as well as a pistol. However, it soon became apparent that rifles were too heavy and awkward to be practical, so the riders stopped carrying them. Some riders carried horns to signal the relay station of their approach, and in hot, dry areas a canteen of water was also standard equipment.

There is no record of the exact number of stations along the Pony Express route, but historians estimate that there were about 190. Many of them had colorful names such as Log Chain, Big Sandy, Plum Creek, Mud Spring, and Chimney Rock. The station keeper had complete responsibility for the facility. Not only did he have to supervise the care of the livestock and the maintenance of the station, he also had to order supplies, be certain that a change horse was saddled and ready for the incoming rider, and keep an accurate record of the rider's arrival and departure time. Working at one of the remote stations, often in hostile territory, was a lonesome and dangerous occupation. One could never be certain whether approaching hoofbeats signaled a Pony Express rider, bandits, or hostile Indians.

The leather mochila, with its four pockets, or cantinas, for mail, fit snugly over the saddle. Only one mochila was lost during the entire operation of the Pony Express service. —Courtesy St. Joseph Museum

The distance between stations, determined by the distance a good horse could run at a full gallop over that particular terrain, was usually ten to fifteen miles. In flat country, where the trail was not difficult, stations were farther apart; in the mountains, they were closer together. Stations were built even where grass and water were not readily available. Some of the worst locations in terms of natural resources and vulnerability to Indian attack were between Salt Lake City, Utah, and Carson City, Nevada. It took brave men to live and work in these isolated, indefensible cabins. Most of the stations could be easily overrun by fewer than a dozen warriors, and in several instances the mutilated bodies of station keepers were tragic evidence of that fact.

All but the best stations had dirt floors. Glass windows were unknown, and the furniture often consisted of empty wooden crates. Food at the smaller stations was little more than sufficient to keep the workers from starvation: cured meats, dried fruit, flour for bread baked in an open fire, molasses, pickles, coffee, and cornmeal.

Patee House, a luxurious hotel in St. Joseph, was the headquarters for the Pony Express organization. —Courtesy Patee House Museum

The home stations were much bigger, with extra sleeping quarters for a couple of riders. Here a rider could eat at a more leisurely pace, chat with the station keeper and his assistants, and above all get a good rest in preparation for his next demanding trip. Runs were usually about seventy to one hundred miles long, during which the rider changed horses from four to seven times. Like relay stations, home stations had horse stalls and a corral. When the rider arrived at a home station, he removed the mochila from his horse and threw it over the saddle of the fresh horse, and the new rider would leap into the saddle and be off.

The home station in St. Joseph, Missouri was comprised of two locations. The horses were housed at Pike's Peak Stables, at Ninth Street and Mitchell Avenue. The riders stayed a few blocks away, at the luxurious Patee House hotel, which housed the Central Overland California & Pike's Peak Express Company headquarters. Pike's Peak Stables had been built in 1858 by a successful businessman named Ben Holladay. Knowing Alexander Majors's reputation for honesty and integrity, Holladay lent the company the building to help launch their exciting project. This home station was most commonly referred to as St. Joseph, but it may also have been called Patee House or Pike's Peak Station.

Traveling west, the next home station was in Seneca, Kansas, about eighty miles from St. Joseph. Other home stations included Big Sandy in Nebraska; Three Crossings in Wyoming; Salt Lake Station in Salt Lake City; Buckland's and Friday's Stations in Nevada; Sportsman's Hall in California, with its comfortable beds, warm bath, and excellent dining room; and finally, Sacramento, normally the last Pony stop.

Home stations were established along the route about every seventy-five miles. The exact placement was determined by the terrain and, where possible, by the availability of an already established facility, such as a fort or a stagecoach stop. The company had to build many of the home stations, as well as relay stations, from scratch, especially in western Utah and Nevada.

Taking the ferry from St. Joseph, the westbound Pony rider landed at Elwood, Kansas, in the lowlands below the bluffs bordering each side of the Missouri. There is a question as to whether a Pony Express relay station existed there. The westbound courier from St. Joseph always started his run during the day, as the ferry service did not run after dark. So what did eastbound riders do if they arrived in Elwood at a very late hour? It is speculated that there was a livery stable there. When a rider arrived after dark, he would leave his horse at the livery stable and row the mail across the Old Muddy to deliver the mochila to St. Joseph. Technically, then, since the rider did not change horses there, the Elwood facility would not qualify as a relay station. At best, it could be considered a "one-way" station.

Once in Elwood, the westbound rider rode about five miles through thick forests to the little town of Wathena. Right outside of Wathena, the trail split into southern and northern branches. The southern branch is believed to be the one used during the early months of the Pony Express service. Part of the long-established Pottawatomie Trail and frequently used by pioneers headed for California and Oregon, the southern route required a ford of Peters Creek, which posed the first dangerous crossing for the Pony rider.

The southern trail had a relay station at Cottonwood Springs (possibly also called Thompson's Ranch), in Brown County, Kansas. Although practically nothing is known about the employees and the structure of the Cottonwood Springs Station, local residents claim that a portion of the original station was incorporated in a house that was later built on the site. That house is still standing, a few miles southeast of Troy.

When the Pony Express started, Russell, Majors & Waddell, probably represented by division supervisor A. E. Lewis, asked hotel owner

Leonard Smith to construct a relay station adjacent to his hotel in Troy. The station consisted of a barn housing five horses. Once it was finished, Cottonwood Springs Station was closed and riders took the northern route to Troy.

Headed to Troy Station, the Pony rider passed a popular lodging place, Thompson's Ranch (because of its proximity to both Troy Station and Cottonwood Springs Station, its name was sometimes applied to the stations). Troy itself was a small community, picturesquely situated on the crest of a hill and consisting of a blacksmith shop, a few grocery stores, and of course, several saloons.

There is an old Pony Express tale that seems to have originated in Troy. Rider Johnny Frye had a number of relatives in the town and apparently a number of girlfriends. As Frye raced through town on his run, two local sisters named Dooley stood by to hand him pieces of cake. After a little experimentation, the young ladies decided that putting holes in the center of the pastries would make it a lot easier for Frye to hold on to them. This, supposedly, was the birth of the American doughnut.

Just west of Troy, the north and the south forks of the trail merged and the rider headed over rolling hills to Cold Springs Station, also referred to as Lewis or Syracuse Station. Again we run into some disagreement among historians as this station is sometimes not included in the list of relay stations. Cold Springs Station (not to be confused with Cold Springs Station in Wyoming or Nevada) was a small, crude cabin in which a woman and her family lived. She cooked meals, her two daughters served them, and her two sons tended the stock. Located in the small town of Syracuse, long since vanished, the structure was described disparagingly by Sir Richard Burton as "a log-hut, which ignored the duster and the broom."

The road to the next relay station, Kennekuk, headed southwest for a while. It was broad and well marked, so the rider could make good speed, even in the dark of night. At this point we must pause to consider a bit of educated speculation concerning a change of route in the later period of the Pony Express. In March 1861, a contract between the government and the Overland Mail Company stated that the eastern terminus of the Pony Express service could be in either St. Joseph, Missouri, or Atchison, Kansas. According to Frank A. Root, who lived in Atchison at the time and worked as the assistant to the local postmaster, during the final weeks of the Pony Express most of the mail passed through the Atchison Post Office. If that was the case, Lancaster Station, ten miles west of Atchison, would have been a Pony Express station, and from there the rider would head for Kennekuk.

The settlement of Kennekuk, named in honor of a Kickapoo chief, was a relatively busy community, as a stagecoach trail and the military road from Leavenworth joined just a little east of town. At the height of its development in 1860, the town had a population of one hundred and boasted two hotels, a livery barn, a blacksmith shop, a post office, a couple of churches, a wagon shop, and a harness shop. It also housed the headquarters of the local Indian agent.

Tom Perry and his wife ran the Kennekuk Station and also served meals to travelers passing through town. Mrs. Perry was a fine enough cook to receive a laudatory remark from Mark Twain, who noted her delicious food and excellent coffee. It is unclear whether or not Kennekuk was a home station. While it certainly had the facilities to provide boarding for a rider, it was only about thirty-five miles from St. Joseph, along good roads most of the way. So Kennekuk was most likely a relay station. A Pony Express rider would spend only two or three minutes there, not enough time to enjoy a cup of Mrs. Perry's coffee, which is too bad, since it would have gone well with the doughnuts he picked up in Troy.

A fast and pleasant ride over more rolling hills and farms, wooded with walnut, elm, oak, and cottonwood, brought the speeding rider to Kickapoo Station, also known as Goteshell or Plum Creek Station, about twelve miles west of Horton, Kansas. The station, maintained by Kansas pioneer Noble Rising and W. W. Letson, was situated on a one-hundred-fifty-thousand-acre Kickapoo reservation. Rising's son, Dan, was a Pony Express rider on routes in Kansas and Nebraska.

Most authoratative sources list Log Chain Station, in Nemaha County, Kansas, as the next station west. Some historians claim that another station, Granada, existed between Kickapoo and Log Chain. But this is unlikely, as it would make the distance between relay stations far too close. Perhaps Granada was an alternate name for Log Chain. Those who cite it as a separate stop are presumably in error.

The small relay station of Log Chain sat nestled in a grove of beautiful elm, hickory, and walnut trees. Some historians think that it got its name from the many chains left scattered about after pulling wagons out of the muddy-bottomed Locknane Creek. Others believe Log Chain was merely a corruption of the name of the creek. The station was originally a large, twenty-four-by-forty-foot house and seventy-foot-long barn built by Noble Rising, the station keeper at Kickapoo. But a rider had no time to enjoy its amenities. A two-minute stop to change horses, perhaps a quick drink of water on a hot day, and he was off.

About eight hours after the first-leg westbound Pony rider left the St. Joseph ferry, perhaps hot or cold, undoubtedly hungry, thirsty, and bone tired, he arrived at the very welcome home station at Seneca, Kansas, seventy-seven miles west of St. Joseph. This little town on the Nemaha River consisted of a number of very well-constructed buildings, which the rider could spot from the top of a hill. Although Seneca is well documented as the first home station west of St. Joseph, verified by early Pony Express riders, later riders stated that they stayed at Guittard Station and Marysville as home stations. The Pony route went through a number of changes over time to adjust and refine it for maximum efficiency.

Seneca Station was part of a two-story hotel built in 1858 by John E. Smith. The hotel also served as a stagecoach station and was filled with guests almost every night. Pony riders enjoyed this home station not only for its comfortable accommodations, but also because Mrs. Smith was an excellent cook. One visitor to the hotel stated, in contrast to the description of Cold Springs Station, that the floors were kept clean enough to eat off of. The hotel was large, with many windows and a big porch surrounded by shade trees. Unlike most Pony stations, Seneca was a wonderful place to work, especially since it was also relatively safe from Indian attacks.

As the incoming rider came to a stop in front of the station, he passed the mochila to the new rider, who would take it along the next leg. While the first-leg rider settled in for a well-deserved rest, the new rider was racing to his first relay station, Ash Point, on the western edge of Nemaha County. It was a small station in the town of Ash Point, which was at the height of its prosperity in 1860, with a population of thirty. Founded by James Parsons and Josiah Blancett, the short-lived town included several homes, a general store, post office, and even a small hotel. John O'Laughlin (known as Uncle John), the proprietor of the general store, was also the Pony Express station keeper.

According to the writings of Sir Richard Burton, Ash Point was a place where "Hang-dog Indians were seen squatting, standing and stalking about." Luckily the rider's stay was limited to about two minutes. Not long after the termination of the Pony Express service, the little town disappeared.

About an hour later and twelve miles farther, the courier arrived at Vermilion Creek, on the Guittard Ranch in Marshall County, Kansas, the location of the Guittard relay and sometimes home station. Housed in George Guittard's spacious, two-story home, the station was one of the best known on this segment of the Pony Express Trail. Guittard was an emigrant from French-speaking Alsatia who moved his family to Kansas in 1858 to establish a ranch. His thirty-eight-by-forty-three-foot house had many windows and six large rooms, some of which he sometimes rented out. One of the rooms contained the hotel desk and also served as a stagecoach waiting room as well as a Pony Express station. Guittard's son Xavier was the station keeper. The adjacent barn was capable of housing twenty-four horses and held a fully equipped blacksmith shop.

Sir Richard Burton, who had passed through Guittard's ranch in August 1860, wrote that he saw his first Pony Express rider arrive there. He also described the house: "The house and kitchen [were] clean, the fences neat; the ham and eggs, the hot rolls and coffee were fresh and good. . . . The menu sometimes included roast chicken and beef. Fresh vegetables were also available at times."

Leaving Guittard Station, the young rider entered a changing landscape. The lush, rolling hills had now become a more desolate plain, with stone ledges appearing more frequently. The trail headed slightly northwest and brought the rider to the Big Blue River. On its banks sat the town of Marysville, also called Palmetto City. According to Sir Richard Burton, the town attracted a number of less-than-genteel citizens and thrived "by selling whiskey to ruffians of all descriptions." An emigrant described the town: "[T]he buildings [were] scattered in patches across the valley from the river bank to the bluffs. The buildings are all frame, with the single exception of a large two-story stone dwelling situated on the north-eastern extremity of the town."

The stone dwelling, built in 1859, was a combination home and livery stable and operated as the Pony Express station. Once again, historians disagree about the status of Marysville Station. Some believe it was used as a home station; if so, the riders would probably have stayed at the nearby American Hotel. Yet its closeness to the Seneca home station would suggest otherwise. Nevertheless, in 1931 a marker at the Marshall County Courthouse designated Marysville a home station.

After leaving Marysville, the Pony Express rider rode to the banks of the Big Blue River, where he would normally ford the two-and-a-half-foot-deep, fifty-foot-wide river. During flood conditions, however, the rider would avail himself of the services of Robert Shilbey, who operated a rope-drawn ferry, probably built by Frank Marshall. From there

An early artist's sketch of the Marysville Pony Express station
—Courtesy Kansas State Historical Society.

it was a ten-mile run to the next and last station in Kansas. The Pony courier raced along the west bank of the Little Blue River, heading almost due north. The river's grassy, cottonwood-lined banks were once a favorite grazing spot for thousands of buffalo. The rider knew that these would be the last trees he would see for a long while. Soon he rode into the Little Blue Valley, a treeless corridor about two miles wide with low bluffs on each side. Yet there was a pleasant stop just ahead, one of the best stations for hundreds of miles.

Hollenberg Station, sometimes called Cottonwood Station because it was near Cottonwood Creek, was a large, wooden farm-style building with a pointed shingled roof. It was built by G. H. Hollenberg, who left Germany in 1849 to seek his fortune. After traveling to California, Australia, Peru, and New York City, a doctor suggested he move west for his health. In 1854 he came to Kansas Territory and in 1857 constructed the building as a stagecoach stop and hotel. It was the first substantial structure in Washington County.

By 1860 Hollenberg had a thriving business, selling clothes, food, livestock, and feed to passing emigrants headed for Oregon, California, and Utah. A couple dozen people could be accommodated on the second floor of his building, and at times more than a hundred travelers

The Hollenberg Pony Express station was originally built as a stagecoach station. Today it is the only original and unaltered Pony Express station still standing. It is located in Hanover, Kansas. —Courtesy Kansas State Historical Society

were camped on his grounds. The ground floor of the house contained a small post office, a kitchen, a dining room, and a bedroom for the Hollenberg family. The place also had an enormous barn, capable of stabling a hundred horses, so in 1860 Pony Express division superintendent A. E. Lewis contracted with Hollenberg to use his facility as a home station. Riders and station keepers slept in its large attic, which ran the entire length of the building.

After Hollenberg Station, it was goodbye to comfort and civilization for the Pony Express rider. A quick seven-mile ride north took him out of Kansas and into the vast, treeless wilderness of the Platte Valley in the untamed territory of Nebraska, where the buffalo roamed and the Indians ruled. From this point on, the rider would have to call upon all his skill, stamina, speed, and courage in order to survive

Entering the southwest corner of Nebraska the rider traveled almost due north through Gage County, then headed northeast into Jefferson County, where he arrived at a small, isolated station called Rockhouse. The station was about three miles northeast of Steele City (a very loose use of the word *city*), where the Oketo Cutoff merged with the main emigrant trail. Thus it was sometimes called Oketo Station.

The next relay station in Nebraska was Rock Creek Station, also referred to as Pawnee, Turkey Creek, or Elkhorn Station, or the Lodi Post Office. Approximately six miles southeast of Fairbury, this relay station consisted of a few log cabins and a stable and corral for the horses. In 1859 David McCanles erected a toll bridge across Rock Creek and nearby built a large, sixteen-by-thirty-six log cabin with a big stone fireplace and a large attic. This was the structure used as a Pony Express station.

At one time the Rock Creek area had a wealth of animal life. Large herds of buffalo and wild horses were a common sight, and turkeys were everywhere. But in 1861, because of settlers' relentless hunting and trapping, the area had become a virtual wasteland, and it was difficult for the station keeper to get fresh meat. This little station, however, could lay claim to a bit of fame. It was here a young stock tender named James Butler Hickok, better known as Wild Bill Hickok, began his career as a gunfighter. His story is told in chapter 12.

The rider continued up the Platte Valley, changing horses at Virginia City Station, also called Grayson's or Whiskey Run Station, about four miles north of Fairbury. Then, on to Big Sandy, where Dan Patterson owned a house that operated as both a home station for Pony riders and an inn for weary stagecoach travelers. The station, about three miles east of Alexandria, might have been referred to as the Daniel Ranch or the Ed Farrell Ranch, but the most common name was Big Sandy Station. Later in 1860, Dan Patterson sold the station to Asa and John Latham, who continued to run it for the Pony Express.

As the trail again neared the Little Blue River, the rider changed horses at Millersville Station, also known as Thompson's Station because the station keeper was George B. Thompson. From there the hoofbeats kept pounding until pausing briefly at Kiowa Station, where Jim Douglas was in charge, about ten miles northwest of Hebron, Nebraska. About one mile east of the station, the trail arrived at the Little Blue and for a while followed its western bank, heading northwest.

According to some historians, the rider may have stopped at a station called Oak Grove. It was a small station, reportedly next to a general store owned by Russell, Majors & Waddell. The name of the station's manager, Al Holiday, is recorded in the 1861 mail contract. At that time there were a number of large ranches in the area, including the Roper, Emory, and Eubank Ranches, and E. S. Comstock's ranch, which went by the name Oak Grove Ranch. It is possible that Oak Grove may have been confused with Little Blue, a stagecoach station about four miles away.

The next stop, Liberty Farm, was a home station, right on the north bank of the Little Blue River, about half a mile northeast of Deweese, Nebraska. In 1860 James Lemmons ran the station; later, Chas Emory took over. Here the rider eagerly relinquished the mochila to his well-rested replacement.

There is disgreement about whether the next station, Spring Ranch (or Lone Tree), existed. If it did not, it would have meant a twenty-five-mile ride between Liberty Farm and the next recorded station, Thirty-Two Mile Creek, an unlikely scenario. In the early 1860s there was a small community called Spring Ranch with a nearby stage stop, which Sioux burned to the ground in August 1864. That building may have been the Pony Express station.

As the trail began to veer westward, approaching the great Platte River Valley, it was time to watch for Indians. About six miles southeast of Hastings, Nebraska, the lone rider could spot the long one-story building that was Thirty-Two Mile Creek Station, also called Dinner Station. Here he might pause for a cool drink of water and perhaps a few words with station keeper George A. Comstock and his family, then mount a fresh horse and be on his way. Not very far from the station was a trading post, to the great comfort of the inhabitants of Thirty-Two Mile Creek Station. The facility was abandoned during the fierce Indian raids of 1864.

In what was described as one of the loneliest places in Nebraska stood a small relay station known by any of five names: Summit, Sand Hill, Water Hole, Fairfield, or Gills. The first two were the most commonly used. About a mile and a half south of Kenesaw, on the crest of the divide between the Little Blue and Platte Rivers, the station's remote location made it an easy target for Indian war parties, who destroyed it in 1864. After Sand Hill the trail was covered with loose sand, making the going a little slow on horseback; wagons had to use double teams to get through it.

Next came Hooks Station, also known as Dogtown, Valley City, Kearney, or Hinshaw's Ranch, a home station. This was the end of Division One and the jurisdiction of A. E. Lewis, and the beginning of no-nonsense Jack Slade's territory. Slade was an appropriate match for the rugged country that lay ahead.

It is not certain, but most historians believe that from Hooks Station Pony Express riders made a routine stop at Fort Kearney, on the north bank of the Platte River. Fort Kearney was one of the few military camps dedicated to keeping the western trail safe for emigrants. Built in 1848, it consisted of a group of low buildings made of adobe with nearly flat roofs. In the center was a hospital tent, a few workshops, and a stable. Named in honor of Colonel Steven Watts Kearney, the fort saw few travelers at first. But during the great gold rush to California in 1849, thousands of emigrant wagons came through, and the tide did not cease—in 1861, eight hundred wagons and ten thousand oxen passed through the fort in one day. For Pony Express riders, a stop at the fort lasted only a few minutes. They probably stopped there for special mail deliveries and pickups. While Fort Kearney was most likely not an official Pony Express station, it is possible there was a station in Doby Town, two miles west.

The first station in Slade's division was Seventeen Mile, also known as Platte Station. In 1859 the Leavenworth & Pike's Peak Express Company had established a stagecoach station along the Platte River about five miles southeast of Odessa, Nebraska. In 1860, the Pony Express made this facility a relay station. The trail here was marked by chuckholes, which were a danger to galloping riders, especially at night.

About six miles southwest of Elm Creek, in Phelpe County, the rider came to Garden Station (perhaps called Craig's, Biddleman, or Shakespeare Station). A quick switch of the mochila and he was off to Plum Creek Station, a small log cabin near Fort McPherson, about ten miles southeast of Lexington. It was here that the famous chronicler Sir Richard Burton ate a buffalo steak for the first time; he found it distastefully dry. It was also here that fourteen settlers were killed during Indian raids. The Pony rider knew to keep his eyes sharp and his horse galloping through this stretch.

From there it was on to Willow Island (or Willow Bend or Willow Springs) Station, six miles southeast of Cozad, near the south end of the Platte River Bridge. This station consisted of a small adobe house, stables, and a store, which Sir Richard Burton said had a "drinking shop." Next came Midway, a home station three miles south of Gothenburg, Nebraska, on the Harry Williams Ranch in the heart of the Platte Valley. Its name came from its location, midway between Atchison, Kansas, and Denver, on the stage route. The station, sturdily built of heavy timber, was also referred to as Pat Mullay's Station, Smith's East Ranch, Cold Water Station, or Heavy Timber Station.

From Midway the new rider was off in a cloud of dust to Gilman's Station in Lincoln County, where in a flash the mochila was switched. Then it was up the Platte Valley and across a broad, hilly prairie with bluffs and trees on each side of the river. Soon he arrived at Sam Mattache's Station, also known as Dan Trout's or Joe Bower's Station,

The Midway Pony Express home station, near Gothenburg, Nebraska, in the heart of the Great Platte Valley. —Courtesy Nebraska State Historical Society

or Broken Ranch, or Fort McPherson—all these are names that have at one time or another been connected with this relay station.

An hour later the rider stopped at Cottonwood Springs, also known as McDonald's Ranch or simply Cottonwood, a two-story log cabin next to the springs of that name. The relay station was run by a one-legged man named Boyer. Boyer did a great deal of trading with the local Indians, who called him Hook-sah, which means "cut leg." Then a fifteen-mile trek took the rider around lagoons covered with flags and water rushes to Cold Spring relay station on Box Elder Creek. To the south towered a range of red clay buttes that rose to nearly perpendicular bluffs at the edge of the valley.

The next stop was a home station, Freemont Springs (also called Buffalo Ranch), near Hershey, Nebraska, on the south fork of the Platte River. Here the station keeper's wife was struggling to raise a flock of chickens. The station's construction was unique in the area—a beamed roof connected two hulls, forming a veranda, the coolest part of the house.

The new rider's first stop was O'Fallon's Bluff (or just O'Fallon's), where a sign notified weary travelers that they were now four hundred miles west of St. Joseph, Missouri—which meant there were still fifteen

Cottonwood Springs Pony Express station in Nebraska. There was also a Cottonwood Springs Station in Kansas and a Cottonwood Station in Wyoming.
—Courtesy Nebraska State Historical Society

hundred miles of Pony Express Trail ahead. Officially called Dansey's Station, but sometimes referred to as Elkhorn or Halfway House, O'Fallon's Bluff Station was in a remote area near Sutherland, Nebraska. It was known as the best place between the Missouri River and the Rocky Mountains for ambushing Indians to hide.

Heading southwest, the rider stopped at Alkali Lake Station (sometimes called Pike's Peak Station), about two miles southwest of Paxton. Its location would suggest that it was a relay station, but it may have operated for a while as a home station. Then it was on to Sand Hill, or Gill's as it was also called, near Ogallala, for a quick switch of horses, and off again on an hour's ride to Diamond Springs, on the south fork of the Platte River, about a mile west of Brule. Here again there is some controversy as to whether Diamond Springs was a home station, or whether Beauvai's Ranch, which had several sturdy cabins, was the home station. But there is little evidence to support the theory that Beauvai's Ranch, at the famous South Platte River crossing called Fort Laramie Crossing, Upper Ash Hollow Crossing, or California Crossing, was a Pony station at all.

The new courier soon entered Colorado, the most mountainous part of the trail. A wildly scenic area dotted by twenty-four hundred lakes, it was also a land where the burning heat could quickly disable a fatigued rider or a sudden blizzard freeze him to death. There were only two Pony Express stations in Colorado. The first one was Frontz's, or South

California Crossing on the South Platte River. (Painting by W. H. Jackson) —Courtesy Scotts Bluff National Monument

Platte Station, also referred to as Butte Station, just west of what is today the state line. Little is known about Frontz's Station, but the second station in Colorado, Julesburg, was among the most famous stations on the entire trail.

The rowdy town of Julesburg, about a mile and a half southeast of Ovid, Colorado, was just a group of rugged shacks interspersed with saloons. It was named for its founder, Jules Reni, a hard-drinking French-Canadian fur trapper, who established it in 1859 as a trading post. Because it was so far from civilization and its laws, Julesburg became a favorite hangout for outlaws and other shady characters. When the Central Overland California & Pike's Peak Express Company made the settlement a stage and Pony stop, "Old Jules" became the station keeper, but was shortly replaced by a man named George Chrisman. Julesburg served as a home station.

From Julesburg, the rider headed northwest, out of Colorado and through the western end of Nebraska, making a quick change of horses at Nine Mile Station (also Lodge Pole), two miles southeast of Chappell, Nebraska. He changed again at Pole Creek Number 2 Station, near the settlement of Lodgepole, and then at Pole Creek Number 3. This station was not much more than a large hole dug in the side of a hill, with a crude wood facade. There were two bunk beds for the station attendants, a couple of boxes for chairs, a tin washbasin, a water pail, and a single public towel.

The location of the station called Midway (not to be confused with Pat Mullay's Midway) is a mystery, but it is presumed to have been about three and a half miles south and one mile west of Gurley, Nebraska. In fact, its very existence is uncertain. Other historical sources refer to a station called Thirty Mile Ridge. Perhaps these are the same station.

There are no such questions concerning the next stop, Mud Springs Station, a place not much more inviting than Pole Creek Number 3. Though it was a home station, it was just a sod shack with no extra sleeping accommodations; when Sir Richard Burton stopped there for the night, his bedroom was a large wooden box. Mud Springs was also vulnerable to Indian attacks. In 1865 it was the site of a fierce battle between the U.S. Army and a large Indian war party. The station, run by James McArdle, later served as an early telegraph office.

The next two stations were at well-known landmarks, Courthouse Rock and Chimney Rock. One historic map shows a station between these two, called Junction, but there is no supporting evidence for its existence. Maintaining a full gallop, the rider continued to Ficklin's Springs, or Ficklin's Station (also known as Ash Hollow), named after the general superintendent, then on to Scotts Bluff (Fort Mitchell), a home station.

The first station the relief rider encountered was the last station in Nebraska, Horse Creek, on the west bank of the creek of that name, two miles east of Lyman. An hour's ride brought the rider to the first station in Wyoming, where the trail would climb a steady grade for over 350 miles, through thick forests, plunging ravines, and vast plateaus seven thousand feet above sea level. Here, in the deadly frost of winter, a ravenous pack of wolves could run down a rider and quickly tear him and his horse to pieces.

A grueling fifteen-mile ride brought the rider to Cold Springs Station (also Spring, Spring Ranch, Torrington, or Junction House), about two miles southeast of Torrington. A quick change of horses and he was off for Bordeaux (or Beauvais), about ten miles west. As he approached the sky-scraping Laramie Mountains, in the middle of utter wilderness there suddenly appeared, at an elevation of 4,230 feet, Fort Laramie. Though it wasn't a home station, it was still a very welcome sight.

The fort stood near the Laramie River. It was a large log cabin, 180 feet by 120 feet, with 11-foot-high walls and two towers. Both river and fort were named for French trapper Jacques La Ramee, who in 1818 established a permanent camp on the site. In 1836 the American Fur Company built a large adobe trading post, which was called Fort John. The fort contained many buildings within its four-foot thick walls, including an office, a general store, a warehouse, a meat house, a smithy, a carpentry shop, a large kitchen, and living quarters. It was like an enclosed small town in the wilderness.

Weary emigrants and other travelers were glad to reach Fort Laramie— it was a place to rest, get a good meal, make repairs, and replenish supplies. Here, one could buy steel beaver traps from England, mirrors from Germany, colored beads from Italy, calico cloth from France, gunpowder from Delaware, and the famous Hawken plains rifles from St. Louis,

Tens of thousands of pioneers on their way to Oregon, California, and Utah stopped at Fort Laramie to rest and buy supplies. For the Pony Express rider, the fort provided a sense of security in the middle of a vast wilderness. Although it was quite comfortable, it operated merely as a relay station for the Pony Express. (Painting by W. H. Jackson) —Courtesy Scotts Bluff National Monument

Sutler's Store at Fort Laramie offered an abundant array of goods to frontier travelers. —Courtesy Fort Laramie National Park Site

as well as food and whiskey. But prices were very high: sugar cost $2 per cup and five-cent tobacco went for $1.50.

In 1849 the U.S. government bought Fort Laramie to use as a military outpost to protect travelers on the great trail west. Ironically, the presence of the army led to greater unrest in the area, which continued for more than two decades. This made the area a danger zone for the Pony rider.

After Fort Laramie, the rider stopped at Nine Mile Station (aka Sand Point, Ward's, or Central Star), then rode on to Cottonwood (or Cottonwood Creek), splashing across the creek's icy waters. The last stop in Division Two was a home station, Horseshoe Station. The station keeper here was the division superintendent himself, notorious gunslinger Jack Slade, along with his wife, Molly, and their children. It is likely that Horseshoe Station had little trouble with bandits.

The first stop in Division Three, which comprised perhaps forty-six stations supervised by J. E. Bromley, was Elkhorn Station. While nothing to write home about, Elkhorn was better than the next station, La Bonte, where the station keepers lived in a dried-brush enclosure. On the way to the next station the rider had to ford two streams, La Bonte Creek and Wagonhound Creek. Historical records are vague about the next three stations. Did the rider stop at a place called Bed Tick Station? Who really knows? The same goes for La Prele (or Lapierelle) Station and Box Elder Station.

Along the rugged mountain trail the Pony Express courier rode, the Medicine Bow Mountains to the south; ahead of him lay the Deer Creek Range and the Haystack Range, both of which he had to cross, sometimes in a swirling snowstorm. After the previous stations, Deer Creek Station must have felt like a metropolis. There was the office of the Indian agent, Major Twiss, as well as a store, a saloon, and a post office. Deer Creek may have been a home station.

Ten rough miles brought the rider to Little Muddy (also called Glen Rock) Station, built of stone without mortar. Next came a stop at Bridger Station, then it was off to Platte Bridge (or North Platte, or Casper) Station, a well-made structure built in 1859 at a then astounding cost of $40,000. It is unclear whether or not this was a home station, but because of its proximity to Deer Creek and Willow Spring, it was probably just a relay station. After Platte Bridge, the rider crossed the North Platte River and rode toward the Rattlesnake Range, which topped eight thousand feet in elevation, arriving about an hour later at Red Butte Station, which was also probably a relay station. Sir Richard Burton described the terrain:

> After ten miles of severe ups and downs, which, by the bye, nearly brought our consort, the official's wagon, to grief, we halted for a few minutes at an old-established trading-post, called "Red Buttes." The feature from which it derives its name lies on the right bank of, and about five miles distant from, the river, which here cuts its way through a ridge. These bluffs are a fine bold formation, escarpment of ruddy argillaceous sandstone, and shells, which dip toward the west; they are the eastern wall of the mass that hems in the stream, and rear high above it their conical heads and fantastic figures.

At Willow Spring Station, by a narrow stream about two feet wide and ten inches deep, in an area destitute of timber, a new rider took over. From there the trail became a very steep climb, and the pony had to work very hard to maintain speed. After a quick change of horses at Horse Creek, it was on to Sweetwater (also called Independence Rock) Station, which was no more than shack with a bunk and a horse shed with no corral. It was abandoned in mid-1860 in favor of a better location, possibly Devil's Gate. The Pony Express Trail did not go through the famous landmark of Devil's Gate, a rocky channel impassable on horseback.

After Devil's Gate was Plant's Station, then, in a curious twist of names, came Split Rock, operated by a French Canadian named Plante.

Sir Richard Burton gives a most colorful description of Split Rock Station and its surroundings:

> After fording the swift Pina Pa, at that point about seventy feet wide and deep to the axles, we ran along its valley about six miles, and reached at 9:15 P.M. the muddy station kept by M. Plante, the usual Canadian. En route we had passed by the Devils Gate, one of the great curiosities of this line of travel. . . . We supped badly [at the station]. . . . [A] very plain young person, and not neat . . . supplied us with a cock whose toughness claimed for it the honors of grand paternity. Chickens and eggs there were none; butcher's meat, of course, was unknown, and our hosts ignored the name of tea; their salt was a kind of saleratus, and their sugar at least half Indian meal. When asked about fish, they said that the Sweetwater contained nothing but suckers, and that these, though good eating, cannot be caught with a hook. . . . [A]fter a look at the supper, which had all the effect of a copious feed, I found a kind of outhouse, and smoked till sleep weighed down my eyelids. . . .
>
> The breakfast was a little picture of supper; for watered milk, half baked bread and unrecognizable butter, we paid the somewhat "steep" sum of $0.75.

After Split Rock the rider ended his run at Three Crossings, the home station of a young rider named William F. Cody, better known as Buffalo Bill. The site was so named because the Sweetwater River made such sharp turns here that a rider heading east or west had to cross it three times. The station was nestled near the Sweetwater River, with the Gas Hills to the north and the Green Mountains to the south. The station keepers were a Mormon couple named Moore, who ended their journey to Utah upon learning that the men in Salt Lake City had more than one wife. Moore and his wife, who was an excellent cook and a spotless housekeeper, simply settled where they were, at Three Crossings.

Hoofbeats resonated on the barren plain as the next rider came into Ice Slough (or Ice Springs) Station. Not far from the station was a bog, where black, sulfurous water oozed up from the ground. Just below the surface lay an eighteen-inch layer of ice from which clear, delicious water could be drawn. After a few words to the station keeper the courier was off on an hour's ride to Warm Springs Station, not far from Sulphur Creek, which races down from the Antelope Hills.

Presumably the Pony rider knew where the next station, St. Mary's (or Rocky Bridge, or Foot of the Ridge) was, but historians are uncertain. It may have been between Warm Springs and Rock Creek, or between Rock Creek and South Pass. In any case, the rider had good

Three Crossings Station, on the Sweetwater River in Wyoming
—Courtesy St. Joseph Museum

reason to want to reach St. Mary's because it may have been a home station. William Ried ran this station, which was not, in the opinion of Sir Richard Burton, the most appealing place: "[T]he station rather added to than took from our discomfort: it was a terrible, unclean hole, milk was not procurable within thirty-five miles; . . . there was no sugar and the cooking was atrocious."

After a hard ride, any meal was better than none, no doubt, and a crude, grimy bed was better than a saddle. In any case, the rider's home station may not have been at St. Mary's, anyway, but at Rock Creek, about which there is almost no information.

Traveling on a barely perceptible but ever-rising slope, the rider soon reached one of the most famous landmarks in the West, South Pass, the halfway point on the Oregon Trail. South Pass Station, on the Continental Divide, was also known as Upper Sweetwater Station or Burnt Ranch. The first Pony Express station west of the Great Divide was Pacific Springs, another facility Burton found less than luxurious:

The shanty was perhaps a trifle more uncomfortable than the average; our only seat was a kind of trestled plank, which suggested a certain obsolete military punishment, called riding on a rail. . . . The night was, like the day, loud and windy, the log hut being somewhat crannied and creviced, and the door had a porcelain handle, and a shocking bad fit—a characteristic combination. We had some trouble to keep ourselves warm.

Luckily for the rider, Pacific Springs was just a relay station. After a two-minute stop at Dry Sandy, which was run by a Mormon couple, the courier was off to Little Sandy, near a creek by the same name. The keepers there were an English couple, also Mormon. Next it was Big Sandy Station, then an hour's ride southwest to a small station just east of Slate Creek, which went by one of three names, Big Timber, Big Bend, or Simpson's Hollow.

Soon the rider was on his way to one of the most famous rivers in the Rocky Mountains, the Green River, a favorite rendezvous spot for mountain men in the early 1800s. During the dry season, the river could fall to a depth of three feet. But after heavy rains, its swiftly running waters were crossable only by ferry. The ferry, which Pony riders used along

The Green River, in southwestern Wyoming, ca. 1907
—Courtesy Wyoming Division of Cultural Resources

with emigrants, was not much safer than fording the river, as pioneer James Wilkins testified:

> Some Mormons have established a ferry here, a very unsafe flat boat, a heavy wagon comes near sinking it, for which they charge $4 per wagon, but there is no help for it. We passed the ferry for a miracle without accident, as a more crazy thing to call a boat I never saw. It required one man to bail all the time, while another at every trip kept stuffing in bits of rag.

Green River Station was a comfortable home station where three English women served good home cooking. Once again, we have a description from Burton:

> The station was the home of Mr. Macarthy, our driver. . . . The station had the indescribable scent of a Hindu village, which appears to be the result from the burning of bois de vache and the presence of cattle: there were sheep, horses, mules, and a few cows, the latter so lively that it was impossible to milk them. The ground about had the effect of an oasis in the sterile waste. . . . We supped comfortable at Green River Station, the stream supplying excellent salmon-trout. The Kichimichi, or buffalo-berry, makes tolerable jelly, and alongside of the station is a store where Mr. Burton (of Maine) sells "Valley Tan" whiskey.

There is little accurate supporting information about the nine stations after Green River. They are all officially listed as relay stations, but this would represent an awfully long distance without a home station. One of them must have been a home station, perhaps Muddy Creek.

Riding about ten miles southwest brought the new rider to Michael Martin's Station, then it was on to Ham's Fork. A Scottish Mormon named David Lewis ran Ham's Fork Station, where he lived with his two wives and their children. The next relay station was Church Buttes, near the dramatic land formation of that name, said to resemble a Gothic cathedral. Farther down the trail was Millersville, named in honor of A. B. Miller, a partner in the firm of Russell, Majors & Waddell. The relay station there was part of a trading post run by a man named Holmes.

After Millersville the rider headed toward the southwest corner of Wyoming, to the station at Fort Bridger. Fort Bridger was the second of two forts built by the famous trailblazer Jim Bridger in 1844, and it tended to disappoint those who saw it for the first time. Built of rough logs covered with sun-baked mud, it provided the barest of living conditions. Emigrant Joel Palmer offered an excellent firsthand description of the fort:

It is built of poles and daubed with mud; it is a shabby concern. Here are about twenty-five lodges of Indians, or rather white trappers' lodges occupied by their Indian wives. They have a good supply of robes, dressed deer, elk and antelope skins, coats, pants, moccasins, and other Indian fixens, which they trade low for flour, pork, powder, lead, blankets, butcher-knives, spirits, hats, ready made clothes, coffee, sugar, etc. . . . Their wives are mostly of the Pyentes and Snake Indians. They have a herd of cattle, twenty-five or thirty goats and some sheep. They generally abandon this fort during the winter months.

By 1860 conditions at Fort Bridger had improved somewhat, but not much. It probably didn't matter to the Pony riders, as it was only a relay stop.

Nearing the end of the trail in Wyoming, the rider made brief stops at Muddy Creek Station, which a French Canadian operated with his wife; Quaking Asp (also Aspen or Spring Station); and the last relay station in the Rockies, Bear River, about eighty miles east of Salt Lake City. A man named Myers ran Bear River Station along with his fifth wife and a helper named Briggs. From there the Pony Express Trail went "downhill" from the Rockies, into the bleak, vast, burning deserts of Utah and, soon, Nevada. It was a totally unforgiving land, where many a frontiersman met his end from Indians or nature's ravages.

— 11 —

STATION TO STATION:
UTAH, NEVADA, AND CALIFORNIA

I N UTAH, ABOUT twenty-six Pony stations spanned a distance of 275 rugged miles. Bringing the mail through this desolate region at high speed was not a task for the fainthearted. The mountain passes could be choked with fifteen-foot snowdrifts in winter, and the desert expanses could simmer at temperatures in excess of 110 degrees, with no water for miles around.

The Pony rider was now headed southwest, just north of the Uinta Mountains, the only major range in the United States that runs east and west, a mighty fortress with five of its snowy peaks soaring above thirteen thousand feet. The trail through Utah and Nevada Territories presented a grave challenge to even the sturdiest rider, especially during the early months of the service, before all the stations were in place. At that time, some of the riders—and their ponies—had to make extraordinary rides, such as George Washington Perkins, who described his first run:

> My run on that record breaking ride was 57 miles. We did not have stations then to change our horses. I had to make it with just one horse and I made the run in mighty good time considering the distance, but I killed the poor horse doing it. He was so stiff the next morning we couldn't get him out of the stable. For later runs I had a change of mounts every six or eight miles.

Threading his way through the six-hundred-foot-high hills for about eight miles, the Pony Express rider arrived at the first station in Utah Territory, Needle Rock (aka the Needles), just west of Yellow Creek. This portion of the trail had quite a history: the ill-fated Donner-Reed party used it in 1846, then the Mormon pioneers in 1847, and finally General Johnston's army took this route in 1857 when he attempted to subdue the Mormon establishment in Salt Lake.

Zigzagging through the hills for eight more miles, the rider arrived at the home station, Head of Echo Canyon Station. Echo Canyon was

The Uinta Mountains —Courtesy Wyoming Division of Cultural Resources

so named because of the reverberations that bounced off its red rock walls. The station was a primitive log cabin run by a Frenchman, thus its other name, Frenchie's. Nearby was a unique sandstone formation thought to resemble a castle, so some of the riders referred to the station as Castle Rock. About midway between Head of Echo Canyon and the next station, Halfway Station, was a large cave, called Cache Cave, which may have been used as an emergency stop, perhaps during unusually severe storms.

Seven miles past Echo Canyon was Halfway Station (also called Daniels or Emery Station). For a while the station keeper, a man named Daniels, was having a great deal of trouble with horse thieves stealing the stock. The thieves even had the audacity to sell the horses back to the Pony Express Company. Daniels finally put a stop to it by branding the horses with an XP (for express).

Now the rider was traveling in canyons bordered by six-thousand-foot mountains, which could cause snow to pile up during winter storms and effectively trapped the heat in the summer. Weber Station (also known as Bromley's, Echo, Pulpit Rock, or Hanging Rock), about ten miles west of Halfway Station, was built by division superintendent James

This early photograph of the Head of Echo Canyon Pony Express Station (Frenchie's) in Utah was taken by A. J. Russell in 1868. —Courtesy Al Mulder, Utah Crossroads

Weber Pony Express Station, built by division superintendent James E. Bromley, appears on the extreme right of the photograph. —Courtesy David C. Bagley

E. Bromley in 1854. Bromley used this station as a headquarters from which he operated his division; he also acted as station keeper. It was a relatively large, stone structure containing a general store, an inn, a saloon, a blacksmith shop, and a jail. The station also acted as a supply depot, growing vegetables and storing locally grown wild hay. Yet it was just a relay stop for the riders.

After leaving Weber Station, the Pony rider crossed the Weber River at Forney's Bridge, built in 1858. The rider then began a steep climb up Bachelor's Canyon to the top of Dixie Hollow. But there were times when, because of flooding or deep snowdrifts, Bachelor's Canyon was closed; the rider would then continue through the Weber Valley to the Brimville Emergency Station (also called Henneferville and possibly Carson House; it is possible that Carson House was a separate station after Brimville, though there is little evidence to support this). From Brimville the rider could usually make it safely through Little East Canyon to Dixie Hollow.

Snyder's Mill (or East Canyon) Station, also known by several other names. Some conflicting reports state that this station was a sturdy stone structure; the wooden front may have been added later. —Courtesy Oakland Museum of California

The next stop was East Canyon Station. This relay station may have been known by as many as *seven* other names: Dixie, Dixie Hollow, Dixie Creek, Bauchmann's, Big Mountain, Dutchmann's Flat, and Snyder's Mill. It stood by a creek just east of the nine-thousand-foot-tall Big Mountain. A man named James McDonald operated the station.

An eight-mile ride through barren, rocky terrain brought the rider to Weaton Springs (or Winston Springs, or Bauchmann's) Station, about which little is known except that it was surrounded by pine trees. Then it was another eight miles, riding north of Big Mountain, to Mountain Dale (or Dell) Station. This relay station was run by Ephrain Hanks, who was related to Nancy Hanks, the grandmother of Abraham Lincoln. Some historians believe the station was at Hanks's cabin along Freeze Creek, west of Little Mountain.

On the last, nine-mile leg of his run, the rider passed over Little Mountain, its face scarred with the wheel marks of thousands of emigrant wagons on their way to California. Past Donner Hill and Emigration Canyon, he could see the valley of the Great Salt Lake, where the comfortable home station in Salt Lake City awaited him.

It was a lucky rider who was assigned to this home station. East of Main Street between First and Second Streets South, the station had all the amenities of civilization. The beds were clean and the food was excellent, facts corroborated by Sir Richard Burton, Horace Greeley, and Mark Twain, who had been guests there. A. B. Miller was the station keeper.

Descending Little Mountain, the Pony Express rider could see the vast Salt Lake Valley, where he would find a comfortable home station in Salt Lake City. (Painting by W. H. Jackson) —Courtesy Scotts Bluff National Monument

After a fast nine-mile run due south along State Street, the fresh rider changed horses at Trader's Rest (or Traveler's Rest) Station, in present-day Murray, Utah. This was the first station in Howard Egan's division. Ten miles south of Trader's Rest came Rockwell's relay station at Hot Springs Brewery Hotel. Porter Rockwell, who had served as a personal bodyguard to Brigham Young in the 1830s, ran this station. In 1850 Rockwell was appointed territorial marshall, which certainly gave him excellent credentials for guaranteeing the security of the Pony Express station. There is some debate as to whether Rockwell was a station keeper or a special agent for the Pony Express. His assistant was a Mormon named Absalom Smith.

After Rockwell's, the land became extremely barren and barely livable. Water was so scarce that some stations had to have it brought in by pack mule. At Joe's Dugout (Joe Butcher's), operator Joe Dorton, having failed to find water after drilling a deep well, arranged to have water brought in from Utah Lake and sold for twenty-five cents a bucket. An industrious man, Dorton also ran a small grocery store that was frequented by soldiers from Camp Floyd. The station also included a two-room brick home, a log barn, and a small dugout where a young Indian helper lived—thus the station's name.

About eight miles southwest of Joe's, the rider made a quick stop at the Camp Floyd relay station. Contrary to its name, the Pony Express station may actually have been in Fairfield, adjacent to the fort, at John Carson's Inn, an adobe building built in 1858. Thus Camp Floyd Station was also referred to as Carson's Inn, Carson House, Cedar City, Fairfield, and Fort Crittenden. The fort's name was changed from Camp Floyd to Fort Crittenden when Secretary of War John B. Floyd joined the Confederacy.

With a relatively large population of four thousand, plus an additional three thousand soldiers at the fort, Fairfield was the third largest city in the territory, supporting seventeen saloons. At the start of the Civil War, the fort was abandoned and destroyed, and by September 1861 this formerly flourishing town harbored a mere eighteen families.

Ten miles west of Fairfield, the rider came to the bone-dry East Rush Valley Station (also called Pass, Five Mile Pass, and No Name Pass Station). About nine miles due west was Rush Valley (or Faust's, or Meady Creek) home station, which stood in an arid, flat, desolate landscape with not a single tree as far as the eye could see. Originally erected by George Chorpenning in 1858, this two-story but extremely small stone structure was later sold to Henry J. "Doc" Faust and used to raise horses for the Pony Express. Faust also served as the station keeper and lived on the land until 1870.

A surprising visitor to this dismal site was Horace Greeley, the famous *New York Tribune* editor. Knowing Greeley would want to spend his evening reading but wanting to converse with his famous visitor, Doc Faust kept all the candles hidden. According to some historians, however, this incident actually took place at Prairie Gate (Pleasant Valley) Station in Nevada.

The next westbound rider entered the worst part of the trail and the worst desert in North America, an area also known as "Paiute Hell." The country was mostly bare, rocky mountain ranges and countless miles of parched sand, with blinding dust storms and bewildering mirages in the brutal heat of summer. There were expanses where the choking alkali dirt was so thick it looked like snow.

The trail began to climb west of Rush Valley, leading up to the relay station at Point Lookout (also known as General Johnson's Pass or Jackson's Station), where the station keeper was a Mr. Jackson. The rider's view from the top of the lookout was not encouraging. Before him lay nothing but more scalding alkali wasteland.

The trail now skirted the south end of Scull Valley. The next possible station, Government Creek, is questionable. There is some circumstantial evidence that such a station existed about eight miles west of Point Lookout. It was another eight torturous miles to Simpson's Springs (also Egan's Springs, Pleasant Springs, or Lost Springs). Named after the Camp Floyd topographical engineer and trailblazer Captain James H. Simpson, this stone relay station enjoyed a rare amenity, good-quality water. After taking a quick refreshing drink from George Dewers, the station operator, the rider was on his way again, galloping southwest.

Eight more burning miles brought the courier to Riverbed Station, which, as its name implies, was built in a dry riverbed—an indication of how seldom it rained. It is interesting to note that it was very difficult for the Pony Express to keep station workers here, perhaps because of its remote location, or the strange sounds the wind made, or the mirages. Three former operators, William Hosiepool, Oscar Quinn, and George Wright, claimed they were afraid of the "desert fairies."

Desert fairies may have been more acceptable than the primitive conditions of Dugway Station, ten miles to the southwest. According to Horace Greeley, it was "about the forlornest spot I ever saw." The relay station was nothing more than a large hole dug into the side of a hill, with a wooden front door and an adobe chimney—not very defensible against Indian attack. Several wells had been drilled there, all in vain, so water had to be hauled in from Simpson's Springs. Historians are unsure

An early photograph of the Riverbed Pony Express station in Utah. It was difficult to keep station keepers here because they were terrified of the "desert fairies." —Courtesy David C. Bagley

as to the exact location of the next relay station, Black Rock, but it was about fourteen miles west of Dugway. After a quick change of horses, the hot, weary rider headed his horse southwest, along the Thomas Range, skirting the southern edge of the salt flats. Ten miles later he arrived at Fish Springs Station (or Fresh Springs, Smith's Springs, or Fish Creek). A man named Smith ran this home station, a true oasis in the desert. Here was a pool of clear water filled with sparkling minnows, where wild ducks and other waterfowl splashed.

As the incoming rider eased into his rest period, the replacement rider speeded due west. Depending on weather conditions, he either rode over the pass through the Fish Spring Range, a route of about nine miles, or took the fourteen-mile route around the mountains, to Boyd's Station. There, Bid Boyd, the station keeper, was waiting with a cup of water and a fresh horse. At this relay station, as at so many others in Utah and Nevada, living conditions bordered on the primitive. Part of the station was dug out of a hill, and the other walls were made of lava rock. The bunks were built into the walls and the furniture consisted of wooden boxes. Adding to this the dreary, isolated surroundings, life for the station workers—which included a station keeper, a blacksmith, and perhaps a spare rider—was monotonous at best, their simple routine broken for a few minutes each day by the passing riders.

With little time to chat, the rider hurried off on his appointed route. After a quick stop at Willow Springs Station in Caleo, eight miles north-west of Boyd's Station, it was a fast six miles northwest to Willow Creek Station. There is some question regarding the existence of this station, but Pony rider Nick Wilson spoke of it in his memoirs, as did Sir Richard Burton in his records. According to Burton, the station keeper there was an Irish Mormon named Pete Joyce.

The rider picked up another fresh horse at Canyon Station (or Burnt Station or Overland Canyon), another hole in the side of a hill with a log front. Then it was fourteen more hot, dusty miles through Overland Canyon to the end of his ride at Deep Creek (also called Ibapah or Egan's Station), the last stop in Utah. This most wonderful home station was a large brick house, home of division superintendent Howard Egan, who ran the station along with Harrison Sevier and Matthew Orr. It had a large barn and corral and produced hay, grain, beef, and mutton for other stations along the route.

The new rider may have glanced wistfully back at the comfortable station as he galloped away. Before him lay Nevada, more than 110,000 square miles of rugged, mostly uncharted wasteland. Its 420 miles of

Willow Springs Pony Express Station in Caleo, Utah —Courtesy David C. Bagley

The remains of Canyon Station (Burnt Station). The original station was burned down during an Indian raid; it was rebuilt with stones. —Courtesy David C. Bagley

An early photograph of Deep Creek Station, the last Pony Express station in Utah. It was a comfortable home station and residence of Major Howard Egan.
—Courtesy David C. Bagley

torturous, winding trails were filled with hiding places for ambushing bandits or hostile Utes and Bannock warriors. Here temperatures can range from a high of 122 degrees to a low of negative 50 degrees, and a lost soul could wander for a week without ever finding an inhabited outpost. Yet even here, the Pony Express courier was expected to carry the mail through—on schedule.

The rider headed roughly northwest across what would become the Goshute Indian Reservation. During the first few months of the Pony Express, this section of the run was a brutally long and dangerous one, since there was not a relay station until Antelope Springs, at least fifteen miles away. Later a station called Prairie Gate (or Pleasant Valley) was built about eight miles west of Deep Creek. Prairie Gate opened none too soon; Antelope Springs Station existed for only a couple of months before Paiute warriors burned it to the ground. Just northwest of Antelope Springs stood Spring Valley Station, whose keeper was either Constant Dubail or a man named Reynal. This station was used only during the last few months of the Pony Express service. It was here that rider Elijah N. "Uncle Nick" Wilson had a disastrous encounter with some Paiute warriors, described in chapter 13.

A section of the Pony Express Trail, leading to the Antelope Springs relay station in Nevada. This was a very dangerous portion of the trail when the Paiute War broke out in the spring of 1860. —Courtesy David C. Bagley

At the northern end of the Egan Mountains, the rider reached the home station at Schell Creek, also known as Fort Schellborne, which George Chorpenning and Howard Egan built in 1859. It acquired the title of "fort" when a cavalry company was stationed there to protect the trail after the Pyramid Lake massacre. In the summer of 1860, a fierce battle took place there between the soldiers and a Paiute war party. According to Sir Richard Burton, Francais de France Constant Dubail was the station keeper at the bullet-scarred log cabin.

For a few months, the first stop for the fresh rider was Egan, or Egan's Canyon, Station, established in the spring of 1860; but by October 5, 1860, when Burton saw the station, all that was left was part of a stone chimney, a few pieces of burnt wood, and evidence of buried bodies. Goshute war parties had attacked it repeatedly and killed several Pony Express personnel. Burton called the trail through Egan Canyon "vile."

In spite of the dangers, the Pony Express rider kept heading west until he reached Butte Station. This relay station, also known as Bates or Robber's Roost, was also burned during the Paiute war, but by October 1860 it had been rebuilt. An English Mormon identified only as

Thomas ran the two-room sandstone, wood, and mud structure. Burton described it thus:

> It is about as civilized as the Galway shanty, or the normal dwelling-place in Central Equatorial Africa. Outside the door—the hingeless and lockless backboard of a wagon bearing the wounds of bullets—and resting on lintels and staples, which also had formed parts of locomotives, a slab [acted as a] stepping-stone over a mass of soppy black soil strewed with ashes, gobs of meat offal, and other delicacies.
>
> The inside reflected the outside. The length was divided by two perpendiculars, the southernmost of which, assisted by a halfway canvass partition, cut the hut into unequal parts. Behind it were two bunks for four men; standing bedsteads of poles planted in the ground . . . and covered with piles of ragged blankets. The floor, which also frequently represented bedsteads, was rough, uneven earth, neither tamped nor swept, and the fine end of a spring oozing through the western wall kept part of it in a state of eternal mud. A redeeming point was the fire-place, which occupied half of the northern short hall; . . . its inglenooks boasted dimensions which one connects with an idea of hospitality and jollity. . . . There was no sign of Bible, Shakespeare, or Milton; a Holywell Street romance or two was the only attempt at literature.

The rider made a quick stop here to change horses, and another about an hour later, at Mountain Springs Station, in the Maverick Springs Mountains. Then, if the rider approached them at sunset, the Ruby Mountains would appear as deeply red as the jewel for which they were named. The Ruby Valley relay station was operated by William "Uncle Billy" Rogers and Frederick William Hurst. It had been one of George Chorpenning's mail stations in 1859. Unlike most of the rest of Nevada, Ruby Valley had rich soil, so the station was able to provide food and hay for other Pony Express stations. Because of the relatively lush surroundings, there was also a Shoshone camp as well as an army camp nearby.

Climbing up steep hillsides and winding through twisting canyons, the rider finally arrived at Jacob's Well Station in Huntington Valley. Named after General Frederick Jacobs and the well he dug here, this station was not open until October 1860. Before that, the rider had to continue for another strenuous hour until he reached Diamond Springs Station in the Diamond Mountains. William Cox, a Mormon, ran this station, which received its name from the nearby crystalline springs. The springs continue to flow to this day.

From there it was on to Sulphur Springs Station, more than fifteen miles west. Little is known about the original station, but in July 1861 a new station was built at Sulphur Springs. In a wink of an eye, the rider was off again, heading southwest through endless hills and across acres of desert in Indian territory. After perhaps as far as twenty miles, he reached the last station in Howard Egan's division, Roberts Creek. Built as a home station for the Pony Express in the spring of 1860, Roberts Creek Station was shortly thereafter attacked by warring Indians and burned. It was immediately, if only partially, rebuilt.

West of Roberts Creek Station, the Pony rider entered Bolivar Roberts's division. For the first fifteen months of the Pony Express, riders had to make an exhausting thirty-five-mile run from Roberts Creek to the next station, Dry Creek. But by July 1861, Camp, or Grub's Well, Station had been built halfway between the two. From there it was about seventeen southwesterly miles to Dry Creek Station. Also built specifically for the Pony Express in the spring of 1860, Dry Creek soon fell victim to the bloody Paiute war. Its keeper, Ralph Rosier, was killed and his partner, John Applegate, badly wounded. Their harrowing story was told in chapter 9. The new station keeper was known as Colonel Totten. Dry Creek probably served as a home station.

There is disagreement among historians about whether or not Cape Horn Station existed. If it did exist, it was only a relay station. The next relay station was Simpson's Park (named for Captain James H. Simpson), another small oasis in an otherwise barren land, with good water, plenty of trees, and lush grass. Unfortunately, barely two months after the station's construction, on May 20, 1860, Indians attacked it, killing station keeper James Alcott, scattering the livestock, and burning the structure to the ground. It took a while to rebuild; in the meantime, the Pony rider continued on.

The next station, Reese River, also known as Jacob's Spring or Jacobsville (for its keeper, George Washington Jacobs), was one of those George Chorpenning built in 1859. It too was put to the torch by warring Indians. It was later replaced with an adobe structure. Obviously, the Paiute war devastated the western portion of the Pony Express route. Nevertheless the riders kept going, with or without a place to change horses.

It was a long ride from Reese River to the home station at Smith's Creek. In the last few months of Pony service, another station, Dry Wells, aka Mount Airy, was constructed in the Shoshone Mountains, halfway in between. Smith's Creek home station, in the Desatoya Mountains, was, according to Sir Richard Burton, very comfortable, but it was not always peaceful. In addition to Indian attacks, there was frequent fighting among the workers. In one instance, station keeper H. Trumbo shot a rider named Montgomery Maze; fortunately, Maze survived. In an even more serious incident, William Carr got into a violent argument with fellow worker Bernard Chessy and afterward shot him dead. Officials hanged Carr in Carson City.

The new rider's first relay station may have been Castle Rock, if it in fact existed. The next was Edwards Creek, then Cold Springs home station, which Bolivar Roberts and J. G. Kelly built in March 1860. Several men ran this station, including Jim McNaughton and John Williams, along with Kelly. But no sooner had they started operation than a band of Paiute attacked, killed one of the men, and stole the horses. Two weeks later the Indians returned and finished the job, burning down the station. The Pony workers rebuilt the station, this time out of stone, putting gun holes in the structure's thick walls.

The next rider's first stop was a small station called Middlegate, or Middle Creek. There may have been another relay station, which some sources refer to as Westgate, following Middlegate. After that the trail split into a southern route, used during the first year, and a northern route, used in the final seven months of the Pony Express service. From Middlegate Station, a rider on the southern route headed only slightly southward then west, making the usual sharp turns around mountains, canyons, and the like, to Sand Springs relay station, operated by James

Alternate routes on Pony Express Trail between Middlegate and Miller's Stations in Nevada

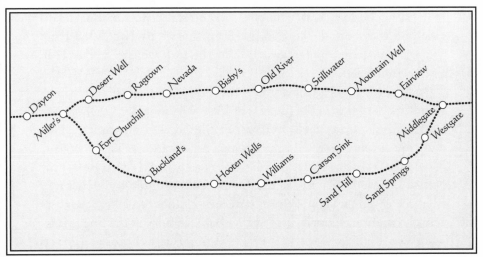

McNaughton. Burton described this station, too, in a less than favorable way:

> Sand Springs deserved its name . . . the land is cumbered here and there with drifted ridges of the finest sand, sometimes 200 feet high and shifting before every gale. Behind the house stood a mound shaped like the contents of an hour-glass. . . . The water near this vile hole was thick and stale with sulphury salts: it blistered even the hands. The station house was no unfit object in such a scene, roofless and chairless, filthy and squalid, with a smoky fire in one corner, and a table in the centre of an impure floor, the walls open to every wind, and the interior full of dust. Of the employes, all loitered and sauntered about . . . except one, who lay on the ground crippled and apparently dying by the fall of a horse upon his breast bone.

After a blessedly quick stop at Sand Springs, the southern-route rider was off to Sand Hill to change horses. Another hour or so in the saddle brought the courier to the Sink of Carson Station, an adobe structure where reasonably good water was available. Then it was on to Williams Station (also known as Honey Lake), managed by J. O. Williams and his two brothers. This was the site of the Pyramid Lake massacre, described in chapter 9.

The next stop on the southern route was Desert Station (possibly called Hooten Wells), and after that the rider reached the home station, which for the first few months of the Pony Express was Buckland's Station. Samuel S. Buckland established a ranch and a trading post at this site in 1859, and when the Pony Express was created the following year, Bolivar Roberts hired Buckland to run a home station there. Several months later, after the Pyramid Lake massacre, a company of soldiers built an adobe fort, Fort Churchill, several miles west of Buckland's ranch on the shore of the Carson River; shortly afterward, the Pony Express transferred its home station to the fort, which Captain F. F. Flint commanded.

Pony riders followed the northern, or "Stillwater Dogleg," route from Middlegate starting in the summer of 1861, when the Butterfield Overland Mail Company took over part of the Pony Express route. This more direct route took the rider through relay stations called Fairview, Mountain Well, Stillwater (possibly nonexistent), Old River, Bisby's (or Busby's), Nevada, Ragtown, and Desert Well. Ragtown got its name from the common sight of freshly washed clothes of passing pioneers spread out on the grass or draped over bushes to dry in the bright sunlight.

The two routes merged back into the main route at the next relay stop, Miller's (or Reed's) Station, about thirty miles east of Carson City, Nevada. The station was built in 1849 to service the vast number of pioneers traveling along the California Trail, and it was one of the first places Russell, Majors & Waddell established as a relay station.

As the Pony rider approached Carson City, he began to encounter a few fairly well-populated towns. The next relay station (Dayton Station, also called Spafford's Hall) was in Dayton, a town of about twenty-five hundred residents. From there the rider spurred his horse on to Carson, or Carson City, a Pony Express home station and the headquarters of the western superintendent, William Finney. Mormon pioneer Orson Hyde founded Carson City in 1855.

From Carson City, the fresh rider rode an hour to his first stop, Genoa Station, sometimes referred to as Old Mormon Station because of the large colony of Mormons living there. Looming ahead was the towering, white-capped Sierra Nevada. It would be the hardest climb of the entire trail to the last stop in Nevada, Friday's, or Lakeside, Station, high up on the Kingbury Grade. No swift riding at this point; it was a great labor for even the stoutest pony to carry its load over the seven-thousand-foot summit.

Originally established as a Pony Express home station, Friday's was operated by Martin K. "Friday" Burke and James Washington Small. It was one of the larger posts along the trail, consisting of a large single-room log cabin, a two-and-a-half-story hostelry, a dining room, a kitchen, a storeroom, a woodshed, and a very large stable and hay barn.

After the most rigorous of rides, the land leveled off and began to descend into another world: California, where the rain was plentiful, vast pine forests abounded, and streams rushed down the mountainside. The sagebrush and greasewood were behind.

The early Pony Express riders made a quick stop at a temporary station called Woodford's. But after only a few weeks, William Finney established a shorter route that bypassed that station. The next stop, Fountain Place Station, was the home of Garret Washington Fountain, who purchased the land in 1859 and built a sturdy log cabin there. The following year the cabin became a Pony Express relay station.

From there it was on to Yank's Station, which was a relatively large complex. When Ephrain "Yank" Clement and his wife, Lydia, bought the place in 1859, they enlarged the hostelry into a three-story, fourteen-room hotel and stage stop. They also added a large stable and hay barn and a corral. Amid the neighboring saloons, general store, blacksmith shop, and meat-processing plant, the hotel was very successful. Yank's served as a Pony Express relay station from the beginning to the end of the service.

Strawberry Station, established in 1856 as a hostelry, supposedly received its name from the fact that one of its managers, a Mr. Berry, regularly charged riders for hay and then fed their horses straw. This station was very comfortable but was only a relay post. From there, an hour's ride brought the Pony courier to Webster's relay station, also called Sugar Loaf House because of nearby Sugar Loaf Mountain. After that, the rider changed horses at Moss Station (also Moore's, Mess, or Riverton Station), then he was off to one of the most comfortable of all the home stations, Sportsman's Hall. Also referred to as Twelve Mile Station because it was twelve miles from Placerville, Sportsman's Hall was known for its fine food, clean and comfortable accommodations, and picturesque setting. Brothers John and James Blair ran the station.

A fresh rider now took to the saddle and headed due west for the last stretch of the two-thousand-mile route. Sacramento was now a mere fifty-six miles away. His first stop was Placerville, also known as

Alternate routes on Pony Express Trail between Placerville and Sacramento, California

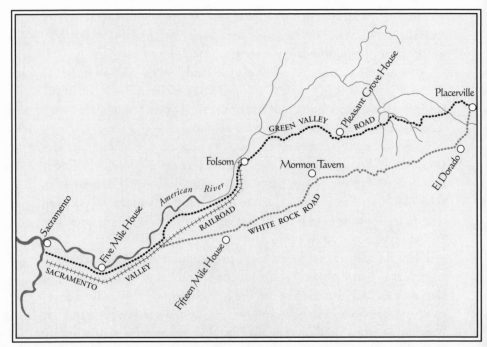

Hangtown, managed by Louis Lepetit. Because it had a telegraph office, Placerville was the western terminus for any telegrams the Pony Express carried.

With the rest of the mail, the rider kept going toward Sacramento, following one of two routes. For the first several months of the service, the rider followed a southern route along the White Rock Road to Five Mile House, five miles east of Sacramento. After that time, they took the Green Valley Road, a northerly route, from Placerville to Five Mile.

On the White Rock Road route, the rider went south to El Dorado Station, where he stopped to change horses. El Dorado, meaning "The Guilded One," was originally known as Mud Springs because local ranchers' large herds of cattle and horses made a muddy quagmire of the nearby springs. In the mid-1840s this was an important campsite on the old Carson Trail; by 1850 it had developed into a mining center and a crossroads for freight and stage lines. But for the Pony rider it was just a two-minute stop.

Sacramento, California, was still a sleepy little town in the 1860s.
—Courtesy California State Library

From El Dorado the rider was off to Mormon Tavern, also called Sunrise House, about a half mile west of the small settlement of Clarksville. Franklin Winchell, who had expanded the station, may also have managed it. Next there was an eleven-mile dash along the White Rock Road to Fifteen Mile House. This structure was originally an inn in 1855, when A. M. Plummer ran it. A few years later a man named Henry Detering bought the property and began to improve it. The enlarged structure contained a dining room, a kitchen, a parlor, a bar, a dance hall, and numerous bedrooms. But the Pony Express rider used it merely to change horses and move on the next station, Five Mile House, or Mills Station, the last relay station before Sacramento.

Riders on the northern route changed horses at Pleasant Grove House (possibly called Duroc Station) on the Green Valley Road, after which they proceeded to Folsom Station. Starting July 1, 1860, Folsom became the terminus for the Pony Express when the Sacramento Valley Railroad laid tracks to that town, and the train then carried the mail to Sacramento. But for a few months, the Pony riders galloped on to Five Mile House and then to Sacramento.

Interestingly, while the steamboat was the main form of transportation of the Pony Express mail between Sacramento and San Francisco, three additional relay stations were established between these two towns in the event that the rider missed the boat. The three stations were, east to west, Benicia, Martinez, and Oakland. If he made the boat, the weary rider could relax all the way to San Francisco.

TWO EXTRAORDINARY MEN

MANY OF THE MEN who worked on the rugged, lonely, and danger-ous Pony Express Trail were unsung heroes. But two Pony Express employees, James Butler "Wild Bill" Hickok and William F. Cody, also known as Buffalo Bill, attained world fame—in fact, their names have become synonymous with the American West.

Immortalized in the folklore of the American West, Hickok's larger-than-life image captured the imagination of his contemporaries as well as historians, writers, and filmmakers. In the late 1860s James F. Meline of Fort Kearny, Nebraska, described Hickok as "Six feet tall, lithe, ac-tive, sinewy, [a] daring rider, [a] dead shot with pistol and rifle, [with] long locks, fine features and mustache, buckskin leggings, red shirt, broad-rim hat, twin pistols in belt, rifle in hand."

In contrast to the rough-and-ready image of the frontiersman in the 1860s, Hickok could have "gained unquestioned admittance to the floor of most fancy dress balls in metropolitan cities" according to Theodore R. Davis, a commercial artist for *Harper's Weekly* magazine.

> I have seen "Wild Bill" appear in an immaculate boiled shirt, with collar and cuffs to match—a sleeveless, suave jacket of startling scar-let, slashed with black velvet. The entire garment being over orna-mented with buttons which if not silver, seemed to be. The trousers might be either black velvet or buckskin and like his jacket fitted with buttons quite beyond useful requirement. The French calf skin boots worn with this costume fitted admirably, and were polished as if the individual wearing them had recently vacated an Italian arm chair throne on a side street near Broadway. The long wavy hair that fell in masses from beneath a conventional sombrero was glassy from a re-cent anointment of some heavily perfumed mixture. As far as dress went, "Wild Bill" was to border plainsmen what "Beau" Neil was to the Army of the Potomac—faultlessly clad under surprising circum-stances.

*James Butler
"Wild Bill" Hickok*
—Courtesy Adams
Museum & House, Inc.,
Deadwood, S.D.

The more human side of this legend can be glimpsed by the observations of young Miguel Otero, son of a local businessman near Hays City, Kansas. Hickok used to take Miguel and his brother buffalo hunting. Later the boy recalled, "when we were under his care on a buffalo hunt, his entire time and attention were centered on us. In a chase he would cut out a cow and maneuver the animal so that either my brother or I could get an easy shot and down the buffalo."

Interestingly, Hickok's roots can be traced back to a couple of tenant farmers working for William Shakespeare. His ancestors came to America in 1635. Hickok's great-grandfather settled in Pittsfield, Massachusetts, where he served as a minuteman and responded to Paul Revere's famous ride on April 22, 1775. Hickok's father, William Alonzo Hickok, was born in Vermont. He had plans to join the ministry, but these were frustrated when he contracted typhoid. William and his bride, Polly Butler Hickok, moved from Vermont to Maine, and finally, in 1836, to Homer, Illinois.

James Butler Hickok was born May 27, 1837, in Troy Grove, Illinois. He had three older brothers and two younger sisters. Life was difficult for the Hickok family. The year James was born, a financial panic had left his father penniless. The family struggled to operate a small farm, where they harbored runaway slaves in a hidden cellar that was, according to James's nephew, Howard L. Hickok, "a dry earthen room, probably six-foot square" and lined with hay.

In 1852 William's illness, exacerbated by the physical stress of heavy labor, took its toll, and the Hickok family was left without a father. James and his brothers Horace and Lorenzo took on the task of managing the farm. The eldest, Oliver, had left home to seek his fortune in the goldfields of California. After his father died, James, who exhibited an interest in firearms at an early age, provided food for his family by hunting squirrels, rabbits, deer, and prairie chickens. Working on neighboring farms, he eventually saved enough money to buy a handgun, and he soon developed the marksmanship that would later bring him world fame.

But like his brother Oliver, James Hickok had a bit of wanderlust. At seventeen he traveled to Utica, Illinois, where he found a job as a driver of a canal boat. But his temper soon got him fired—he threw his boss into the canal for mistreating the livestock. Sometime in 1856, on hearing about land opportunities in Kansas, Hickok and his brother Lorenzo headed to the new frontier. Lorenzo left his brother en route and returned home upon hearing their mother was sick, but Hickok continued on to Kansas. When he docked in Leavenworth, his boat was greeted by a large mob of proslavery men who prevented the passengers from disembarking. Hickok, thinking fast, picked up a box of cargo and slipped into the line of stevedores unloading the boat.

Soon after his arrival in Leavenworth, Hickok decided to join General James H. Lanes's Free State Army. Because of his skills with a gun, Hickok became one of the general's bodyguards. About this time, Hickok came across a raw-boned man who was about to beat up an eleven-year-old boy. Without hesitation Hickok stepped in and saved the boy. The lad was William F. Cody, eventually known as Buffalo Bill. From that time on, they remained close friends.

Hickok's reputation for fairness and courage began to spread, and in March 1858, at age twenty-one, he was elected constable of Monticello, Kansas. Meanwhile, he was also taking care of a small farm he had purchased. Later that year, Hickok took a job as a teamster with the great freighting enterprise of Russell, Majors & Waddell.

When the Pony Express was started in 1860, Hickok, too tall and heavy to be a rider, served Russell, Majors & Waddell as a wagon and stagecoach driver, delivering supplies to the relay and home stations. In the summer of 1861, he worked as a Pony Express station worker at the Rock Creek Station in Nebraska. It was during this time that Hickok had the famous shootout with David McCanles (also spelled M'Kandlas) and his gang, an incident that catapulted Hickok into notoriety. The story has become distorted with time, and there are several renditions of it.

One of the first major descriptions of the episode appeared in the February 1867 *Harper's New Monthly Magazine.* The article was written six years after the fact by Colonel George Ward Nichols, who claimed he had heard it from Hickok, by then known as "Wild Bill." Hickok had had other dealings with McCanles, the captain of a gang Hickok describes as "desperadoes, horse thieves, murderers, regular cut-throats . . . the terror of everybody on the border," even before their deadly confrontation.

According to the *Harper's* story, sometime in 1861 Hickok was guiding a detachment of Union cavalry through southern Nebraska to the Kansas line at the time. As Hickok entered the cabin of an old friend, Mrs. Waltman, "she turned white as a sheet and screamed: 'Is that you, Bill? Oh God! They will kill you! Run! Run!'" The "they" was McCanles, a Confederate in the extreme, and his gang, who had just gone down the road looking for Hickok and his party of Yankee cavalry. Hickok, in the cabin, had just loaded his revolver when he heard McCanles return, shouting, "There's that d—d Yank Wild Bill's horse; he's here and we'll skin him alive. Surround the house and give no quarter!"

Hickok grabbed a Hawkins rifle from over the cabin door, and when McCanles poked his head inside, Hickok stood with the rifle ready. "Come in here, you cowardly dog!" Hickok shouted. McCanles "jumped inside the room, his gun leveled to shoot," but Hickok was too fast for him—he shot him through the heart. When the gang members outside realized what had happened, a shout arose. Then, according to Hickok, "there was a few seconds of that awful stillness, and then the ruffians came rushing in at both doors. How wild they looked with their red, drunken faces and inflamed eyes, shouting and cussing! But I never aimed more deliberately in my life."

Hickok killed four men, but the other five gang members came at him, firing shotguns. Hickok knocked one out and shot another one dead, but the other three grabbed him and threw him down on the bed.

"I fought hard," Hickok said. "I broke with my hand one man's arm. I was struck with the stock of a rifle, and felt the blood rushing out of my nose and mouth. Then I got ugly. . . . I remember that I got hold of a knife, and then it was all cloudy-like, and I was wild, and I struck savage blows, following the devils up from one side to the other of the room and into the corners, striking and slashing until I knew that every one was dead."

Nichols's version of the Hickok-McCanles shootout in *Harper's New Monthly Magazine* grabbed the public's attention and spread like wildfire, making Hickok a legend. Similar stories followed. But historians such as William E. Connelley of the Kansas State Historical Society present a radically different account of what happened at Rock Creek. In Connelley's version of that July afternoon in 1861, the shootout took place inside the Rock Creek Pony Express station, not at Mrs. Waltman's cabin, and Hickok's defense was far from single-handed.

In Connelley's version, McCanles rode to Rock Creek Station with his son, Monroe; his cousin, James Woods; and James Gordon, a man in his service. McCanles had sold the building at Rock Creek to Russell,

The Rock Creek Pony Express Station in southern Nebraska. It became famous as the site of a gunfight between Hickok and the McCanles gang. (Painting by W. H. Jackson) —Courtesy Scotts Bluff National Monument

Majors & Waddell, but they had failed to pay him for it. McCanles had come to demand payment from the station keeper, Horace Wellman.

McCanles directed his companions to wait by the barn and rode up to the station with a short double-barreled shotgun, at least two revolvers, and perhaps a bowie knife. McCanles confronted Wellman, who insisted he did not have McCanles's money. McCanles then demanded Wellman relinquish the station, the horses, and everything else on the premises. Wellman disappeared inside the house, only to be replaced by Mrs. Wellman, who defied McCanles to take the station.

At this point, Hickok appeared. He pushed Mrs. Wellman aside and confronted McCanles, who said, according to Connelley, "What the h— Hickok have you got to do with this? My business is with Wellman, not you." The two men continued to argue, with McCanles threatening to come in after Wellman. Hickok stepped back into the house, where he began to talk to Wellman about how best to defend the station. Soon McCanles stepped into the doorway and, seemingly at a loss, asked for a drink of water. Hickok handed him a dipper, then walked away toward the curtain that divided the room in half.

McCanles told Hickok to stop and turn around, but Hickok disappeared behind the curtain. As the men continued to argue, a shot was suddenly fired from behind the curtain, the bullet piercing McCanles's heart. Since Wellman was there with Hickok, it is conceivable that he may have been the one who fired. The wounded man staggered backward into the yard and fell into his son's arms, where he died.

When Woods and Gordon saw McCanles drop, they ran to the cabin and tried to enter through separate doors. As Woods stepped over the threshold, Hickok shot him twice with a revolver. He stumbled outside and collapsed in a clump of weeds, where his suffering was ended by, most historians think, Mrs. Wellman and her hoe. Meanwhile, Gordon turned and ran toward the barn, but Hickok shot and wounded him twice before he disappeared in the underbrush by the creek. Hickok pursued him, firing until his revolvers were empty.

When Hickok returned to the station to reload, he was met at the front door by Mrs. Wellman, brandishing her hoe and crying, "Come, let's kill all of the —!" She indicated Monroe McCanles, who was still kneeling beside his father's body, dazed. As the woman approached with the bloody hoe, the boy leapt to his feet and dashed away.

During the commotion, which had brought to the scene other Pony Express workers from nearby, Hickok called out to Joe Baker, one of the stock tenders at the barn, and accused him of being part of the

McCanles gang, a charge Baker denied. Just as Hickok cocked his pistol, Baker's stepdaughter ran out and pleaded for Baker's life. At this Hickok relented, instead beating the man senseless with the butt of his pistol, saying, "Well you've got to take that anyway."

A short while later Hickok and some others found the wounded Gordon under a tree. Hickok handed a shotgun to one of the bystanders and said, "Put that fellow out of his misery. That will show me that you don't belong to the McCanles gang." The man obeyed.

There are many other versions of this incident, some less reliable than others. Although the *Harper's* story undoubtedly took some liberties with the truth, it and others served to spread Hickok's Wild West image far and wide. He continued to live up to his reputation during the Civil War, when he helped guide General William T. Sherman's tour of the West in 1866 and scouted for General Winfield Scott Hancock and Lieutenant Colonel George Armstrong Custer in 1867–68.

Hickok, who was called Bill as early as the mid-1850s, may have picked up the nickname "Wild Bill" for his daring fighting for the Union troops during the Civil War. Others say he picked up the name during one or another of his numerous confrontations.

According to Nichols's story in *Harper's,* Hickok once joined General Price's Confederate army as a spy for five months. During a battle in Missouri in 1862, some Union soldiers recognized Hickok and shouted out, "Bully for Wild Bill!" The Rebel sergeant at his side suddenly realized Hickok's duplicity and cried out, "By God, I believe yer a Yank!" whereupon Hickok shot him.

After the war Hickok continued his wild ways, at times just skirting the right side of the law. On July 21, 1865, he killed David Tutt, a gunfighter of no little skill, in Springfield, Missouri. According to the *Harper's* article, there was already bad blood between the two because of Hickok's interest in Tutt's sister. The evening before the shooting, Tutt won Hickok's pocket watch in a poker game. Humiliated, Hickok warned Tutt not to wear the watch in public. The next day Tutt pulled out the watch as he crossed the town square. When he spotted Hickok he drew his gun, but Hickok shot first.

As is the case with so many events in Hickok's life, there are other versions of this story. One claims a rivalry between the two men over a woman named Susannah Moore. Needless to say, the truth is veiled in the mists of time.

Hickok was arrested and brought to trial. On August 16, 1865, a jury found Hickok ". . . not guilty in the manner and form charged." Less than a year later, he was appointed a U.S. deputy marshal at Fort Riley, Kansas, responsible for bringing to justice those who committed crimes against the government or on government property. Over the next few years, Hickok had a variety of exciting and dangerous jobs, including scouting for Indians for the army under the colorful and controversial General George A. Custer.

On August 23, 1869, Hickok was elected sheriff of Hays City, Kansas, a row of saloons along the Kansas Pacific Railroad. Established in 1867, the town was so wild and lawless it could not keep a justice of the peace. "There was no Sunday west of Junction City," Hickok was quoted as saying, "no law west of Hays City and no God west of Carson City." Immediately after becoming sheriff, Hickok posted a notice in town prohibiting anyone from carrying a gun. Several days later, he killed a lawbreaker. After that few men challenged him.

In 1873, William "Buffalo Bill" Cody pursuaded Hickok to join his Wild West show, based in Rochester, New York. But Hickok did not take to show business, and he left the troupe after less than a year and returned to his beloved West.

Wild Bill Hickok met his end at a card table in a saloon in a dirty little shanty town called Deadwood in the Black Hills of what is now South Dakota. Hickok had recently married Agnes Lake, whom he left home in Cheyenne in the spring of 1876. He came to Deadwood to mine gold in the newly discovered fields in the area, hoping to return to Agnes with money in his pocket. Deadwood was overrun with gunmen and gamblers intent on relieving honest miners of their hard-earned gold dust. When Hickok came on the scene, these outlaws plotted against him, fearing he might repeat his performances as a peace officer.

Hickok may have had a premonition of his pending death. He became morose and frequently spoke of death, stating that he believed he would not leave Deadwood alive. He wrote his wife on the day before he was killed:

> Agnes Darling.
>
> If such should be we never meet again, while firing my last shot, I will gently breathe the name of my wife—Agnes—and with wishes even for my enemies I will make the plunge and try to swim to the other shore.

On August 2, 1876, during a poker game in a dilapidated bar known as Carl Mann's Saloon Number 10, a man named Jack McCall (possibly a hired assassin) killed Wild Bill Hickok with a gunshot to the back of his head. Although McCall was acquitted in an unauthorized court in Deadwood, he was officially tried and hanged on January 3, 1877, in Laramie, Wyoming.

The words engraved on a monument dedicated to James Butler Hickok, erected by the state of Illinois in 1929 at his birthplace of Troy Grove, are testimony to his preeminence as a hero in American history:

JAMES BUTLER "WILD BILL" HICKOK

PIONEER OF THE GREAT PLAINS, BORN HERE MAY 27, 1837,
ASSASSINATED AT DEADWOOD AUGUST 2, 1876. SERVED HIS
COUNTRY AS A SCOUT AND SPY IN THE WESTERN STATES TO
PRESERVE THE UNION IN THE CIVIL WAR. EQUALLY GREAT WERE
HIS SERVICES ON THE FRONTIER AS EXPRESS MESSENGER AND
UPHOLDER OF LAW AND ORDER. HE CONTRIBUTED LARGELY IN
MAKING THE WEST A SAFE PLACE FOR WOMEN AND CHILDREN;
HIS STERLING COURAGE WAS ALWAYS AT THE SERVICE OF
RIGHT AND JUSTICE.

Although Wild Bill Hickok was a legend, his friend William Frederick Cody, whom the press dubbed "Buffalo Bill" when he was just twenty-two, eclipsed him in fame. The excitement, adventure, and color of the American West seemed to have been embodied in Cody, who ultimately mingled with not only the highest levels of American society, but with European royalty.

Born to Isaac and Mary Ann Cody on February 26, 1846, on a remote farm in Scott County, Iowa, William Frederick Cody was the fourth of eight children. In the spring of 1852, several years after Bill's older brother, Samuel, died in a riding accident, Isaac Cody moved his family to Kansas, where he operated a trading post near the Kickapoo Indian Agency. There young Billy's cousin, Horace Billings, taught him how to ride.

While still a boy, Bill Cody met Alexander Majors, who befriended him. At the young age of nine, Cody, against his mother's wishes, left home to herd cattle for Russell, Majors & Waddell for twenty-five dollars per month. The next year, he got into a tussle with a local bully and stabbed him in the leg. Afraid of the boy's father, Cody ran away with a wagon train carrying supplies to Fort Kearney, Nebraska.

In 1857, when Cody was eleven, another tragedy struck his family. While giving an antislavery speech, Isaac Cody was suddenly stabbed by a man with a bowie knife and later died from his wounds. In May of that same year, Cody became, according to a story in the Fort Leavenworth newspaper, the "youngest Indian slayer on the plains" when he killed an Indian at Plum Creek on the South Platte River. He was working on a cattle drive with a group of cowboys when they were surprised by a band of Indian warriors, who killed three of the men. As the cowboys tried to escape along the riverbank, with Cody in the rear, one of the Indians came up on them. Without hesitation, Cody raised his rifle and killed the Indian. The lad became an instant hero.

It was on this same trip that Cody made the acquaintance of Wild Bill Hickok. They met after a loud, burly, and unkempt member of the wagon train who enjoyed picking on the eleven-year-old Cody hit the boy in the face one night at dinner. In retaliation, Cody threw a pot of boiling coffee on the man, who came tearing after him, intent on killing him. Suddenly a tall, muscular man stood between them. It was Hickok. He swung his fist and knocked the bully to the ground.

The chastened man demanded to know what business this was of Hickok's. According to Cody, he answered, "It's my business to protect that boy, or anybody else, from being unmercifully abused, kicked, and cuffed, and I'll whip any man who tries it. . . . [I]f you ever again lay a hand on that boy—little Billy there—I'll give you such a pounding that you won't get over it for a month of Sundays." It was the beginning of a lifelong friendship.

Some have suggested that William Cody never rode as a Pony Express rider, noting that he is not listed in the official records. But there is a preponderance of evidence, including eyewitness reports, that Cody did in fact make the famous mail runs. Not only did Cody make the claim in his autobiography, as did his sister in her book about him, but Alexander Majors himself stated in his autobiography that Cody was a Pony rider.

Cody served two tours of duty as a Pony rider. In the spring of 1860, already a hardened frontiersman at age fourteen, he approached George Chrisman, the station keeper at Julesberg, Colorado, asking for a job as a rider. Cody had some experience riding the trail for Russell, Majors & Waddell, delivering messages between wagon trains headed for Utah, and he'd seen his share of Indians and violence. Chrisman agreed to hire the lad, but because he was so young, he assigned him to a short run of forty-five miles, between Julesberg and one of the home stations in Nebraska, probably Mud Springs. Cody rode the route for two months,

William F. Cody at fifteen. At this tender age Cody was already a Pony Express rider and had experienced several battles with hostile Indians.
—Courtesy American Heritage Center, University of Wyoming

maintaining the required schedule, until he received a message that his mother was seriously ill and he went home.

When his mother recovered, Cody again applied for a Pony Express rider position, this time to Jack Slade. In spite of Slade's cynicism about the boy's ability, he assigned Cody to one of the toughest routes, between Red Butte and Three Crossings in Wyoming. The trail was seventy-six miles long and lonely. There were hostile Indians and road bandits along the way, and the rider had to cross the North Platte River, which in places was twelve feet deep and riddled with quicksand. But Cody was determined to succeed. While in the Pony service, young Cody had a number of dramatic adventures and hair-raising escapes, which are described in chapter 13.

While some of Cody's exploits were the creations of dime novelists and publicity agents, there is no doubt about the courage and dedication he showed while in the service of the Pony Express. After leaving

Cody, age twenty-two, was an expert scout, trapper, and hunter. His skill hunting buffalo earned him the name Buffalo Bill. —Courtesy American Heritage Center, University of Wyoming

the Pony, Cody became an Indian scout for the army and soon became renowned as an expert frontiersman. He was best known for his buffalo hunting, hence the nickname Buffalo Bill. He did much of this hunting for the Kansas Pacific Railroad, which hired him in 1867 to provide fresh meat for the large crews building the new lines across the West. He also sometimes hunted buffalo for the army. He was always ready and willing to show off his shooting skills, especially in front of women.

While working as an army scout, during the Civil War and again from 1868 to 1872, Cody accepted many assignments no one else would take. He once rode 355 miles in fifty-eight hours, through dangerous Indian territory and with no trail to follow, to deliver some dispatches. During his army service, his reputation as an expert rider, fearless Indian fighter, and exceptional marksman continued to grow. Eventually his fame would spread throughout the world with his Wild West show, which toured all over the United States and Europe.

It was novelist Ned Buntline, real name Colonel E. Z. C. Judson, who first persuaded Cody to come east and perform on the stage. Cody's

Cody, right, with the famous general George A. Custer, left, and a Russian duke who had asked to join Cody in a buffalo hunt.
—Courtesy American Heritage Center, University of Wyoming

debut appearance was in 1872, when he played himself in *Scouts of the Plains,* which Buntline had written just days before its scheduled opening in Chicago. There was little time to rehearse, so when the curtain opened, Cody drew a blank. Finally Buntline called out, "Where have you been Bill? What kept you so long?" Catching sight of a well-known Chicagoan named Milligan in the audience, Cody blurted out, "I have been out on a hunt with Milligan!" The audience applauded vigorously, and the show went on.

It was the beginning of a forty-five-year stage career. For many years, Cody performed during the winter and continued scouting for the army in the summer. In 1883 he launched his own show, "Buffalo Bill's Wild West," and it became spectacularly successful. In 1887, the show played at Queen Victoria's Golden Jubilee. By the end of the nineteenth century, Buffalo Bill was one of the most recognized men in the world.

Cody continued to perform in his Wild West show until 1916, although, at seventy-one, he often had to be helped onto his horse backstage. In January 1917, Cody suffered a nervous collapse in Denver, Colorado. The great Indian fighter, hunter, scout, and Pony Express rider died January 10. Cody's family received condolences from presidents, generals, and fans from all walks of life. Former President Theodore Roosevelt called him "an American of Americans."

— 13 —

HEROES ON HORSEBACK

IN THE EARLY MONTHS of the Pony Express, there appeared on the front pages of various western newspapers numerous grim headlines and stories reflecting the dangerous conditions confronting both the riders and the station keepers:

> BART RILES, THE PONY RIDER, DIED THIS MORNING FROM WOUNDS HE RECEIVED AT COLD SPRINGS.

> THE MEN AT DRY CREEK STATION HAVE ALL BEEN KILLED AND IT IS THOUGHT THOSE AT ROBERTS CREEK HAVE MET WITH THE SAME FATE.

> SIX PIKE'S PEAKERS FOUND THE BODY OF THE STATION KEEPER HORRIBLY MUTILATED, THE STATION BURNED AND ALL THE STOCK MISSING FROM SIMPSON'S [PARK STATION].

> EIGHT HORSES WERE STOLEN FROM SMITH'S CREEK ON LAST MONDAY, SUPPOSEDLY BY ROAD AGENTS.

There are few documents recording the personal heroism that was almost routine among the loyal personnel of the Pony Express. The mail had to go through, and practically no circumstances, no matter how difficult or grave, dissuaded the riders and station keepers from performing their duties.

Soon after the start of the Pony Express service, the fame of the young riders—some merely boys—began to spread throughout the country. They were considered a very special class of citizens. Although they were young and small in stature, they tackled a big job, getting the mochila, which filled with mail weighed about twenty pounds, across miles of wilderness. As stories about these swift, brave riders circulated, their image became bigger than life. Newspapers praised them and built them up to the level of epic heroes.

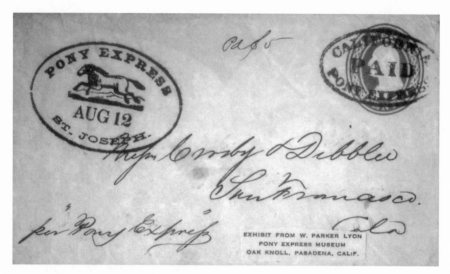

EXHIBIT FROM W. PARKER LYON
PONY EXPRESS MUSEUM
OAK KNOLL, PASADENA, CALIF.

An original envelope with Pony Express postmarks
—Courtesy American Heritage Center, University of Wyoming

Much was expected of the riders, both in terms of their duty and in their personal life. In fact, every employee of the Central Overland California & Pike's Peak Express Company was required to take the following pledge:

> I [name], do hereby swear, before the Great and Living God, that during my engagement, and while I am an employee of Russell, Majors & Waddell, I will, under no circumstances, use profane language; that I will drink no intoxicating liquors; that I will not quarrel or fight with any other employee of the firm, and tiat in every respect I will conduct myself honestly, be faithful to my duties, and so direct all my acts as to win the confidence of my employer. So help me God.

Those who seriously violated this oath could expect to be terminated, with the loss of back pay. This is not to say that the Pony Express riders were saints. But in most cases, they were devoted to their task and proved their loyalty again and again.

Mark Twain, who in 1860 was traveling by stagecoach across the country, captured the thrill of seeing a Pony rider in *Roughing It*:

> We had a consuming desire from the beginning, to see a pony rider; but somehow or other all that passed us, and all that met us managed to streak by in the night and so we heard only a whiz and a hail, and

Thomas Owen King, Pony Express rider and later, Mormon bishop of Almo, Idaho
—Courtesy Historical Department, Church of Jesus Christ of Latter-day Saints

the swift phantom of the desert was gone before we could get our heads out of the window. But now we were expecting one along any moment, and would see him in broad daylight. Presently the driver exclaims:

"Here he comes!"

Every neck is stretched further and every eye strained wider away across the endless dead level of the prairie, a black speck appears against the sky, and it is plain that it moves. Well I should think so! In a second it becomes a horse and rider, rising and falling, rising and falling—sweeping toward us nearer and nearer growing more sharply defined—nearer and still nearer, and the flutter of hoofs comes faintly to the ear—another instant a whoop and a hurrah from our upper deck, a wave of the rider's hands but no reply and man and horse burst past our excited faces and winging away like the belated fragment of a storm!

So sudden is it all, and so like a flash of unreal fancy, that but for a flake of white foam left quivering and perishing on a mail sack after the vision had flashed by and disappeared, we might have doubted whether we had seen any actual horse and man at all, maybe.

Thomas Ryon, top, and Ira and John Draper, bottom, Ira left, are listed at the Nebraska State Historical Society as having been Pony Express riders, though they do not appear on the St. Joseph Pony Express Museum list of riders. —Courtesy Nebraska State Historical Society

The Pony Express horses were bred and maintained for speed and endurance. Capable of sustaining top speed for ten miles or more, the horses were often called upon to run even longer distances. When a crucial message had to be delivered in record time, these gallant animals were sometimes ridden to death. High-quality horses were important not only for keeping the run on schedule, but also to give protection to the riders. Fed wholesome grain and attentively cared for, Pony Express horses could outrun any Indian horse.

But even with the finest horses it was often extremely difficult to complete a run. The most taxing conditions raged against the all-too-human riders. Bad weather, warring Indians, road agents, rugged terrain, and personal fatigue could discourage even the hardiest soul from completing his task. But in almost every case, the dedicated riders prevailed. Some of their stories were nothing short of miraculous.

William Campbell was a case in point. During his tenure as a Pony rider, Campbell faced just about every difficulty one could imagine on the trail. Born in 1842 and raised in Illinois, Billy Campbell traveled with his brother to Kansas City to seek his fortune at the age of sixteen. Soon the brothers crossed paths with Russell, Majors & Waddell, who hired them as bullwhackers for $25 a month plus rations, mostly bacon and beans. Once out on the trail, the young men added buffalo meat and other game to their diet. They were assigned to the huge trains that shipped supplies along the famous Santa Fe Trail.

Life on the trail was exciting for the Campbell brothers, and there was a great deal to learn about being a bullwhacker. It wasn't long before the young adventurers had a brush with death. Billy described the incident:

> As we were passing along some sand-hills in the Arkansas River Valley, the first thing we knew some old buffalo bulls came charging over one of the hills and then about five hundred cows and younger buffalo appeared. They were going pell-mell to escape from a band of more than a hundred Pawnee Indians that were right on their heels.
>
> Every Indian was on his pony, and stripped for action. As soon as the buffaloes had got out of the hills on to the plain, each red hunter would single out a choice young cow and, with his trained pony clinging close to the fleeing creature, would finally get right alongside, and sink arrow after arrow into the cow till she dropped to the ground.
>
> The buffaloes and Indians were heading towards our train. Our cattle began to get excited. Our wagons were being huddled together. The drivers were trying to hold their lead oxen to prevent a stampede. The frantic buffalo began to run right in among us. We managed,

however, to hold things pretty level, until the buffalo storm had swept by. When it had passed we saw about a hundred and fifty dead buffaloes scattered over the plain. Not a rifle had been fired. It was all the skilful work of Indians with their ponies and bows and arrows.

In early 1860, the company asked Billy Campbell to help build and supply relay stations east of Salt Lake City for the Pony Express. When young Campbell saw the Pony Express riders dash by on their fleet horses, it stimulated his sense of adventure. Now eighteen, Campbell mustered up the courage to ask Alexander Majors for a job as a rider.

He was tall and heavy for a rider—the company preferred that riders weigh less than 125 pounds. But Majors, perhaps impressed with the young man's enthusiasm and determination, agreed to give him a chance. Campbell was thrilled: "I took the pledge he extracted of all the boys; received my little leather-bound Bible (which I have yet), and after thanking him, went out walking on air—a full fledged pony rider."

The romance of the job soon vanished, and Campbell realized that being a Pony rider was far more strenuous than freighting. His first run was between Fort Kearny and Fort McPherson (Plum Creek), Nebraska, a distance of about a hundred miles. At that time the stations hadn't all been built, and some of the relay stops were as much as thirty miles apart, a long distance for a horse galloping at top speed.

Campbell had his share of adventures along the trail. Once his favorite horse, Ragged Jim, jumped into a buffalo wallow in the dark and Campbell was tossed head over heels, along with the mochila, to the ground. In the excitement, Ragged Jim turned around and raced back to the previous station, leaving his rider stranded on the remote trail. Fortunately, a stagecoach heading in Campbell's direction saw the horse, and the driver caught him and took him along. It wasn't long before the coach came upon Campbell, carrying the mochila. Soon horse and rider were flying along the trail again, trying to make up for lost time.

Some of Campbell's misadventures were much more serious. One night when he was riding his route, Campbell came upon a pack of large wolves feeding on a horse they had just killed. When the rider dashed by, a number of the beasts took off after him, intending to bring down his horse. Unfortunately, Campbell had not brought his gun on that run and the next station was several miles away. The savage wolves were closing in on him, and there would be no way to fight them off if the horse was brought down. Then Campbell remembered the horn he used to alert the station keeper of his arrival. He took it and blew a mighty blast at the wolves. Startled, the pack stopped a moment, then continued their chase. As they grew closer Campbell again blew the horn, and again the wolves fell back. He was able to keep this up until he made it safely to the station.

On another run, Campbell was caught in a furious snowstorm. For an entire day and night he had to battle through the blinding blizzard, the snow piled up three feet with drifts over his head. The trail was completely buried, so Campbell had to watch for the tops of tall dry weeds to keep his direction. At night he had to depend totally on the natural directional sense of his gallant horse, which struggled on with great difficulty. Half frozen and exhausted, Campbell reached the home station only to find that there was no relief rider there. This meant another twenty miles through the freezing stosm. Off he went on a fresh horse, plowing through the snowdrifts with the icy wind blowing gusts of snow like frosted clouds.

Weather conditions never stopped a rider from completing his run. Several riders almost froze to death riding through blinding snowstorms. —Courtesy Wyoming Division of Cultural Resources

By the time Campbell reached the next station, he had been out in the storm for twenty-four hours. He was nearly frozen to death and beyond exhausted. "After a good meal, I went to bed and slept like a log from four in the afternoon until ten the next morning," Campbell later said.

On May 23, 1934 (or 1932 according to some sources), William Campbell, who had risen to the position of state senator, died. He had been the last surviving Pony Express rider, and one of the most courageous. His death closed the book on one of the greatest enterprises of the American West.

Nick Wilson was only fifteen when he started riding for the Pony Express, but in the short time he rode the trail, he must have aged considerably from the frightening experiences he had. Elijah Nicholas Wilson was born in Adams County, Illinois, in 1845. When he was five his family migrated to Utah, settling in the small community of Grantsville. At age seven, Nick was responsible for watching his father's sheep as they grazed.

It is unclear why he did it, but in 1856, at the age of eleven, Nick went off to stay with the Shoshone Indians, living as the adopted son of Chief Washakie's mother. He became very attached to the tribe, learning their ways and language. In later years he published a book entitled *"Uncle Nick" among the Shoshones.*

When he heard about the Pony Express, Nick Wilson, now fifteen, was raring to go. At first he was rejected because of his age. But after observing his outstanding horsemanship (he could stick like glue to just about any horse) and considering his intimate knowledge of Indians, a station keeper named Faust and division superintendent Howard Egan agreed to hire the lad.

After taking his oath, Wilson heard the instructions given to all Pony riders. At no time, except when carrying the mail, should he ever be more than a hundred yards from a relay station. He must be prepared to make his run at top speed, day or night, rain or snow, Indians or no Indians. Once he started his run, he should never, under any circumstances, turn back. These words must have sounded awesome to a boy of fifteen. But Nick Wilson was no ordinary boy.

It is ironic that nearly all of the life-threatening experiences of Nick Wilson, who had lived with the Shoshone, were with Indians. Most of these occurred while he was a Pony Express rider. His run was between Schell Creek Station (or Fort Schellborne) and Deep Creek Station in Utah, in Howard Egan's division. When Wilson took the job, the local

Paiute had been on a killing and burning rampage, and the boy had already had one terrifying encounter at Willow Creek, as described in chapter 9.

Not long after that incident, Wilson was riding along his route when four Indian warriors suddenly jumped out from behind some large rocks. Instinctively the young rider whirled his horse around to make a run for it. But three other Indians blocked the trail, their bows and arrows and one gun aimed at him. There was nowhere to run. He stopped; death appeared imminent. The chief, a mean-looking, one-eyed warrior, grabbed the reins of Wilson's horse and ordered him to get off. The chief then took Wilson's revolver.

There was one slender ray of hope: Wilson recognized Tabby, an Indian who had been a friend of his father. But Tabby remained flint-faced, showing not the slightest sign of recognition. The chief, asserting that the Pony Express riders had no right to cross their lands, said that he and his people intended to drive out the white man, burn the stations, and kill the riders.

With this said, the chief rejoined his band, and they talked heatedly for several minutes. For all Wilson knew, they were arguing about which was the most brutal way to kill him. Finally one of the warriors approached Wilson and asked him for some tobacco. The boy gladly gave them all he had. After they all had a smoke, Tabby walked up to Wilson. He explained that the other braves were intent on killing him, but it took a unanimous vote to do so, and he would not agree. Wilson was free to turn back, but he must never ride this trail again or he would certainly be killed.

At this point, even the most dedicated Pony Express rider would be justified in turning back—it was either that or die. Nick, however, was made of tougher stuff. He appealed to Tabby. The mail's got to go through, he insisted. He said that if they let him pass, he would never ride there again. To the gutsy young rider's amazement, Tabby returned with the Indians' approval, leading the boy's horse. Wilson thanked the old Indian and took off as fast as his horse would carry him. He also kept his word never to ride that trail again. Major Egan assigned him another route farther west, in Nevada, and another rider took over that one.

This was Nick Wilson's second narrow escape as a Pony rider. Yet his most serious brush with death at the hands of Indians was yet to come. Enmity between whites and Indians was fueled not only by major clashes, such as the Pyramid Lake massacre, but also by individual brutal acts. In one incident, a white man shot a defenseless old Indian who was up on a hill trapping ground squirrels to feed his family. The old man's body was left beside the trail. Often, innocent Pony riders paid for such deeds. Nick Wilson was one of those riders.

One day on his usual run, Wilson, dashing into the Spring Valley relay station, learned that the old station keeper (perhaps a man named Constant Dubail) had fled, fearing an Indian attack. Two young boys, whose father and mother had died of cholera on their way out west, were doing their best to tend the station. They asked Wilson to share a quick meal with them. He agreed, figuring he might be able to evaluate the situation and report it to his boss. He turned his pony loose to graze with some other horses behind the stable.

A few minutes later, Wilson and the two youngsters were surprised to see two Indians driving the horses across a meadow. They dashed after them, firing their revolvers as they ran. The Indians dove behind a grove of trees. Wilson ran ahead of the younger boys, and just as he approached a large cedar one of the Indians sent a flint arrow whistling through the air. It hit its mark, embedding deep into Wilson's skull, about two inches above his left eye. The Indians disappeared with the horses.

The two boys tried desperately to pull the arrow out of Wilson's head, but the shaft broke, leaving the flinthead in his skull. Certain that Wilson was as good as dead, the boys rolled him under the shade of a cedar tree and ran to the next station for help. Wilson lay there all night, easy prey for wolves, mountain lions, or wandering war parties.

The next morning some men came with the boys to give poor Nick a decent burial. To their astonishment, he was still alive. They carried him into the station and sent for the closest doctor, who was in Ruby Valley, a considerable distance. All the doctor could do was to remove the arrowhead and tell the boys to keep a wet cloth on the wound. He did not seriously expect Wilson to live. For six days the young victim lay in a coma.

Major Egan, Wilson's superintendent, came by to check on his fallen rider. Seeing Wilson's condition, he sent for the doctor and demanded that he make a better effort. Despite further treatment, Wilson lay near death for another eighteen days. Then he began to recover, and it was only a matter of weeks before the intrepid young man was back in the saddle. Of course the wound left a terrible scar; Wilson always wore a hat after that.

After his service with the Pony Express, Wilson took a job delivering mail from Salt Lake City to Montana, and several years later, in

Elijah Nicholas Wilson at age fifty-nine. As a young Pony rider Wilson was shot in the forehead with an Indian arrow at the Spring Valley relay station. Afterward he always wore a hat to cover the scar.
—Courtesy St. Joseph Museum

1865, he married Matilda Patton. The couple later settled in Bloomington, Idaho, where Wilson successfully operated a mercantile store, a blacksmith shop, a sawmill, and a ranch. He was a valuable peacemaker between whites and Indians in the area. But he still had a thirst for adventure.

In 1888 Wilson took his family to Jackson Hole, Wyoming, driving the first wagon over Teton Pass. But he paid a dreadful price for the experience. An epidemic of diphtheria broke out among the wagon train with which he was traveling, and Wilson worked tirelessly to tend the sick and dying. Six of Wilson's ten children died; members of the train buried three of them before he learned of their deaths.

After settling in Wyoming, Wilson lived a peaceful life. In 1893 he was ordained as a bishop of the Mormon Church. He often received visits from Chief Washakie, who warmly recalled the days when young Nick lived among the Shoshone. The courageous Pony Express rider

Chief Washakie of the Shoshone, one of the most famous of the peacemaking chiefs. His camp in west-central Wyoming was a refuge for Pony Express riders.
—Courtesy Wyoming Division of Cultural Resources

died on December 26, 1915, in the little town named in his honor, Wilson, Wyoming.

Jack Keetley was another sturdy young man who routinely performed extraordinary tasks. Born on November 28, 1841, perhaps in England, he spent most of his childhood in Marysville, Kansas. At age nineteen he became a Pony Express rider and continued in its service to the end. Keetley rode in A. E. Lewis's division, between Marysville, Kansas, and Big Sandy, Nebraska. He had incredible stamina, as he illustrated with one mail run that few other riders could match. After completing his normal eastbound run, due to some unknown circumstance, presumably a missing or indisposed relief rider, he agreed to make the next run, which went all the way to Elwood, Kansas, on the Missouri River. Some historians claim he rode from Rock Creek, Nebraska, to St. Joseph. Either way, it was a nearly two-hundred-mile ride.

But still he did not rest. Eating while at a full gallop, this steely young man took the westbound mochila as well, running all the way back to Seneca, Kansas. Keetley rode an astounding total of 340 miles,

Pony Express rider Jack Keetley rode in A. E. Lewis's division. With incredible stamina, he rode 340 miles in thirty-one hours. —
Courtesy St. Joseph Museum

completed in thirty-one hours without a significant stop. As he rode into the Seneca home station, the station attendant and his helper gently eased the rider down off his horse. He had ridden the last several miles sound asleep.

Sometime after his service as a Pony Express rider, Keetley married Margaret Ochiltree. Meanwhile, he had skillfully parlayed his horse and saddle into a tract of mining property, then, using his six-shooter as payment for materials and labor, he built a cabin on the property. A year later he sold the land and the cabin for an incredible $17,000. Keetley spent the rest of his career managing mines, namely the Little Bell Mine and the Silver King Mine near Park City, Utah. He died at age seventy-one in Salt Lake City, on October 2, 1912.

Another Pony rider of strength and endurance was Bill James. William James was born in Lynchburg, Virginia, in 1843, and his family moved to Utah when he was five years old. Joining the Pony Express at seventeen, James had a regular run between Simpson's Park and Cold Springs in Nevada. His sixty-mile route, which lay in the Smoky Valley

Range, in the heart of Shoshone country, was considered the loneliest and most dangerous run of Bolivar Roberts's division. Riding a California mustang, James carried the mochila over the summits of two mountains, whether it was a scorching day or a raging snowstorm at night. In his fastest run, Bill James made the 120-mile round-trip in twelve hours, including horse changes.

Jim Moore was another extraordinary rider. On June 8, 1860, Moore happened to be visiting Midway home station in Nebraska's Platte Valley when the westbound rider arrived carrying important government documents to California. For an unknown reason there was no other rider available, and although it was not his route, Moore did not hesitate to pick up the mochila and dash westward on one of the longest routes of the Pony Express Trail. Racing his horse at an average of eighteen miles per hour, the rider pounded the trail hour after hour, in the burning heat of the day, through the desolate barren expanses of the Platte Valley.

One hundred and forty miles later, a tired and hungry Moore rode into Julesburg Station in Colorado, where what waited for him was not the food and rest he so sorely needed, but a mochila of urgent news for Washington, D.C. The eastbound rider had been killed the day before, and there were no other relief riders available. Yet the mail had to go through, at any cost. That was the promise of the Pony Express.

Without a second thought, Moore was back in the saddle and off on the eastbound run. This meant another 140 miles, a nonstop ride through the blackness of night and the threat of warring Indians. By this time Moore's hunger and exhaustion must have been almost unbearable, but he kept going, stopping only to change horses, until he reached Midway Station.

Jim Moore had ridden 280 miles, tiring about twenty horses, in an amazing fourteen hours and forty-six minutes—a feat worthy of the name Pony Express rider. Moore's effort also contributed to the record eastbound run from Sacramento to St. Joseph of eight days and nine hours.

The adventures of young William Cody rank among the most exciting in the annals of the mail service. One run, in particular, was one of the extraordinary feats in Pony Express history. On a summer day in 1860, Cody left Red Butte headed west, carrying the mochila filled with mail. After crossing the North Platte, he rode at a full gallop, trying to maintain the average of fifteen miles per hour that was required to meet the schedule. Stopping at the relay stations for fresh horses and quick drinks of water, he kept up the fast pace over rolling hills and into the stark, barren land of the Platte Valley. His final stop was the home station at Three Crossings, where he could have a hot meal and a good night's sleep.

As he approached the station, Cody was tired, having been in the saddle for over five hours. But his relief rider was nowhere in sight. It turned out that the rider had been killed in a drunken brawl the night before, and there was no replacement for him. The mail had to be carried on to Pacific Springs Station, another seventy-two miles west, entailing a rugged ride up the mountain to South Pass. Cody took a few minutes to gulp down the meal the station keeper's wife had prepared, then mounted a fresh horse and took off at a full gallop.

Wearing out horse after horse, he kept going. Finally, after an exhausting eleven-hour run, he arrived at Pacific Springs. At fourteen, Cody had done not only a man's job, but an extraordinary man's job. But his challenge was not over. Sitting down for his well-earned meal at the station, Cody learned that there was no rider to carry the mochila that would soon arrive with the eastbound rider.

As tired as he was, Cody decided to take the run back to Red Butte, riding throughout the blackness of night. After what must have felt like an eternity, Cody arrived with the mochila in Red Butte, thoroughly exhausted after twenty-two almost continuous hours in the saddle. He had ridden about three hundred miles, averaging nearly fourteen miles per hour. Over the years, historians have disputed the total distance Cody actually traveled; estimates have varied from 296 miles to a record 388 miles. It has been suggested that mileage was added to his run in order to give to Buffalo Bill the record for the longest ride ever made by a Pony Express rider. Whatever the actual distance, it was a stupendous achievement.

Cody had many other adventures with the Pony Express, although determining which were fact and which myth is difficult. One story holds that during one of his mail runs to Three Crossings Station, Cody suddenly found himself nearly surrounded by a band of Sioux warriors. They attacked, and Cody's only chance was to outrun them. With bullets and arrows whizzing by, Cody laid flat on his pony and spurred the animal to a gallop. But when he arrived at the station he found, to his horror, the station keeper dead and all the horses stolen.

With the Sioux not far behind, Cody urged his tired horse on and headed for the next station. Fortunately he found a relief rider there and was able to turn the mail over to him safely. At that point, according to one version of the story, he gathered some men and went after the Sioux. The Pony riders surprised the Indians in their camp, retrieved their stolen horses, and took a few extra ones as payment for their trouble, all without losing a single man.

In another tale, Cody had been hunting grouse to bring back to Horseshoe Station, Jack Slade's headquarters in Wyoming. He had stopped to roast a couple of birds for lunch when he heard a horse whinnying. Concerned that it might be Indians, the youth hid his horse in a clump of trees and went to investigate. He soon spotted several white men going into a dugout hidden among the rocks and trees. Without thinking, Cody scurried to the dugout and knocked at the door. When the door opened, Cody recognized two of the men: they were bullwhackers who had deserted their outfit, killed someone, and joined up with robbers. Cody realized he had entered a den of thieves.

After questioning Cody, the group's leader sent two of his men with Cody to fetch the boy's horse. Cody led the two bandits to his campsite, and one of them took the horse. As they started back, Cody picked up the two grouse he'd roasted and followed the man who was leading his horse. The other man was right behind him. Cody dropped one of the birds, and when the man behind him stooped down to pick it up, the youth pulled out his revolver with lightning speed and hit the man on the head with it, knocking him senseless. Then he spun around and put a bullet through the second man, killing him instantly. Cody then leaped onto his horse and was out of there like a flash.

During another of his Pony Express rides, Cody was asked to deliver a large amount of money. Realizing that he would be an easy mark for road bandits, the boy filled a mochila with wads of paper and put the money in a second mochila that he hid under his saddle blanket. Along the trail, two highwaymen stepped out from behind some rocks, leveled their guns at Cody, and demanded he surrender the mochila. At first the lad protested, but when the men threatened to kill him he loosened the leather pouch and flung it right at one of the bandits, who dodged it with some amusement. Suddenly Cody drew his pistol and shot one of the bandits. Before the other could react, the lad spurred his horse around and knocked him to the ground, trampled his horse over him, and galloped away. He arrived at the next relay station to deliver the money and the mail on time.

J. G. Kelly, who at barely a hundred pounds was one of the lightest Pony riders, also had his share of adventures. He had worked with Bolivar

Roberts in establishing the trail along the mosquito-infested Carson River, then became a rider, operating out of Cold Springs (also called East Gate), Nevada, twenty miles east of Carson Lake. The spring of 1860 marked the beginning of the bloody Paiute war, and Kelly's route passed through Paiute country.

On one occasion, Kelly was making fast tracks on his mail run when he came upon a wagon train. Although it must have been a pleasant sight on an otherwise lonely and dangerous trail, the rider could not stop for pleasantries and raced by at top speed. Suddenly, with no warning, members of the wagon train began firing at him. Bullets whizzed by his head. Miraculously, he was not hit, and he soon outdistanced the train.

On his return trip, Kelly encountered the same train. He carefully approached it and, using some salty language normally forbidden under the Pony Express oath, gave the emigrants a good tongue lashing. They explained that they had mistaken Kelly for an Indian. Often, a lone Indian would ride ahead of a warrior band to draw gunfire from a wagon train. Then, while everyone was reloading their rifles, the main band attacked.

Another time, while Kelly was at Cold Springs Station, a young Mexican Pony Express rider named Bart Riles approached, slumped in his saddle. As the men at the station helped him down, he told them his story. While riding eastbound down Edwards Creek, on the narrow trail through Quaking Asp Grove, he was suddenly attacked by a band of Paiute. He urged his horse on, but he remained well within rifle range, and a bullet passed through his chest. He turned back for Cold Springs, the nearest station, hanging on for dear life. Riles died several hours after his arrival.

Now Kelly took up the eastbound mail. He completed the run without incident, but on the return trip he once again had to pass through the thicket at Quaking Asp Grove, a two-mile trail wide enough for only a single horse. Even worse, the trail had such sharp turns that often a rider could not see more than ten or fifteen feet ahead. It was a perfect place for an ambush. The young rider drew out his rifle, crouched low on his horse, and made a mad dash through the death trap, every moment expecting to hear Indian war cries and rifle fire.

When Kelly reached the top of a small hill, he looked back at the trail behind him. He noticed some of the bushes moving. Instantly he fired several rounds at the spot. The movement stopped. Without stopping to see what was in the bushes, Kelly rode off, feeling lucky to be alive. The next day, a couple of soldiers were not so lucky; they were ambushed and killed in the very same area. Yet the Pony Express riders continued to ride through that treacherous grove on a routine basis.

Kelly survived another brush with death through sheer bravado. One day while racing headlong down the trail, he rounded a sharp bend and found himself smack in the midst of a Paiute camp. As he stood motionless on his horse, Chief Buffalo Jim approached and spoke in English. Surprisingly, he merely asked for tobacco. Kelly gave him half his pouch, but the chief wanted it all. When Kelly refused, the chief asked to see his gun. Kelly pulled it from the holster, pointed it at the chief, and warned him not to take another step closer. It was a standoff, and the odds were very much against the lone young rider. But the chief, apparently admiring Kelly's mettle, told him to go.

Sometime later, Kelly was assigned to be the assistant station keeper at Sand Springs, Nevada. Though he no longer had to worry about the dangers of the trail, the Paiute war was then at its height, and the Sand Springs relay station was right in the middle of Paiute territory. In May 1860 a band of warriors had raided the station, killing the station keeper and running off the horses. A few weeks later, Indians raided the station again. Everyone was on full alert.

One night, while Kelly was on guard duty, he saw the silhouette of an Indian near the station. He fired a shot but missed. The station workers came running out and saw that, off in the distance, the hillside was dotted with Indian campfires. The next morning the men found a large number of footprints around the perimeter of the station. Had Kelly not fired that shot, who could be certain that any of them would have lived until morning?

For all his close calls, Kelly survived his career with the Pony Express and later served in the Union Army during the Civil War as captain of C Company in the Nevada Infantry. After the war he became an eminent mining engineer and mineralogist in Denver, Colorado.

Another Pony rider who, like Kelly, met danger with pure grit was Howard Ranson Egan, the son of division superintendent Howard Egan. Once, when the rider at Schell Creek Station in Nevada fell ill, young Egan agreed to take his run. Leaping to his saddle, sitting firmly on the mochila, he headed west toward Butte Station just as it was starting to get dark. He was racing along Egan Canyon when he caught sight of a fire up ahead. Suspicious, he cautiously approached. It was a band of Indians. Egan was in a serious predicament: if he turned back and went through another canyon, it would cost a considerable amount of time. But this canyon was too narrow for him to go around the Indians. What to do?

He got as close to them as he could without being seen, then took out his six-shooter and suddenly spurred his horse to a full gallop. Approaching the Indian camp at full speed, he fired his gun and yelled at the top of his voice. As he rode through, the warriors, believing there must be a large group of riders, panicked and scattered in all directions.

Once out of the canyon, Egan took a shortcut to Butte Station and reached safety. Later, an Indian friend of his told him that the warriors had set a trap for him and that there had also been a band of Indians in the other canyon. He explained that the Indians wanted to capture a Pony Express rider so they could find out what was so important in the mochila.

Richard Erastus Egan, son of Major Howard Egan, was an exceptional Pony Express rider. He once traveled 150 miles through a snowstorm without a rest stop.
—Courtesy St. Joseph Museum

Ranson Egan's brother Richard was also a Pony rider. In the winter of 1860 Richard Egan started out on his westward run from Fort Crittenden (Camp Floyd) to Rush Valley Station, Utah, during a blinding snowstorm. As night approached, the snow was already knee-deep to his horse. Soon it was so dark and snowy he could not see the trail. In order to stay moving in the general direction, Egan kept the wind at his right cheek as he traveled all night.

At dawn, after an exhausting ride, he found himself back at his starting point, Fort Crittenden. The wind had changed direction during the night, and he had ridden 150 miles in a vast circle. Undaunted, he immediately mounted a fresh horse and continued on to Rush Valley Station without a rest stop. Talk about tenacity. Another time, Egan agreed to replace a rider who wanted to court his sweetheart and ended up remaining in the saddle for 330 miles.

Near the top of the list of heroes on horseback is the name Robert Haslam, known in history as Pony Bob. Very little is known about his early life. He was born in England in 1840, and his parents brought him to the American frontier at an early age. He signed up with the Pony Express at twenty.

Pony Bob Haslam held the record for the longest and fastest run in the history of the Pony Express. In May 1860, he started out on his normal eastbound route, between Friday's Station, on the southwest shore of Lake Tahoe, to Buckland's Station (marked Nevada Station on some maps), a distance of seventy-five miles. The Pyramid Lake massacre had recently taken place, and Indian war parties were roaming the entire area. Passing through Carson City, he encountered the first sign of trouble. The settlers were fortifying themselves against attack, not a good sign for conditions up the trail.

Haslam reached Reed's Station (also called Miller's Station) only to find that there were no fresh horses. Local people had taken them all to stage a campaign against Chief Winnemucca and his Paiute warriors. Haslam fed his weary horse and urged it on another fifteen miles to Buckland's Station, the end of his seventy-five mile run, where he and the horse could have a well-earned rest.

Upon arriving, Haslam learned that the relief rider, Johnny Richardson, was terrified about the Indians on the warpath and would not make the run. Richardson's was one of the few recorded cases of a Pony Express rider refusing to carry the mail. As it happened, western superintendent W. C. Marley was at the station at the time, and after trying in vain to persuade Richardson to perform his duty, he turned to Pony Bob. Marley offered Haslam a fifty-dollar bonus to take the next run, a winding ninety-mile trek through hostile Paiute territory. As tired as he was, Haslam knew the mail had to go through. Ten minutes later, he was off at a gallop.

The first stretch was thirty-five lonesome, dangerous miles to the Sink of Carson Station (on some maps called Old River Station). Mile after exhausting mile Haslam rode. After the Sink of Carson he had a thirty-seven-mile trek over choking alkali wasteland and parched sand to Cold Springs Station. From there it was another thirty miles to Smith's Creek Station (Castle Rock on some maps). There, with every muscle in his body aching, Haslam delivered his mochila to relief rider J. G. Kelly. Pony Bob had ridden a staggering 190 miles, stopping only to change horses. But this was only the beginning of his amazing story.

About nine hours later, the westbound rider arrived at Smith's Creek. Without hesitation, Haslam, being the only rider there, leaped on a fresh horse and raced away with the mail. Meanwhile, Indian hostilities raged like a prairie fire. Haslam arrived at Cold Springs to a scene of tragedy: Indians had killed the station keeper and taken all the horses. The place was in ruins. Haslam stayed only long enough for his horse to drink, then rode away at top speed. There wasn't even time to bury the poor victim. Haslam had to warn others.

It was getting dark by then. Both sides of the trail were thickly lined with tall sagebrush, providing easy cover for waiting Indians, even those on horseback. Haslam kept a sharp eye on his horse's ears—they instinctively twitched when the animal sensed danger. The stillness of the night, broken every so often by howling wolves, did nothing to calm his fears. He was no stranger to Indian attacks, having been wounded several times. He rode on to Middlegate, then to Westgate, warning the station keepers along the way. He finally arrived at Sand Springs Station (Mountain Well on some maps).

At Sand Springs Haslam reported the Cold Springs raid to the station keeper, either James McNaughton or Montgomery Maze, and convinced him that it was far too dangerous for him to remain there. The two men rode west to the Sink of Carson Station. As it turned out, Sand Springs Station would be attacked and destroyed the very next morning—Pony Bob saved the station keeper's life.

Waiting at the Sink of Carson when the pair arrived were a group of fifteen well-armed but shaken men who had just been attacked a couple of hours earlier by a Paiute war party. The men strongly advised Haslam not to finish his run. But the courier had pledged to carry the mail under all conditions, "Indians or no Indians." After barely an hour's rest, Haslam continued west and arrived at Buckland's Station only three and a half hours behind schedule. Superintendent Marley was so impressed with Haslam's dedication he paid him double the bonus, $100. But this was still not the end of his ride.

There was no rider at Buckland's to carry the mail to Friday's Station (Haslam's normal run). How the frazzled rider was able to stand, let alone take on another exhausting run, is beyond understanding. However, Pony Bob Haslam was an extraordinary fellow. Gallantly, without complaint, he leaped into the saddle and was off. He rode another seventy-five miles, climbing high into the Sierra Nevada. When Pony Bob delivered the mail to his home station, he had ridden an unbelievable 380 miles in under forty hours. Later, when asked about this spectacular feat of courage and endurance, he modestly replied, "I was rather tired, but the excitement of the trip had braced me up to stand the journey."

Pony Bob's matter-of-fact attitude was not mere bravado; it stemmed from his extraordinary riding ability and stamina. He was the natural choice to deliver crucial messages in record time. On November 7, 1860, Haslam was one of the swift riders chosen to ride from Fort Kearny, Nebraska, to Fort Churchill, Nevada, to deliver the news of Lincoln's election. Maintaining breakneck speed, the young rider raced into Fort Churchill shouting, "Lincoln is elected! Lincoln is elected!" In March 1861, Haslam rode from Smith's Creek to Fort Churchill, 180 miles, delivering a copy of President Lincoln's inaugural address in a record-breaking eight hours and ten minutes.

For Pony Bob Haslam, riding was like breathing. When the Pony Express stopped running on October 26, 1861, Haslam kept riding. For the next year he worked for Wells, Fargo & Company as an express rider between Virginia City, Nevada, and Friday's Station, in the High Sierra. His schedule called for him to make a one-hundred-mile round-trip in ten hours.

When the Union Pacific rail line eliminated the need for his services in Nevada in 1869, the company moved him to Idaho, where he covered a one-hundred-mile route, from Queen's River to the Owhyee River, using only one horse. As if he had not had enough adventure as a Pony Express rider, Haslam worked in Idaho during the Modoc Indian war.

On one of his rides he passed a ghastly scene, the mutilated bodies of ninety Chinese workers, strewn along the trail for ten miles, bleaching in the sun. They had been massacred by local Indians. Only one of them had escaped. This experience may have convinced Pony Bob to move on. The decision most likely saved his life, for Indians killed Haslam's replacement on his very first run.

Haslam continued to work for Wells Fargo for several more years, driving a stagecoach between Salt Lake City and Denver. In 1912, this man of iron, who represented the very essence of the Pony Express rider, died at the age of seventy-two, in Chicago.

Less well-known than Pony Bob but just as dedicated a rider was Billy Fisher. He was born in Woolrich, England, on November 16, 1839, the second son of Thomas Frederick and Jane Christon Fisher. The elder Fisher worked in the dockyards as a carpenter and a painter for twenty-one years and also served as president of the local branch of the Mormon Church.

Left to right: John Fisher, John Hancock, and William "Billy" Fisher. Each had many adventures riding the Pony Express Trail. —Courtesy St. Joseph Museum

When Billy was fourteen, the family, which consisted of three sons and two daughters, migrated to America. They traveled to Kansas City, where they bought wagons, oxen, and other provisions and began the long overland journey to Salt Lake City. They arrived on October 28, 1854.

Billy Fisher, twenty-one, was one of the first riders hired by Howard Egan. He was assigned to the route between Ruby Valley Station, operated by Frederick Hurst, and Schell Creek Station, where Peter Neece was station supervisor. It was a lonely and dangerous run in mountainous, barren northeastern Nevada.

The then raging Paiute war did not make the job any easier, yet Fisher was confident. He alluded to this in a letter to his sweetheart, Miss M. Van Etten of Salt Lake City: "The Indians are raising the devil out here now, but I think they will soon stop, as the troops have come to our assistance." The highly intelligent Fisher knew the Indians well. He spoke Bannock and Shoshone fluently, and these tribes considered him one of their most trusted friends. But that would not protect him from the Paiute.

As in the case of some other young riders, Fisher was called upon to make an exhaustive ride that challenged the very limit of his endurance. In July 1860, Fisher carried the news of the Paiute uprising led by Chiefs Leather Head, Pocatello, and Winnemucca from Ruby Valley all the way to Salt Lake City, a distance of three hundred miles. Because the regular trail passed through places where Indian warriors were known to wait in ambush, Fisher often had to circle around especially dangerous spots. He completed his incredible run, including stops to change horses, in only thirty-four hours. Upon receiving the message, the army sent two companies of soldiers to Ruby Valley to protect the Pony Express stations. This important news had been carried across the entire Pony Express Trail in just under eight days, certainly illustrating that the Pony Express service was valuable to the nation.

Fisher was also part of the high-speed team that in November 1860 delivered the news of Abraham Lincoln's election. He covered seventy-five miles of rugged terrain in four hours and five minutes, an average of more than eighteen miles per hour.

The closest call Fisher had with death came not from Indians but from Mother Nature. On January 22, 1861, he was stationed at Rush Valley (also known as Faust's Station), Utah, waiting for the rider from the west. When he arrived, Fisher took off at full speed with the mochila, headed for Salt Lake City. He had not gone a mile when the sky opened up and hurled down a vicious blizzard. The wind raged, and visibility dropped to near zero. He kept his horse going in the bitter cold and miraculously made it to East Rush Valley relay station, where he got a fresh horse and was undoubtedly advised to wait out the storm.

But Fisher didn't hesitate and headed northeast toward Camp Floyd, commanded by General Albert Sidney Johnston. By then, the snow was so blinding that Fisher almost missed the station. The howling winds whipped up clouds of powdered snow, adding to the deluge still rushing down from the sky. At the fort, a hostler warned Fisher he'd never make it through the storm. But the rider was determined that the mail would go through.

Mounting a fresh horse, Fisher started out again into the dark, frigid blizzard. Mile after mile he rode. At one point he was startled as his horse nearly collided with a team of oxen pulling a Russell, Majors & Waddell freight wagon heading to Camp Floyd with military supplies. The wagon boss earnestly admonished Fisher to return with them to the fort, but the young man refused.

Several hours later, Fisher found himself in a grove of cedars—completely lost. Tired, cold, and confused, he got off his horse, sat down against a thick cedar, which partially shielded him from the storm, and tried to figure out what to do. In his memoirs, Fisher described what happened next:

> As I sat there holding the reins, I began to get drowsy. That snow bank looked like a feather bed, I guess; and I was about to topple over on to it and take a good nap when suddenly something jumped on to my legs and scared me. I looked up just in time to see a jackrabbit jumping away through the snow.
>
> Then I sensed what was happening to me. A man who goes to sleep in the snow might keep on sleepin', you know. I jumped up and began to thrash my arms about me to get my blood goin' better. Then I got back on my horse and turned the matter over to him.

Fisher's horse evidently knew more than his rider. It wound its way out of the trees and eventually found its way to the bank of the Jordan River. Recognizing the area, Fisher rode across a bridge into the tiny settlement of Lehi, where a generous woman welcomed the weary and deeply chilled Pony rider into her home. After she gave him some hot coffee and a large beefsteak, he soon felt better and was ready to resume his run. She insisted that he wait for the storm to break, but he explained his duty and was off again into the raging blizzard toward Salt Lake City.

After a few hours, Fisher realized that he had again strayed off the trail, into some hills in the northeast corner of Utah. Looking across a gulch, he saw a dim light. He left his horse and plunged into the hip-deep snow, wallowing through drift after drift, until he finally reached a small farmhouse. The good folks there took him in and set him by the fire. They even went and fetched his horse.

When Fisher stepped out of the cabin, the storm had broken and the stars sparkled in the cold night. He took off for Rockwell's relay station, where he changed horses, then continued to Salt Lake City. Finally there, he handed the mochila to the next eastbound rider and settled down to a nice long sleep in a warm bed. He had spent twenty hours in that ferocious blizzard, nearly freezing to death several times. But he made it through with the mail.

One of the most dramatic portrayals of a dedicated young rider is the story of Billy Tate, who carried the mail near Ruby Valley, Nevada, during the height of the Paiute war. One day as he rode along the trail, Tate was suddenly attacked by an Indian war party. He tried to outrun the Indians, but after a long chase, he found himself surrounded. Hiding behind some rocks, he tried to put up a fight. His body was later found full of arrows. But he had killed seven of his attackers.

His friends were surprised that Tate had not been scalped. But the Indians had great respect for courage, and so in Tate's case they refrained from that final act of mutilation. The mochila had not been touched. Billy Tate had remained true to his Pony Express pledge and had put up a good fight. These actions would have brought honor to any seasoned Pony Express rider, but in the case of Billy Tate it was extraordinary: he was only fourteen years old.

It is possible that someone even younger than Billy Tate rode for the Pony Express. A man named "Bronco Charlie" Miller claimed to have ridden the Pony trail at the tender age of eleven. According to him, in July 1861 he was standing by the Sacramento Pony Express Station when suddenly a riderless horse came running up at a gallop. The station operator told young Charlie that the rider was most likely the victim of an Indian's arrow. Without hesitation the lad pleaded with the station keeper to let him take the mail. He said he knew these parts and could ride with the best of them. The station operator agreed and off went Bronco Charlie, headed for Placerville. Miller claimed that he continued to ride for the Pony Express, between Carson City and Placerville, until it went out of business in November 1861.

There are a number of problems with Miller's story, however. The horse must have been coming from the west, from either the paddle-wheel steamer from San Francisco or the Benicia Pony Express station. In either case, it is unlikely that the rider would have been attacked by Indians. Furthermore, Sacramento was a home station, so why was there no replacement rider there?

Also suspect is Miller's statement that he carried the mail to Placerville. Placerville was merely a relay station. The final stop would have been Sportsman's Hall, a home station, where a replacement rider would have been waiting to continue east. Miller went on to say that he carried the mail between Carson City and Placerville, a distance of well over a hundred miles. It is hard to believe that such a long and difficult route would be assigned to an eleven-year-old boy.

Nevertheless, Charlie Miller is listed as a rider. He may have been a temporary or a replacement rider. If this is true, then Miller was indeed the youngest Pony Express rider. Also interesting, since he died in 1955, at age 105, Miller would also have been the last and oldest surviving Pony Express rider.

It is well and proper to reflect on the colorful exploits of the great Pony Express riders, whose stories have been recorded and perhaps embellished. But we must also remember the dozens of other unglorified riders and station keepers who dutifully struggled to keep the mail going through. They performed their ordinary routine duties with a diligence that is itself heroic.

There were men such as Bill Streeper, who once slowed his horse to lure a band of renegade Indians into a military trap. And David Jay, who at fourteen walked seventy-five miles to Marysville to apply as a Pony Express rider—he was accepted. Henry Avis continued riding as he came to one burned-out station after another, with no replacement horses and warring Indians lurking along the trail, to bring the mail through after a grueling 220-mile run.

Then there was Warren Upson, who routinely carried the mail over the High Sierra, often at night, through raging blizzards, sometimes passing through thirty-foot snowdrifts. And George Washington Thatcher, who after being thrown from his horse was attacked by a wolverine, and with a mighty streak of speed, outran the beast to remount his horse and ride to safety.

Stories of equal fascination could be told by William Page, George Perkins, Charles Miller, and a host of unrecognized but valiant riders.

That is not to say that they were all upright citizens and loyal employees of the Pony Express. Bill Streeper tells of a rider he found on the trail dead drunk. Nell Baughn and William Carr were both hanged for murder. Yet, in the vast majority of cases, the men who kept the Pony Express in operation exhibited superior courage and dedication.

— 14 —
PASSING INTO HISTORY

FROM THE VERY MOMENT of its birth on April 3, 1860, the days of the Pony Express were numbered, for the forces of great events and unfortunate circumstances were converging on the stage of American frontier history.

More than two decades earlier, in 1837, New York University art professor Samuel Morse had invented an electric signaling system that, for several years, was considered little more than a laboratory curiosity. This invention, which used electricity to generate dots and dashes to communicate messages over long distances, was practical, but it took about six years before the government was willing to try it. In 1843 Morse received $30,000 from Congress to build a telegraph line between Washington, D.C., and Baltimore, Maryland. The following year the famous words "What hath God wrought?" flashed across the wire and the telegraph became a reality.

Throughout the rest of the 1840s and 1850s, telegraph lines were strung between major cities along the East Coast. By December 1847, telegraph lines had been connected all the way out to St. Louis. The idea of a transcontinental telegraph line was being actively debated in Congress throughout the 1850s. In the meantime, in 1852, two enterprising New Yorkers, Oliver E. Allen and Clark Burnham, petitioned for and won a franchise from the California legislature to build a telegraph line between San Francisco and Marysville via San Jose, Stockton, and Sacramento.

Although the great San Francisco fire of 1852 nearly put an end to Allen and Burnham's project, on September 13, 1853, the California Telegraph Company completed the system, barely weeks before the state franchise contract was to expire. The feat would have been impossible without the help of a very knowledgeable man named James Gamble. Gamble, with a five-man crew, had worked from sunrise to sunset for more than two months, progressing five or six miles a day through rugged country, to complete the two-hundred-mile line.

January 1854 saw another telegraph line, 121 miles from Sacramento—via Mormon Island, Diamond Springs, Placerville, Colona, Auburn, and Grass Valley—to Nevada City, California, built and operated by the newly formed Alta Telegraph Company. In 1858 an organization called the Placerville, Humbolt & Salt Lake City Telegraph Company was created with the intention of stringing telegraph lines from California to Salt Lake City. However, it was a far bigger job than the company had bargained for, and the project came to an abrupt halt at Fort Churchill in Nevada. The march of progress once again met its match in the vast, unforgiving wilderness.

On the other side of the country, by 1860 the westbound telegraph service reached to the end of civilization—St. Joseph. That year, Charles M. Stebbins, president of the Missouri & Western Telegraph Company, extended a line across the barren wastes to Fort Kearny. When the Pony Express riders stopped at the fort, they could pick up telegrams to Salt Lake City or California. It was an improvement, but a vast distance still separated both ends of the telegraph service. Yet it was just a matter of time before this technology would conquer even the great wilderness.

In these early years, telegraph service was made up of a network of individual systems owned by different small companies. In order to send a telegram a substantial distance, it was usually necessary for the message to be relayed from system to system. This cooperation between individual services gave birth to mergers. One such merger in 1851 resulted in the formation a very large company called the Mississippi Valley Printing Telegraph Company; in 1856 the company changed its name to Western Union Telegraph Company. Its major competitor was the American Telegraph Company.

In 1857 Hiram Sibley, president of Western Union, announced to his board of directors that the time had come to make the great leap and construct a telegraph line all the way across the country. The idea was met with some skepticism. The project would require the cooperation of many other telegraph companies. Undaunted, in December 1859 Sibley presented the idea to members of the North American Telegraph Association. They, too, were less than enthusiastic. There were so many challenges: the vast treeless plain, the mountains, the burning deserts, not to mention the hostile Indians, who would undoubtedly tear down the lines as fast as they would be erected. The poles would be in danger of being trampled by stampeding buffalo. Then there was the huge cost of maintenance. It just would not work.

As he pursued his idea, Sibley continued to meet with resistance. His greatest opposition came from Western Union's archrival, the American Telegraph Company, headed by Robert W. Russell (no relation to William H. Russell). Rather than build a line over the central overland route (essentially the route the Pony Express used), as Sibley proposed, Russell wanted to route the line through New Orleans, across Texas and New Mexico Territory to Los Angeles, then up to San Francisco. In this way, many of the lines would run through their telegraph systems in the South.

In the meantime, in January 1860 Sibley went to Washington to lobby for a bill authorizing the funding for a transcontinental telegraph line. A bill passed on June 16, 1860, called for bids not to exceed $40,000 per year for ten years, with a completion deadline of July 31, 1862. At this point Sibley approached the North American Telegraph Association again. Again he met resistance, whereupon Sibley proclaimed that Western Union would simply take on the task alone.

Sibley immediately put in a bid to the government at $40,000 per year. When three other bidders, one of them Pony Express general superintendent Benjamin Ficklin, mysteriously withdrew their lower bids, Western Union won the contract. Sibley's plan was to build the system from the eastern and western ends of the existing telegraph lines, working toward a central point, namely, Salt Lake City.

During the construction, Sibley contracted the Pony Express to operate as a connection between the uncompleted lines, picking up telegrams from one end and delivering them to the other, to create a seamless flow of communication from the start. Though some historians believe the Pony Express ran only between the east and west telegraph stations in 1861, in fact, the Pony riders traveled the entire route right up to the end of the service. Telegraph lines were often down, so it was not uncommon for Pony riders to carry telegrams to the end of the route.

Sibley hired two men to organize a crew on each end. Edward Creighton headed the eastern crew, and James Gamble the western. Creighton surveyed the prospective route and suggested that the eastern crew start from Omaha, Nebraska, and follow the Platte River past Fort Kearney, then go west to Fort Laramie, along the Sweetwater River, and over South Pass to Salt Lake City. The western crew would construct the line eastward from Carson City through Ruby Valley, Egan Canyon, and Deep Creek, and then on to Salt Lake City.

To further accelerate the work, an even more ambitious plan was developed, using four crews instead of two. On the western section,

Superintendent Gamble would have one of the work crews, supervised by James Street, begin at Salt Lake City and work westward, while I. M. Hubble would manage a team working from Carson City eastward. At the eastern end, Creighton delegated W. H. Stebbins to head up a crew working eastward from Salt Lake City, while Creighton himself would supervise the construction west from Omaha. The task was monumental, but the men were ready to go. The time had come, and the historic race to meet the deadline was on.

The construction of the transcontinental telegraph line, while being the principal cause of the demise of the Pony Express, was only one of a number of causes. Another was the deteriorating financial condition of its parent company. Just before the Pony Express service started, Russell, Majors & Waddell had lost a great deal of money when a huge herd of oxen pulling supply wagons froze to death in a raging blizzard at Ruby Valley, Nevada. Along with losses incurred during the Mormon War, the setback seriously weakened the company financially—it had lost about $150,000. And this was all before it took on the burden of the Pony Express.

The Indian war in the spring and summer of 1860 was another substantial blow to the company. When the fires of war flared, bands of the Paiute, Shoshone, Bannock, Goshute, and other tribes burned many stations to the ground, killed station keepers, and stole horses and equipment. The cost to rebuild it all was $75,000, money the company could ill afford. Then came the awful winter of 1860-61, with its deep snows and unbearable storms, killing and injuring many Pony Express horses. The cost of replacing these animals was also high.

As though these external troubles were not bad enough, internal dissention among the executives of the Central Overland California & Pike's Peak Express Company further debilitated the disintegrating organization. The problems centered mainly around William Russell. In one case, Russell had made an agreement with Robert B. Bradford committing Russell, Majors & Waddell to invest in a stage company that ran between the Missouri River and Denver, Colorado, where gold had recently been discovered. The line turned out to be a losing proposition; the failure put more strain on the company and created resentment among the three partners. There was also a volatile relationship between Russell and Ben Ficklin, the general superintendent. The two men never agreed on company policy, resulting in sometimes explosive confrontations.

In his position with the company, Ficklin wielded enormous authority and basically did things his own way, and his judgment was usually on the mark. But Russell resented Ficklin's ignoring his policy decisions and felt he was left out of the loop. By midsummer 1860, the enmity between the two had become so extreme that Ficklin finally submitted his resignation to Russell. The other partners refused to accept Ficklin's resignation and sent him a conciliatory letter, after which Ficklin withdrew his threat and even sent Russell a letter of apology. But Russell would not relent, and eventually Ficklin did quit. Losing an excellent superintendent certainly did not help the Pony Express's stability.

Still another cause for the Pony Express's failure was the lack of support on the part of the general public. To a certain extent this was understandable—sending mail via Pony Express was terribly expensive, $5 per ounce, the equivalent of about $250 today. Later it was reduced to $1 per ounce, still a prohibitive sum. The average citizen could not afford to send a letter by Pony Express. The service was used mostly by newspapers and businesses.

In the end, the company's income did not meet its basic expenses, which were about $1,000 per day. Its financial statement revealed a dismal picture: the cost of equipment was $100,000; maintenance for sixteen months of operation was $480,000; replacing damages from the Indian war was $75,000; and other expenditures came to $45,000, for a total of $700,000. The total receipts were about $500,000. As word of the red ink spread, the company's creditors began to get nervous and demand immediate payment, putting further pressure on the once great Russell, Majors & Waddell.

In December 1860 came another blow, a scandal involving William Russell. The story appeared in all the newspapers: Russell had been arrested in New York City and charged with accepting stolen government bonds. What extraordinary set of circumstances had led to such a disastrous state of affairs? Had Russell, until now a man of integrity, suddenly become a common thief? Or was there an undercurrent of political intrigue involved? While there is not enough evidence available to satisfactorily resolve all these questions, we do know that William Russell was deeply engaged in a complex web of Washington politics.

In the partnership of Russell, Majors & Waddell, Russell was "the front man," the one who developed all the connections and business relationships. In Washington, he lobbied for government monies, and in the business world he sought corporate funding. Thus he spent a great deal of time in New York City and in the nation's capital, hobnobbing with bankers, businessmen, and politicians. To understand the position in which Russell came to find himself, it helps to examine the political and economic climate in which he was operating.

Throughout the 1850s Washington, D.C., was bustling with business. Large, well-appointed hotels and new retail shops sprang up yearly and prospered. The city enjoyed an enviable sense of security, in spite of the financial crash of 1857, which paralyzed other American cities. As the *Washington Star* observed, "[M]ost of Washington by early 1859 was in better condition than before the blow came. There never was more hard cash in the hands of our fellow citizens than at this time." Washington's prosperity resulted not from the output of local businesses, however, but rather from the overwhelming presence of the federal government and its large-scale spending.

Yet even in the midst of this comforting economic stability, Washingtonians were severely polarized on the issue of slavery. A significant portion of the city's seventy-five thousand inhabitants in 1860 were Southern. Though most of these citizens were inclined to maintain the integrity of the Union, they were of a mind that the government had no right to coerce states into emancipating slaves. Abolitionists were regarded by both Southerners and some Northerners as anarchists ready to rip the country asunder. The intense feeling led to a certain amount of social chaos in the streets.

As the election of 1860 approached, crime ran rampant in Washington, whose police force was inadequate to maintain law and order. Through the 1850s vandalism, prostitution, theft, arson, robbery, and assault increased annually. In 1858 a senate committee declared, "Riot and bloodshed are of daily occurrence. Innocent and unoffending persons are shot, stabbed and otherwise shamefully maltreated and not infrequently the offender is not even arrested."

Nor was crime limited to common folk. Congressmen and senators were also involved in illegal activities. Many were addicted to gambling, some participated in deadly duels, and others caroused with prostitutes, setting a sorry example for their constituencies. In one case a congressman shot a waiter in a hotel and went scot-free. Senator Thomas Benton of Missouri was threatened at gunpoint right on the senate floor. In another instance, Massachusetts Senator Charles Summer was mercilessly beaten with a cane by South Carolina Congressman Preston Brooks. Fistfights broke out during congressional sessions, sometimes resulting in duels. In fact, violence was so rampant that congressmen routinely carried derringers when they ventured to Capitol Hill.

In addition to this general indecorum, Congress was permeated with political intrigue, fueled by the diametrically opposed views among its members and maverick congressmen who attempted to change the political system to conform to their own ideals. It was in this highly charged atmosphere that William Russell operated, befriending some and undoubtedly alienating others. Somewhere in this complex matrix, an opportunity arose for Russell to rectify the eroding conditions of his company.

In this milieu of crime, the stealing of government bonds might not have been viewed as noteworthy by the press nor the public. But the incident had the elements of a scandal, involving as it did a well-known, formerly upstanding business leader. The chain of events leading to the scandal may have started in 1858, two years before the creation of the Pony Express. At that point the government owed Russell, Majors & Waddell about $500,000 for freighting services they had rendered. Unfortunately, the Department of the Interior had used up its appropriations and was unable to pay the debt.

Eventually William Russell approached John B. Floyd, the secretary of war, with the request that his department officially recognize the existence of the debt and issue "firm acceptances," a type of IOU, with a deadline for payment. Normally, these agreements could be presented at a bank as security against a loan. Floyd granted Russell the acceptances, one of many such documents—five million dollars' worth—he issued to various companies between March 5, 1858, and October 1, 1860. Regrettably, Floyd did not have the authority to issue acceptances.

Russell tried to obtain a loan from New York bankers with the acceptances as security. But there was a problem: the due date was only nominal. Russell had agreed not to try to collect payment on that date, so in effect, the acceptances were open-ended and therefore practically worthless. The bankers denied Russell's loan. By now Russell, Majors & Waddell had taken on the burden of subsidizing the Pony Express. Things were getting desperate. Enter the mysterious Godard Baily.

Baily was a law clerk in the Department of the Interior, which was headed by Jacob Thompson, and was married to John B. Floyd's niece. Both Thompson and Floyd were strong supporters of the Confederacy, as was their close associate Senator William Gwin of California. This fact cannot help but suggest the possibility of a plot to trap William Russell in a compromising situation, which would discredit this influential businessman and his company and help drive them to bankruptcy. Even though Russell proclaimed to be proslavery, his competition, the

Butterfield Overland Mail Company, ran its line along a southern route. Floyd also stood to gain politically from Russell, Majors & Waddell's ruination because it would effectively erase the debt the government owed the company.

Baily appeared one day offering Russell the use of "Indian Affairs Trust Fund" bonds, in the amount of $150,000. Russell's New York bankers gave him $97,000 on their face value—not nearly enough. Russell returned to Baily hoping for more, whereupon the clerk made a stunning confession: he had no actual authority to lend Russell the bonds— they were, in effect, stolen. But Russell had already accepted and used the bonds, and his company was still in serious debt. So he made a desperate decision and accepted an additional $387,000 of Indian Affairs Trust Fund bonds from Baily.

One wonders why an ordinary clerk would be instigating such a high-level fraud. There must have been someone behind it, but was it only Floyd? Perhaps Thompson? Gwin? Or President James Buchanan himself? While not in favor of secession, Buchanan's sympathies were with the South on the slavery issue.

Buchanan's choice of the Butterfield company's southern mail route over the central overland route in awarding the 1857 mail contract was criticized as partisan. The southern route was an incredible 40 percent longer than the central route. The *Chicago Tribune* denounced the choice as "one of the greatest swindles ever perpetrated upon the country by the slave-holders." Perhaps even more significant, John Butterfield was a close friend of the president. The suggestion of a presidential plot against William Russell may not be far-fetched.

Baily continued to entice Russell into the iniquitous web, providing him a total of $870,000 in Indian Affairs bonds. The disappearance of the bonds was suddenly discovered on December 24, 1860. Russell was arrested on Christmas Day and held on $200,000 bail. The senior officers of Russell, Majors & Waddell, who had a spotless record, were thoroughly disgraced. But Russell was held in such high esteem by his friends and business associates that they raised the money for his bail, and he was immediately released. In fact, he was so highly regarded, not only in New York and in Washington but also in the West, that when he returned home he was given a testimonial ball, attended by the most notable businessmen and politicians, including governors of states and territories.

Russell maintained that he was innocent of any wrongdoing. He rationalized that the government owed his firm a great deal of money, and the bonds simply provided security for those debts. Yet the damage was done, and word of the scandal quickly spread. Russell had to use most of his personal fortune to pay his panicky creditors, but this was inadequate. The company took a substantial loan from a man named Ben Holladay, the head of a huge stagecoach company—the partners' sterling reputation enabled them to secure some loans in spite of everything.

In an investigation by a congressional committee, Secretary Floyd did not come off well—newspapers ran headlines calling him "Captain of the Forty Thieves"—and he soon left Washington to join the Confederacy. Thomas P. Akers, a Methodist minister and congressman, declared that Russell had been deliberately lured into a scheme approved by President Buchanan. Nevertheless, the Pony Express suffered from the scandal.

Things went from bad to worse for the Central Overland California & Pike's Peak Express Company. Creditors were assailing them from every side, and it was becoming a common joke that the company's initials stood for Clean Out of Cash and Poor Pay. An editorial in the *Sacramento Union* reported:

> There is a strong possibility that the Pony Express will be discontinued. Our correspondent in St. Louis says it is pretty well settled that Russell & Co. will get no mail contract, and, as the Pony Express is now a total loss, almost, to them, there is no inducement to continue it.
>
> Our correspondent adds that the people may thank Postmaster General Holt and our plotting Senator Gwin for it. The former is about 100 years behind the age and should go home and cultivate a tobacco plantation. The latter should be expelled from California just as soon as the votes of the people, through the Legislature, can be brought to bear upon his Senatorial aspirations.

In the meantime, back on the western frontier, Alexander Majors had already begun to prepare for bankruptcy even before the bond scheme was exposed. On October 17, 1860, he signed a deed of trust authorizing the sale of the company's assets for the benefit of its creditors. These included two thousand acres of land in Jackson County, Missouri; town lots in Shawnee and Olathe, Kansas; interest in a Kansas City company; as well as slaves, farming equipment, and other property. The news of Majors's bankruptcy proceedings hit the business community like an earthquake—Russell, Majors & Waddell had been considered an unassailable fortress. By the time the bond scandal hit, the death knell had all but sounded for the great freighting firm.

Still, the Pony Express went on, and the dedicated riders continued to make their runs, even though the company was losing as much as $13 on every letter delivered. The Butterfield line, for that matter, was not doing any better. Ironically, Confederate forces had put a stop to the Butterfield Overland Mail Company's service to California. Southern militia had destroyed bridges, burned down stations, and stolen equipment, making it impossible for the line to operate. The only mail reaching the West Coast was carried by Pony Express riders. It is interesting to note that the Butterfield Overland Mail Company continued to receive government payments even after it stopped running, while the Pony Express service got nothing, in spite of its valuable service to the country. It was the Butterfield company that had been given the government mail contract; the Pony Express never did officially win it.

So now what to do? The government could not simply take the central route away from Russell, Majors & Waddell and give it to Butterfield. It was decided to combine the two companies and have them both operate the central-route mail service. Congress passed the Post Route Bill, which stipulated that the southern route service (i.e., its livestock, wagons, personnel, supplies, etc.) be transferred to the central route. In March 1861, William Russell and William Dinsmore, president of the Butterfield Overland Mail Company, signed an agreement.

In accordance with the agreement, the Pony Express route was divided into two parts, the eastern division, from St. Joseph to Salt Lake City, and the western division, from Salt Lake City to Sacramento. Russell, Majors & Waddell would operate the eastern division, and the Butterfield Overland Mail Company would run the western division. Bulk mail would be carried by stagecoach on a six-day-a-week schedule, and the Pony Express service would operate twice a week, from St. Joseph to Placerville, California. The government would pay the Overland Mail Company $1,000,000 per year; the Overland, in turn, would pay Russell, Majors & Waddell $470,000 per year for operating its half of the route. On July 1, 1861, Russell, Majors & Waddell received its first payment. But it was not enough to save the company from financial ruin. The end was at hand.

In an interesting side note, Russell, Majors & Waddell made a minor arrangement at this point in the Pony Express's history that eventually led to a common historical misconception. Upon establishing the agreement with the Overland Mail Company, Russell, Majors & Waddell hired Wells, Fargo & Company to act as its agent in San Francisco. Its function was merely to receive mail and keep accounts for the West

Coast office. At that point Wells Fargo took it upon itself to establish a pony express service between Placerville—now the end of Russell, Majors & Waddell's Pony line—and San Francisco. Even though Wells Fargo operated this service for only two and a half months, from April 15, 1861, to July 1, 1861, over the years it has come to be believed that Wells, Fargo & Company operated the Pony Express—a total misunderstanding.

Upon signing the agreement with the Butterfield company, having been away from company headquarters for nearly a year, William Russell left Washington, D.C., never to return. On April 26, 1861, the partners held a corporate board meeting at which Russell submitted his resignation. The company's new president, Bella M. Hughes, a former agent for the company and a longtime friend of Russell, accepted the resignation. Although the company made various attempts to revitalize itself with new investments, the efforts failed. On July 5, 1861, the remaining partners started preparations to transfer all company assets to Ben Holladay, to whom they were in deep debt.

Meanwhile, the telegraph crews were making rapid progress. Working from Omaha to Salt Lake City, Edward Creighton's crew actually had a greater distance to cover than did Gamble's, but the western crew had the disadvantage of working in the desert. During the construction period, the Pony Express continued its route. In addition to their regular mail, the riders picked up and delivered telegrams between operational telegraph offices. For example, for a telegram from Omaha to San Francisco, if the line were complete from Omaha to South Pass, a rider would pick up the telegram at South Pass and it would be carried to the first operational telegraph office, say, Ruby Valley; the telegraph operator in Ruby Valley would then send the message over the wire to San Francisco.

During this time, the Pony Express service continued night and day, with not the slightest trace of slowdown in anticipation of the coming telegraph line. When the Civil War broke out, it was the Pony Express that provided the most rapid source of crucial news to the concerned citizens of California. This long human chain that at any moment could fall victim to an Indian attack or the whims of nature was the West's primary source of communication with the East in this time of rapidly unfolding events.

As the riders urged their ponies on, they witnessed the army of workers slowly but surely closing the awesome gap with poles and wire. As the riders passed the crews, they would update them on the progress of the competing crew, adding a little more excitement to the great tele-graph race. The well-managed and highly organized teams worked at a hectic pace, installing about ten miles of line per day. They hoped to complete the nearly two-thousand-mile line before winter came.

The telegraph workers faced some serious obstacles. Supplies had to be hauled great distances—wire and insulators were shipped from the East Coast on boats that sailed around Cape Horn to San Francisco, then taken by wagon across the Sierra Nevada and across the desert. On the eastern end, the materials came by wagon across the Great Plains from the Missouri River. Meanwhile, pole cutters working in the moun-tains had to have supplies, and heavy loads of poles had to be hauled down precipitous trails to the work site. In areas such as the Platte Val-ley and the Nevada desert, which were barren of trees, poles had to be hauled hundreds of miles. Then there were the Indians.

At first the Indians were bewildered. Why was the white man tying an iron string along a row of dead trees? At one point Creighton ex-plained to some of the Indians that the telegraph line was a gift from the Great Spirit to make it possible for people to talk to each other over great distances. They remained skeptical. Then Creighton asked Chief

A Pony Express rider passes a crew of telegraph workers. The comple-tion of the transcontinental telegraph line would signal the end of the Pony Express mail service. (Detail of painting by George M. Ottinger)
—Courtesy Nebraska State Historical Society

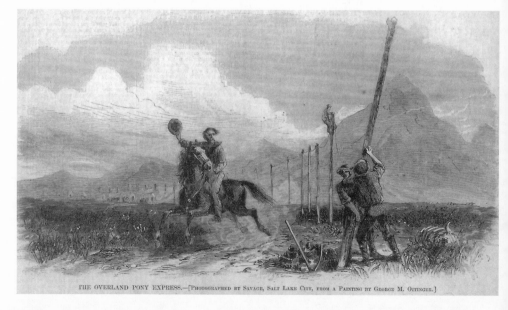

THE OVERLAND PONY EXPRESS.—[Photographed by Savage, Salt Lake City, from a Painting by George M. Ottinger.]

Washakie of the Shoshone to send a message over the telegraph wire to another chief in Wyoming, asking him to meet him at a midway point. The chief agreed, and when Washakie and the other chief met, they were both convinced that the telegraph system had great power.

On October 10, 1861, Creighton's crew completed the eastern section, and Gamble's was not far behind when they hit a stumbling block. They were nearing the last stretch, a section of fifty or sixty miles between Ruby Valley and Schell Creek, but the suppliers could not provide enough poles. The season was getting late, and if the weather turned bad, this small section would hold up the completion of the transcontinental telegraph line until the following spring.

Gamble tried to recruit mountain men and Indians to search the nearby mountains for suitable timber, but they refused, arguing that a sudden storm could trap them in the high country where they could freeze to death. So Gamble approached the workers at Egan Canyon with the assignment, adding that he would accompany them up the mountain himself. The men reluctantly agreed. Within two days, the party had gathered twenty wagonloads of poles, and the western portion of the telegraph line was completed. On October 24, 1861, with the simple connection of two wires, the East and West Coasts were joined with instant communications, and the Pony Express was out of business.

Stephen J. Field, chief justice of California, sent the first message, addressed to President Abraham Lincoln:

> To Abraham Lincoln, President of the United States:
>
> In the temporary absence of the Governor of the State, I am requested to send you the first message which will be transmitted over the wires of the telegraph line which connects the Pacific with the Atlantic States. The People of California desire to congratulate you upon the completion of the great work. They believe that it will be the means of strengthening the attachment which binds both the East and the West to the Union, and they desire in this, the first message across the continent, to express their loyalty to the Union and their determination to stand by its Government on this its day of trial. They regard that Government with affection and will adhere to it under all fortunes.
>
> Stephen J. Field, Chief Justice of California

Horace W. Carpentier, president of the Overland Telegraph Company, sent a second message to President Lincoln:

To His Excellency, the President
Washington, D.C.

I announce to you that the telegraph to California has this day been completed. May it be a bond of perpetuity between the states of the Atlantic and those of the Pacific.

Although the completion of the transcontinental telegraph signaled the end of the Pony Express, the service continued into November to finish delivering all the mail in its possession. During its eighteen months of operation the Pony Express had made a total of 308 complete runs, covering a distance of about 616,000 miles—equivalent to circling the earth more than thirty times. They delivered 34,753 letters through blizzards, rainstorms, and dust storms; over mountains and across deserts and raging rivers; and through hostile Indian territory. Through all that, only one mochila was lost. (Although the details have been blurred by time, it is believed that a letter from the missing mochila was delivered to its destination in 1863. It was marked with a note indicating that the letter had been recovered from a Pony Express mochila some Indians had taken during an attack on a rider.)

The careers of William Russell, Alexander Majors, and William Waddell had hit their high points with the creation of the Pony Express. After the demise of the Pony Express, Russell tried his hand at various businesses without any success. His high-powered friends all but ignored him. He died a disappointed man on September 10, 1872. William Waddell, after paying off all the debts he could, never returned to business. He went back to his family home in Lexington, Missouri. Faced with lawsuits from creditors and troubled by the conflicts of the Civil War, he became ill and went to live with his daughter in Lexington, where he died on April 1, 1872.

Alexander Majors, the sturdiest of the three, sold all he owned to pay his creditors, then established a small freighting company, handling supplies to Idaho and Montana. Unfortunately, bad weather caused these efforts to fail. Later he tried prospecting for silver, also without success. In 1891 Majors was living alone in a small cabin in Denver, trying to write the story of his life when Buffalo Bill Cody, now at the height of his success with his world-renowned Wild West show, looked him up. Cody arranged to have a professional writer help Majors and also paid to have the book, *Seventy Years on the Frontier*, published. Alexander Majors died at the age of eighty-six on January 14, 1900.

The only failure of the Pony Express had been its inability to make a profit. It served our nation well during a difficult time, yet the federal government refused to help support it. Its demise was not due to any lack of effort on the part of its three founders. The fact that they were able to assemble and operate such an incredible service under such challenging circumstances was the ultimate tribute to their courage and ingenuity.

Nor was the Pony's end the fault of the dutiful men who rode the trails and operated the stations. These dedicated men served selflessly and valiantly, sometimes at the cost of their lives. Among them were Bart Riles, James Alcott, Billy Tate, and other riders who may have died while attempting to deliver the all-important mochilas, as well as station keepers Albert Armstrong, Wood Wilson, and others killed while faithfully attending their duties at stations like Egan's Canyon, Schell Creek, Dry Creek, Dugway, Cold Springs, Williams, and Roberts Creek Stations. The incredible rides of Pony Bob Haslam, Bill Cody, Nick Wilson, Jack Keetly, Jim Moore, and other iron men—or iron boys— performed above and beyond any expectations. As much as any other frontier heroes, the men of the Pony Express earned their place of honor in American history.

In October 1861, the Pony Express rider took his place in history. (Painting by W. H. Jackson) —Courtesy Scotts Bluff National Monument

Although most drifted off into oblivion, without a thought of the magnificent service they had rendered to our nation, their memory must be perpetuated and held high for each new generation to admire and emulate. After all, what could be a better symbol of the American spirit than the heroes of the Pony Express? Perhaps their achievement was best expressed by an editorial in the *Sacramento Daily Bee* on October 26, 1861:

> Farewell Pony: Our little friend, the Pony, is to run no more. "Stop it" is the order that has been issued by those in authority. Farewell, thou staunch, wilderness-over-coming, swift-footed messenger. For the good thou hast done we praise thee; and, having run thy race, and accomplished all that was hoped for and expected, we can part with thy services without regret, because, and only because, in the progress of the age, in the advance of science and by the enterprise of capital, thou hast been superseded by a more subtle, active, but no more faithful, public servant. Thou wert the pioneer of a continent in the rapid transmission of intelligence between its peoples, and have dragged in your train the lightning itself, which, in good time, will be followed by steam communication by rail. Rest upon your honors; be satisfied with them, your destiny has been fulfilled—a new and higher power has superseded you. Nothing that has blood and sinews was able to overcome your energy and ardor; but a senseless, soulless thing that eats not, sleeps not, tires not—a thing that cannot distinguish space— that knows not the difference between a rod of ground and the circumference of the globe itself, had encompassed, overthrown and routed you. This is no disgrace, for flesh and blood cannot always war against the elements. Rest, then in peace; for thou hast run thy race, thou hast followed thy course, thou hast done the work that was given thee to do.

Appendix A

PONY EXPRESS STATIONS
(East to West)

LEGEND

Boldface = Original, permanent station
Regular type = Temporary* or alternate station
Italic = Unofficial or uncertain

R = Relay station
H = Home station
R/H = Sometime home station
? = Uncertain
Shaded sections = Alternate routes

*Includes stations built after the service started
and stations that were destroyed and not rebuilt

Name	Other Names	Station Type	State (Today)	Division Supt.
St. Joseph	Patee House	R	Kansas	Lewis
	Pike's Peak	H	Missouri	Lewis
Elwood[1]		—	Kansas	Lewis
Cottonwood Springs[2]	Thompson's Ranch	R	Kansas	Lewis
Troy	Smith's Hotel	R	Kansas	Lewis
	Thompson's Ranch			
Cold Springs	Cold Springs Ranch	R	Kansas	Lewis
	Syracuse			
	Lewis			
Lancaster[3]		R	Kansas	Lewis
Kennekuk		R	Kansas	Lewis
Kickapoo	Goteshell	R	Kansas	Lewis
	Plum Creek			
Log Chain		R	Kansas	Lewis
Seneca		H	Kansas	Lewis
Ash Point	Laramie Creek	R	Kansas	Lewis
	Fogtown			
	Hickory Point			
Guittard	Gantard's	R/H	Kansas	Lewis
	Gutard			
Marysville	Palmetto City	R/H	Kansas	Lewis

[1]May have been used only as a livery stable
[2]Used in early months of service; replaced by Troy Station
[3]May have been used during the final months of service if Atchison, Kansas, was the eastern terminus

Name	Other Names	Station Type	State (Today)	Division Supt.
Hollenberg	Cottonwood	R	Kansas	Lewis
Rockhouse	Oketo Caldwell	R	Nebraska	Lewis
Rock Creek	Pawnee Turkey Creek Elkhorn Lodi Post Office	R	Nebraska	Lewis
Virginia City	Grayson's Whiskey Run	R	Nebraska	Lewis
Big Sandy	Daniel Ranch Ed Farrell Ranch	H	Nebraska	Lewis
Millersville	Thompson's	R	Nebraska	Lewis
Kiowa		R	Nebraska	Lewis
Little Blue	Oak Grove	R	Nebraska	Lewis
Liberty Farm		H	Nebraska	Lewis
Spring Ranch	Lone Tree	R	Nebraska	Lewis
Thirty-Two Mile Creek	Dinner Station	R	Nebraska	Lewis
Summit	Sand Hill Fairfield Water Hole Gills	R	Nebraska	Lewis
Hooks	Dogtown Kearney Valley/Valley City Hinshaw's Ranch Junction City	H	Nebraska	Lewis
Fort Kearney[4]		—	Nebraska	Lewis
Platte	Seventeen Mile	R	Nebraska	Slade
Garden	Craig's Biddleman Shakespeare	R	Nebraska	Slade
Plum Creek	Fort McPherson	R	Nebraska	Slade
Willow Island	Willow Bend Willow Springs	R	Nebraska	Slade

[4]May not have been an official Pony Express station; there may have been a station in nearby Doby Town

Name	Other Names	Station Type	State (Today)	Division Supt.
Midway	Pat Mullay's Smith's East Ranch Cold Water Heavy Timber	H	Nebraska	Slade
Gilman's		R	Nebraska	Slade
Sam Mettache's	Dan Trout's Joe Bower's Broken Ranch Fort McPherson	R	Nebraska	Slade
Cottonwood Springs	McDonald's Ranch Cottonwood	R	Nebraska	Slade
Cold Spring		R	Nebraska	Slade
Fremont Springs	Buffalo Ranch	H	Nebraska	Slade
O'Fallon's Bluff	Dansey's O'Fallon's Halfway House Elkhorn	R	Nebraska	Slade
Alkali Lake	Pike's Peak Alkali	?	Nebraska	Slade
Sand Hill	Gill's	R	Nebraska	Slade
Diamond Springs		?	Nebraska	Slade
Beauvai's Ranch[5]		?	Nebraska	Slade
Frontz's	South Platte Butte	R	Colorado	Slade
Julesburg		H	Colorado	Slade
Nine Mile	Lodge Pole	R	Nebraska	Slade
Pole Creek No. 2		R	Nebraska	Slade
Pole Creek No. 3		R	Nebraska	Slade
Midway	Thirty Mile Ridge	R	Nebraska	Slade
Mud Springs		H	Nebraska	Slade
Courthouse Rock		R	Nebraska	Slade
Junction[6]		R	Nebraska	Slade

[5] There is very little evidence to support this being a Pony Express station

[6] See note 5.

Name	Other Names	Station Type	State (Today)	Division Supt.
Chimney Rock		R	Nebraska	Slade
Ficklin's Springs	Ash Hollow Ficklin's	R	Nebraska	Slade
Scotts Bluff	Fort Mitchell	H	Nebraska	Slade
Horse Creek		R	Nebraska	Slade
Cold Springs	Spring Ranch Spring Torrington Junction House	R	Wyoming	Slade
Bordeaux	Beauvais Diamond Springs	R	Wyoming	Slade
Fort Laramie		R	Wyoming	Slade
Nine Mile	Sand Point Ward's Central Star	R	Wyoming	Slade
Cottonwood	Cottonwood Creek	R	Wyoming	Slade
Horseshoe		H	Wyoming	Slade
Elkhorn		R	Wyoming	Bromley
La Bonte		R	Wyoming	Bromley
Bed Tick	Fetterman Douglas Orin	R	Wyoming	Bromley
Lapierelle	La Prelle	R	Wyoming	Bromley
Box Elder		R	Wyoming	Bromley
Deer Creek		?	Wyoming	Bromley
Little Muddy	Glen Rock	R	Wyoming	Bromley
Bridger		R	Wyoming	Bromley
Platte Bridge	North Platte Casper	?	Wyoming	Bromley
Red Butte	Red Buttes	?	Wyoming	Bromley
Willow Spring		H	Wyoming	Bromley
Horse Creek	Greasewood Creek	R	Wyoming	Bromley
Sweetwater	Independence Rock	R	Wyoming	Bromley

Name	Other Names	Station Type	State (Today)	Division Supt.
Devil's Gate		R	Wyoming	Bromley
Plant's	Plante	R	Wyoming	Bromley
Split Rock		R	Wyoming	Bromley
Three Crossings		H	Wyoming	Bromley
Ice Slough	Ice Springs	R	Wyoming	Bromley
Warm Springs		R	Wyoming	Bromley
Rocky Ridge	Mary's St. Mary's Foot of the Ridge	?	Wyoming	Bromley
Rock Creek	Horse Creek	?	Wyoming	Bromley
South Pass	Upper Sweetwater Burnt Ranch	R	Wyoming	Bromley
Pacific Springs		R	Wyoming	Bromley
Dry Sandy		R	Wyoming	Bromley
Little Sandy		R	Wyoming	Bromley
Big Sandy		R	Wyoming	Bromley
Big Timber	Big Bend Simpson's Hollow	R	Wyoming	Bromley
Green River	Green River Crossing	H	Wyoming	Bromley
Michael Martin's		R	Wyoming	Bromley
Ham's Fork		R	Wyoming	Bromley
Church Buttes		R	Wyoming	Bromley
Millersville		R	Wyoming	Bromley
Fort Bridger		R	Wyoming	Bromley
Muddy Creek	Little Muddy	R	Wyoming	Bromley
Quaking Asp	Aspen Spring Station	R	Wyoming	Bromley
Bear River	Briggs	R	Wyoming	Bromley
Needle Rock	The Needles	R	Utah	Bromley
Head of Echo Canyon	Echo Canyon Echo Frenchie's Castle Rock	H	Utah	Bromley

Name	Other Names	Station Type	State (Today)	Division Supt.
Cache Cave[7]		—	Utah	Bromley
Halfway	Emery Daniels	R	Utah	Bromley
Weber	Hanging Rock Echo Bromley's Pulpit Rock	R	Utah	Bromley
Brimville Emergency[8]	Henneferville Carson House	—	Utah	Bromley
Carson House[9]		R	Utah	Bromley
East Canyon	Dixie Creek Dixie Dixie Hollow Snyder's Mill Dutchmann's Flat Big Mountain Bauchmann's	R	Utah	Bromley
Weaton Springs[10]	Winston Springs Bauchmann's	R	Utah	Bromley
Mountain Dale	Mountain Dell Hank's Big Canyon	R	Utah	Bromley
Salt Lake City	Salt Lake House	H	Utah	Bromley
Trader's Rest	Traveler's Rest	R	Utah	Egan
Rockwell's		R	Utah	Egan
Joe's Dugout	Seven Mile Joe Butcher's	R	Utah	Egan
Camp Floyd	Fort Crittenden Cedar City Carson's Inn Carson House Fairfield	R	Utah	Egan

[7]Used only as an emergency stop
[8]See note 7.
[9]There is very little evidence to support the existence of this station
[10]One map places this station between Weber and East Canyon

Name	Other Names	Station Type	State (Today)	Division Supt.
East Rush Valley	No Name Pass Pass Five Mile Pass	R	Utah	Egan
Rush Valley	Bush Valley Faust's Doc Faust's Meady Creek	H	Utah	Egan
Point Lookout	Lookout Pass Jackson's General Johnson's Pass	R	Utah	Egan
Government Creek[11]	Government Well Davis	R	Utah	Egan
Simpson's Springs	Pleasant Springs Egan's Springs Lost Springs	R	Utah	Egan
Riverbed	Red Bed	R	Utah	Egan
Dugway	Dugout Short Cut Pass	R	Utah	Egan
Black Rock	Butte Desert Station	R	Utah	Egan
Fish Springs	Smith's Springs Fresh Springs Fish Creek	H	Utah	Egan
Boyd's	Butte Desert	R	Utah	Egan
Willow Springs	Six Mile	R	Utah	Egan
Willow Creek		R	Utah	Egan
Canyon	Burnt Overland Canyon	R	Utah	Egan
Deep Creek	Ibapah Egan's	H	Utah	Egan
Prairie Gate	Eight Mile Pleasant Valley	R	Nevada	Egan
Antelope Springs		R	Nevada	Egan
Spring Valley[12]		R	Nevada	Egan

[11]There is very little evidence to support the existence of this station
[12]Used during the final months of the Pony Express service

Name	Other Names	Station Type	State (Today)	Division Supt.
Schell Creek	Fort Schellborne	H	Nevada	Egan
Egan	Egan's Canyon	R	Nevada	Egan
Butte	Bates Robber's Roost	R	Nevada	Egan
Mountain Springs		R	Nevada	Egan
Ruby Valley		R	Nevada	Egan
Jacob's Well[13]		R	Nevada	Egan
Diamond Springs .		R	Nevada	Egan
Sulphur Springs		R	Nevada	Egan
Roberts Creek		R/H	Nevada	Egan
Camp[14]	Grub's Well	R	Nevada	Roberts
Dry Creek		H	Nevada	Roberts
Cape Horn[15]		R	Nevada	Roberts
Simpson's Park		R	Nevada	Roberts
Reese River	Jacob's Spring Jacobsville	R	Nevada	Roberts
Dry Wells[16]	Mount Airy	R	Nevada	Roberts
Smith's Creek		H	Nevada	Roberts
Castle Rock[17]		R	Nevada	Roberts
Edwards Creek		R	Nevada	Roberts
Cold Springs	East Gate	H	Nevada	Roberts
Middlegate	Middle Creek	R	Nevada	Roberts
Westgate		R	Nevada	Roberts
Sand Springs	Mountain Well	R	Nevada	Roberts
Sand Hill		R	Nevada	Roberts
Sink of Carson	Carson Sink Carson River Old River	R	Nevada	Roberts
Williams	Honey Lake	R	Nevada	Roberts

[13]Opened October 1860
[14]See note 12.
[15]There is very little evidence for the existence of this station
[16]See note 12.
[17]See note 15.

Name	Other Names	Station Type	State (Today)	Division Supt.
Desert	Hooten Wells[18]	R	Nevada	Roberts
Buckland's[19]	Nevada	H	Nevada	Roberts
Fort Churchill		H	Nevada	Roberts
Fairview		R	Nevada	Roberts
Mountain Well		R	Nevada	Roberts
Stillwater	Salt Well	R	Nevada	Roberts
Old River		R	Nevada	Roberts
Bisby's	Busby's	R	Nevada	Roberts
Nevada		R	Nevada	Roberts
Ragtown		R	Nevada	Roberts
Desert Well		R	Nevada	Roberts
Miller's	Reed's	R	Nevada	Roberts
Dayton	Spafford's Hall	R	Nevada	Roberts
Carson	Carson City	H	Nevada	Roberts
Genoa	Old Mormon	R	Nevada	Roberts
Friday's	Lakeside	R/H	Nevada	
Woodford's[20]		R	California	Roberts
Fountain Place		R	California	Roberts
Yank's	Hope Valley	R	California	Roberts
Strawberry		R	California	Roberts
Webster's	Sugar Loaf House	R	California	Roberts
Moss	Moore's Mess Riverton	R	California	Roberts
Sportsman's Hall	Twelve Mile	H	California	Roberts
Placerville	Hangtown	R	California	Roberts
El Dorado	Nevada House Mud Springs	R	California	Roberts
Mormon Tavern	Sunrise House	R	California	Roberts
Fifteen Mile House		R	California	Roberts

[18]Hooten Wells may have been a separate station one mile north of Desert Station

[19]Used only during the first few months of service

[20]In service from April 3 to April 28 or 29, 1860

Name	Other Names	Station Type	State (Today)	Division Supt.
Pleasant Grove House	Duroc	R	California	Roberts
Folsom		R	California	Roberts
Five Mile House	Mills	R	California	Roberts
Sacramento	Sutter's Fort	H	California	Roberts
Benicia[21]		R	California	Roberts
Martinez[22]		R	California	Roberts
Oakland[23]		R	California	Roberts
San Francisco		H	California	Roberts

[21]Used only when riders missed the steamboat at Sacramento or San Francisco
[22]See note 21.
[23]See note 21.

APPENDIX B

PONY EXPRESS RIDERS

The identification of many of the riders has been substantiated by the St. Joseph, Missouri, Pony Express Museum. Those who do not appear on the Pony Express Museum list but were obtained from other sources are marked with an asterisk.

Alcott, Jack*

Anderson, Andrew ("Ole")

Anson, John*

Anton (first name unknown)

Aubrey, F. X.*

Avis, Henry

Babbit, Rodney

Ball, Lafaette

Ball, S. W. (or L. W.)

Banks (or Bank), James W.

Barnell, James

Baughm, Jim ("Boston")

Baughm, Mellville (Mel)

Beadsley, Marve

Beatley, James

Becker, Charles

Bedford, Thomas J.

Billman, Charles

Bills, G. R.

Bolwinkle, Lafayette ("Bolly")

Bond (first name unknown)

Boston (first name unknown)

"Black Sam"

"Black Tom"

Black, Thomas

Boulton, William

Brandenburger, John*

Brink, James W. ("Doc")

Brown, Hugh

Brown, James

Bucklin, James (Jimmy)

Buckton, Jim*

Burnett, John

Bush, Ed

Campbell, William

Carlyle (or Carlisle), Alexander

Carr, William (Bill)

Carrigan, William

Carson (first name unknown)

Carter, James

Cates, William A.

Cayton, Francis M.

Clark, James (Jimmy)

Clark, John

Clark, Richard W. ("Deadwood Dick")*

Cleve (or Cleave), Richard

Cliff, Charles

Cliff, Gustavas (Gus)

Cobett, Bill

Cody, William F. ("Buffalo Bill")

Cole, Buck

Combo (or Cumbo), James ("Sawed-Off Jim")

Covington, Edward

Cowad, James

Crawford, Jack

Danley, James*

Dean, Louis

Dennis, William (Billy)

Derrik, Frank

Diffenbacher, Alex

Dobson, Captain Thomas

Dodge, J.

Donovan, Joseph

Donovan, Tom

Dorrington, W. E.

Downs, Calvin

Draper, John*

Draper, Ira*

Drumheller, Daniel

Dunlap, James E.

Eckels, William

Egan, Major Howard

Egan, Howard Ranson

Egan, Richard, E. ("Ras")

Elliot, Thomas J.

Ellis, J. K.

Enos, Charles

Fair, George

Faust, H. J.

Faylor, Josiah

Fisher, John

Fisher, William F.

Flynn, Thomas

Foreman, Jimmie

Frye (or Fry, or Frey), Johnny

Fuller, Abram

Gardner, George ("Irish")

Gentry, James (Jim)

Gilson, James

Gilson, Samuel

Gleanson, James*

Gould, Frank*

Grady, Tom ("Irish Tom")

Hall, Martin*

Hall, Parley*

Hall, Sam

Hamilton, James*

Hamilton, Samuel

Hamilton, William (Billy)

Hancock, Johnny*

Hansel, Levi

Harder, George*

Hardy* (first name unknown)

Haslam, Robert H. ("Pony Bob")

Hawkins, Theodore (Theo)

Haws, Sam

Helvey, Frank

Hickman, William (Bill)

Higginbotham, Charles

Hogan, Martin

Huntington, Clark Allen

Huntington, Lester (Lot)

"Irish Jim"*

James, William (Bill)

Jay, David R.

Jenkins, Will D.

Jennings (first name unknown)

Jobe, Samuel S.

Jones, William

Kates, William

Keetley, Jack H.

Kelley, J. C. (Mike)

Kelly, H.

Kelly, Jay G.

King, Thomas Owen

Koerner, John P.

La Mont, Harry

Lawson, William

Leonard, George

Little, George Edwin

Littleton, Elias ("Tough")

Lytle, N. N.

Macaules, Sye

Martin, Robert (Bob)

Maxfield, Elijah H.

Maze, Montgomery

McCain, Emmitt

McCall, J. G. (Jay)

McCarry, Charlie

McDonald, James (Jim)

McEneamny (or McEarney or McEnearrny), Pat

McLaughlin, David

McNaughton, James (Jim)

McNaughton, William

Meacond, Lorenzo

Mellen, J. P.

Mifflen, Howard

Miller, Charles B.

Miller, Charlie ("Bronco Charlie")*

Moore, James (Jim)

Murphy, Jeremiah H.

Myrick, Newton

Orr, Mathew

Orr, Robert

Packard, G.

Page, William

Paul, John

Paxton, Joe ("Mochila Joe")

Perkins, Josh (or George) W.

Pridham, William (Bill)

Ranahan, Thomas ("Irish Tom" or "Happy Tom")

Rand, Theodore ("Little Yank")

Randall, James

Reynolds, Charles A.

Reynolds, Thomas J.

Richards, William Minor

Richardson, H.*

Richardson, William Johnson

Riles, Bart

Rinhart, Jonathan

Rising, Don C.

Roff, Harry L.

Ruffin, C. H.

Rush, Edward

Ryon, Thomas*

Sanders, Robert

Sangiovanni, Guglielmo G. R.

Scovell, George

Seerbeck, John*

Selman, Jack

Serish, Joseph

Shanks, James ("Doc")*

Sinclair, John

Spurr, George

Streeper, William H. (Billy)

Strickland, Robert C.

Strohm, William

Sugget, John W.

Tate, William (Billy)

Thatcher, George Washington

Thomas, J. J.

Thompson, Bill

Thompson, Charles F.

Thompson, Charlie ("Cyclone Charlie")

Thompson, James M.

Tough, W. S.

Towne, George

Trotter, Bill*

Tuckett, Henry

Tupence (or Topance), Alexander

Upson, Warren ("Boston")

Van Blaricon (or Von Blaircorn), William E.*

Vickery, Bill*

Wade, John B.

Wallace, Henry

Warley (or Worley), Henry

Weaver, Cap*

Wescott, Daniel (Dan)

Whalen, Michael M. ("Whipsaw")

Wheat, George Orson

Willis (or Wills), H. C.

Wilson, Elijah (Nick)

Wilson, Slim*

Wintle, Joseph E. (or B.)

Worley, Henry

Worthington, James

Wright, George*

Wright, Mose

Zowgaltzd (or Zowgal or Zowgalty), Jose

Sites of Interest

Scenic wonders abound along the Pony Express Trail. Although time and manmade construction have eliminated much of the actual trail, some segments can still be seen, along with natural wonders such as Chimney Rock, Courthouse Rock, Independence Rock, Scotts Bluff, and Devil's Gate. To experience the surviving remnants of the Pony Express firsthand, here's a list of places to visit and agencies that can provide information.

For general information:

National Pony Express Association
P.O. Box 236
Pollock Pines, CA 95762
(916) 622-5205
www.xphomestation.com/npea.html
Comprehensive site dedicated to the Pony Express.

Places to visit:

Fort Bridger Pony Express Station
P.O. Box 35
Fort Bridger, WY 82933
(307) 782-3842
Museum and gift shop.

Fort Kearny State Historical Park
1020 V Rd.
Kearney, NE 68847
(308) 234-9513
www.ngpc.state.ne.us/parks/ftkearny.html
Museum, outdoor exhibits, and gift shop.

Fort Laramie National Historic Site
Fort Laramie, Wyoming 82212
(307) 837-2221
www.nps.gov/fola

Fort Sedgewick Depot Museum
114 E. First St.
Julesburg, CO 80737
(970) 474-2061
Former site of the Julesburg Pony Express Station.

Gothenberg Pony Express Station
1617 Ave. A
Ehmen Park
Gothenberg, NE 69138
(308) 537-3505
www.ci.gothenburg.ne.us/attractions_lodges.htm#pony

Hollenberg Station State Historic Site
Box 183 RR 1
Hanover, KS 66945-9634
(785) 337-2635
www.kshs.org/places/hollenbg.htm
The only unaltered, original Pony Express station.

Marysville Pony Express Station
Marysville Pony Express Barn
106 S. Eighth
Marysville, KS 66508
(913) 562-3825

Patee House Museum
Twelfth and Penn
P.O. Box 1022
St. Joseph , MO 64503
(816) 232-8206
www.stjoseph.net/ponyexpress/
Contains the reconstructed offices of Russell, Majors & Waddell. Museum store.

Pony Express Museum
914 Penn St.
St. Joseph, MO 64503
(816) 279-5059 or (800) 530-5930
www.ponyexpress.org
Includes the Pony Express stables. Information, books, brochures, and driving route available.

Rock Creek Station State Historical Park
Rt. 4, Box 36
Fairbury, NE 68352
(402) 729-5777
www.ngpc.state.ne.us/parks/rcstat.html
Includes station site, interpretive center, picnic areas, campgrounds, and hiking and nature trails.

St. Joseph Museum
P.O. Box 128
St. Joseph, MO 64502-0128
(816) 232-8471 or (800) 530-8866
www.stjosephmuseum.org

FOR INFORMATION ON TRAIL SITES:

Bureau of Land Management (BLM)
Nevada State Office
1340 Financial Blvd.
Reno, NV 89502
(775) 861-6400

Salt Lake District Office
Pony Express Resources Area
2370 South 2300 West
Salt Lake City, UT 84119
(801) 977-4300

Wyoming Office
Historic Trails Office
2987 Prospector Dr.,
Casper, WY 82601
(307) 261-7600

All offices: www.blm.gov/nhpl/index.htm

California Office of Tourism
801 K Street, Suite 1600
Sacramento, CA 95814
(800) 462-2543

Colorado Tourism
1625 Broadway, Suite 1700
Denver, CO 80202
(800) 303-1670

Kansas Division of Travel and Tourism
400 SW Eighth Street, 5th Floor
Topeka, KS 66603
(800) 2-KANSAS

Missouri Division of Tourism
P.O. Box 1055
Jefferson City, MO 65102
(800) 519-0100

National Park Service (NPS)
Long Distance Trails Office
325 South State St., Suite 324
Salt Lake City, UT 84145-0155
(801) 539-4093
www.nps.gov/poex/

Nebraska Department of Economic Development
Travel and Tourism Division
P.O. Box 94666
Lincoln, NE, 68509
(800) 228-4307

Nevada Commission of Tourism
Capitol Complex
Carson City, NV 89710
(800) 638-2328

Scotts Bluff National Monument
P.O. Box 27
Gering, NE 69341-0027
(308) 436-4340

Utah Travel Council
300 North State St.
Salt Lake City, UT 84114
(800) 220-1160

Wyoming Division of Tourism
I-25 at College Drive
Cheyenne, WY 82002
(800) 255-5996

WEB SITES:

www.xphomestation.com/penht.html
Pony Express National Historic Trail information.

www.americanwest. com/trails/pages/ponyexp1.htm

www.sfmuseum.org/hist1/pxpress.html
A page of history from the San Francisco Museum.

www.usps.com/history/his2.htm
Postal Service history.

www.ukans.edu/heritage/owk/128/trails.html
Kansas Historic Trails.

http://ngpc.state.ne.us/parks/cody.html
Buffalo Bill Ranch.

www.webpanda.com/white_pine_county/historical_society/pony_exp.htm
Pony Express stations in White Pine County, Nevada.

http://comspark.com/chronicles/ponyexpress.shtml

BIBLIOGRAPHY

Abbey, Edward. *A Thirst for the Desert.* Washington, D.C.: National Geographic Society, 1973.

Alter, S. Cecil. *James Broger: Frontiersman, Scout and Guide.* Salt Lake City: Shepard Book Co., 1925.

Andrews, R. B. "The Pony Express Rides Again." *Travel,* February 1941.

Bailey, W. F. "The Pony Express." *The Century Magazine* 56 (October 1898).

Bennion, Owen C. "Good Indian Spring." *Utah Historical Quarterly* 52 (1984).

Biggs, Donald C. *The Pony Express: Creation of a Legend.* San Francisco: privately printed, 1956.

Bishop, L. C., and Paul Henderson. *California, Oregon, and Mormon Emigrant Roads.* Map. 1959.

Bloss, Roy S. *Pony Express: The Great Gamble.* Berkeley, Calif.: Howell-North Press, 1959.

Boder, Bartlett. *The Pony Express.* Vol. 11, no. 2. St. Joseph, Mo.: St. Joseph Museum, 1959.

Bradley, Glen D. *The Story of the Pony Express.* Chicago: A. C. McGlurg & Co., 1913.

Brewer, William H. *Up and Down California in 1860–1864.* Berkeley: University of California Press, 1966.

Brown, Dee. "Along the Santa Fe Trail." *American History Illustrated,* October 1980.

———. "The Day of the Buffalo." *American History Illustrated,* July 1980.

———. "The Pony Express." *American History Illustrated,* November 1976.

Bureau of Land Management/U.S. Department of the Interior. *Pony Express in Nevada.* Booklet BLMNVG1890048200. 1981.

Bureau of Land Management, Rock Springs (Wyo.) District Office. "South Pass Tales: Adventures in the Past." Pamphlet BLM-WY-AE-91-023-4332. 1991.

Bureau of Land Management, Salt Lake City District Office. *Desert Crossroads.* Booklet. N.d.

Burton, Richard F. *City of the Saints.* London: Longman & Roberts, 1927.

Capps, Benjamin. *The Great Chiefs.* New York: Time Life Books, 1975.

Carter, Kate B. *Utah and the Pony Express.* Centennial ed. Salt Lake City: Daughters of the Pioneers Museum, 1960.

Chapman, Arthur. *The Pony Express.* New York: G. P. Putnam's Sons, 1932.

Cline, Gloria Griffin. *Exploring the Great Basin.* Norman: University of Oklahoma Press, 1963.

Cody, William F. *The Life of Hon. William F. Cody, Known as Buffalo Bill the Famous Hunter, Scout and Guide: An Autobiography.* New York: Indian Head Books, 1991.

Colton, Ray C. *The Civil War in the Western Territories.* Norman: University of Oklahoma Press, 1959.

Connelly, William E. *Wild Bill: James Butler Hickock.* Vol. 17. Topeka: Kansas State Historical Society, 1926–28.

Coy, Owen C. "The Pony Express Ante-dated." *The Grizzly Bear Magazine* 20 (February 1917).

Dary, David. *The True Tails of the Old Time Plains.* New York: Crown Publications, 1979.

Davis, Sam P. *The History of Nevada.* Reno, Nev.: Elms Publishing Co., 1913.

Driggs, Howard R. *Westward America.* New York: G. P. Putnam's Sons, 1942.

———. *The Pony Express Goes Through.* New York: Frederick A. Stokes Co., 1935.

Edwards, Mike. "Colorado Dreaming." *National Geographic,* August 1984.

Egan, Howard. *Pioneering the West 1846–1878: Major Howard Egan's Diary.* Salt Lake City: Shelton Publishing Co., 1917.

Erskine, Gladys. *Broncho Charlie.* New York: Crowell Publishers, 1934.

Farney, Dennis. "The Tallgrass Prairie: Can It Be Saved?" *National Geographic,* January 1980.

Fike, Richard E., and John W. Headly. *The Pony Express Stations of Utah in Historical Perspective.* Booklet. Salt Lake City: Bureau of Land Management, 1979.

Findley, Rowe. "The Pony Express." *National Geographic,* July 1980.

Fisher, Richard Swainson. *Johnson's New Illustrated Family Atlas of the World.* New York: Johnson & Ward, 1866.

Fonter, Eric, and John A. Garraty. *The Reader's Companion to American History.* Boston: Houghton Mifflin Co., 1991.

Forbis, William H. *The Cowboys.* Alexandria, Va.: Time Life Books, 1973.

Franzwa, Gregory M. *The Oregon Trail Revisited.* Tucson: Patrice Press Inc., 1965.

Froneck, Thomas. "Winterkill (The Donner Party)." *American Heritage,* December 1976.

Godfrey, Anthony, and U.S. Department of the Interior/National Park Service. *Historic Resource Study: The Pony Express National Historic Trail.* La Crosse, Wisc.: US West Research, 1994.

Greeley, Horace. *An Overland Journey from New York to San Francisco.* New York: Knopf, 1964.

Green, Constance, and M. C. Laughlin. *Washington: Village and Capital, 1800–1878.* Princeton, N.J.: Princeton University Press, 1962.

Hafen, Leroy R. *The Overland Mail to the Pacific Coast, 1848–1869.* Cleveland: Ams Press, 1969.

Hagen, Olef T. "The Pony Express Starts from St. Joseph." *Missouri Historical Review* 43 (October 1948).

Hale, Edward Everett. *Kansas and Nebraska.* New York: Ayer Company Pubs., 1977.

Harris, Foster. *The Look of the Old West.* New York: Viking Press, 1955.

Hartung, A. M. "The Pony Express and the Old West." *The Cattlemen* 30 (December 1943).

Hawthorne, Hildegarde. *Ox-Team Miracle: The Story of Alexander Majors.* New York: Longmans, Green & Co., 1950.

Holbrook, Stewart Hall. *Wild Bill Hickock Tames the West.* New York: Random House, 1952.

Honnell, William Rosecrans. "The Pony Express." *Kansas Historical Quarterly* 5 (February 1936).

Hopkins, Sarah Winnemucca. *Life Among the Paiutes.* Boston: Putnam Publications, 1883.

Howard, Robert West. *Hoofbeats of Destiny.* New York: New American Library, 1960.

Inman, Henry, and William F. Cody. *The Great Salt Lake Trail.* Williamstown, Mass.: Corner House Publications, 1978.

Jaybusch, David M., and Susan C. Jaybusch. *Pathway to Glory: The Pony Express and Stage Stations in Utah.* Salt Lake City: Treasure Press, 1994.

Jensen, Lee. *The Pony Express.* New York: Grosset & Dunlap, 1955.

Josephy, Alvin M., Jr. *The Civil War in the American West.* New York: Alfred Knopf, 1991.

Kansas State Historical Society. *Inscriptions on Kansas Historical Markers 1940–1941.* Booklet. Topeka: November 1941.

La Farge, Oliver. *A Pictorial History of American Indians.* New York: Bonanza Books, 1980.

Lamar, Howard R., ed. *The Readers' Encyclopedia of the American West.* New York: Thomas Y. Crowell Co., 1977.

Lavender, David. *The American Heritage History of the West.* New York: Bonanza Books, 1965.

———. *The Rockies.* New York: Harper & Row, 1968.

Laxalt, Robert. *Nevada.* New York: W. W. Norton & Co., 1977.

Lewin, Jacqueline. "The Pony Express Trail in Kansas." *The Happenings* (St. Joseph Museum newsletter) 18 (1991).

Loeb, Julius. "The Pony Express." *The American Philatelist* 41 (November 1930).

Loving, Mabel. *The Pony Express Rides On.* St. Joseph, Mo.: Bobidoux Printing Co., 1961.

Majors, Alexander. *Seventy Years on the Frontier.* Lincoln: University of Nebraska Press, 1989.

Mattes, Merril J. "Potholes in the Great Platte River Road." *Wyoming Annals,* Summer/Fall 1993.

Mattes, Merril J., and Paul Henderson. "The Pony Express Across Nebraska." *Nebraska History* 41 (June 1960).

McLoughlin, Denis. *Wild and Woolly: An Encyclopedia of the Old West.* New York: Barnes & Noble, 1975.

Milner, Clyde A., Carol A. O'Conner, and Martha A. Sandweiss. *The Oxford History of the American West.* New York: Oxford University Press, 1994.

Moize, Elizabeth A. "Daniel Boone: First Hero of the Frontier." *National Geographic,* December 1985.

Monaghan, Jay. *The Overland Trail.* Indianapolis: Bobbs-Merrill Co., 1947.

Moody, Ralph. *Riders of the Pony Express.* New York: Dell Yearling, 1958.

Morehead, C. R. "The Pony Express." *Journal of American History* 11, no. 4 (1917).

Morgan, Dale L. *The Great Salt Lake.* Lincoln: University of Nebraska Press, 1947.

———. *The Humboldt: Highroad of the West.* New York: Rinehart & Co., 1943.

Morris, Richard B. *The Life History of the United States.* Vols. 1–5. New York: Time Inc., 1963.

Museum Graphic, Special Centennial Edition (1960), St. Joseph Museum, St. Joseph, Mo.

Museum Graphic 21, no. 2 (Spring 1969), St. Joseph Museum, St. Joseph, Mo.

O'Connel, Robert L. "Post Haste." *American Heritage*, September/October 1989.

O'Conner, Richard. *Wild Bill Hickok.* Garden City, N.Y.: Doubleday Books, 1959.

Olson, Jamie C. *History of Nebraska.* Lincoln: University of Nebraska Press, 1955.

Oregon-California-Mormon Trail Through Matrona County. Booklet. N.d. Fort Casper Museum, Casper, Wyoming.

Oregon-California Trails Association and Bureau of Land Management, Casper, Wyoming District Office. *Oregon Trail Loop Tour.* Brochure. July 1993.

Paxson, Frederic L. *History of the American Frontier, 1763–1893.* Cambridge, Mass.: Riverside Press, 1924.

Petty, Robert O. "Where Have All the Prairies Gone?" In *Wilderness U.S.A.* Washington, D.C.: National Geographic Society, 1973.

"The Pony Express Rides Again." *Kansas Historical Quarterly* 25 (Winter 1959).

Powell, Allen Kent. *Utah History Encyclopedia.* Salt Lake City: University of Utah Press, 1994.

Randall, J. G., and David Donald. *The Civil War and Reconstruction.* Lexington, Mass.: D. C. Heath & Co., 1969.

Reid, James D. *The Telegraph in America.* New York: Derby Press, 1879.

Reinfeld, Fred. *The Pony Express*. Lincoln: University of Nebraska Press, 1966.

Rideing, William H. "History of the Express Business." *Harper's New Monthly Magazine,* August 1875.

Root, Frank A., and William E. Connelly. *The Overland Stage to California.* Topeka, Kansas: privately published, 1901.

Rosa, Joseph G. *They Called Him Wild Bill.* Norman: University of Oklahoma Press, 1974.

Russell, Don. *The Lives and Legends of Buffalo Bill.* Norman: University of Oklahoma Press, 1960.

"Sacramento-Placerville Routes on the Pony Express Trail, 1860." Map. N.d. National Pony Express Association, Marysville, Kansas.

Settle, Raymond W. "Origin of the Pony Express." *Missouri Historical Society Bulletin* 16 (April 1960).

———. "The Pony Express: Heroic Effort, Tragic End." *Utah Historical Quarterly,* April 1959.

Settle, Raymond W., and Mary Lund Settle. "The Early Careers of William Bradford Waddell and William Hepburn Russell." *Kansas Historical Quarterly,* Winter 1960.

———. *Empire on Wheels.* Palo Alto, Calif.: Stanford University Press, 1949.

———. *The Pony Express Saga.* Harrisburg, Pa.: The Stackpole Co., 1955.

Shapiro, Max S., and William Jaber, eds. *Cadillac Modern Encyclopedia.* New York: Cadillac Publishing Co., 1973.

Simpson, J. H. *Report of Exploration across the Great Basin of the Territory of Utah in 1859.* Reno: University of Nevada Press, 1983.

Smith, Waddell F. *The Story of the Pony Express.* San Francisco: Hesperian House, 1960.

Society of California Pioneers Quarterly 2, no. 2 (June 1925).

Starr, Kevin. *Americans and the California Dream: 1850–1915.* New York: Oxford University Press, 1973.

Sutton, Fred E. "Last Financial Statement of the Pony Express." *Pony Express Courier* 2, no. 5 (October 1935).

Swanberg, W. A. *Sickles the Incredible.* New York: Charles Scribners, 1963.

———. "Was the Secretary of War a Traitor?" *American Heritage,* February 1963.

Tarpy, Cliff. "Home to Kansas." *National Geographic*, September 1985.

Thompson, Robert Luther. *Wiring a Continent*. New York: Arno Press, 1972.

Townley, John M. *The Pony Express Guidebook*. Desert Rat Guidebook Series, vol. 3. Reno, Nev.: Great Basin Studies Center, 1989.

Twain, Mark. *Roughing It*. New York: Harper & Bros., 1872.

U.S. Department of the Interior. *California and the Pony Express Trails Feasibility Study*. NPS D-2A, Denver, Colo.: 1987.

U.S. Post Office Department. *The Saga of the Pony Express*. Washington, D.C.: Government Printing Office, 1960.

Visscher, William L. *A Thrilling and Truthful History of the Pony Express*. 1908. Reprint, Chicago: Rand McNally & Co., 1946.

Wetmore, Helen Cody. *Last of the Great Scouts*. New York: Tom Doherty Associates, 1996.

Wexler, Alan. *Atlas of Western Expansion*. New York: Facts on File, 1995.

Williams, Frances R. "Hollenberg Pony Express Station." *Daughters of the American Revolution Magazine* 87 (February 1953).

Young, Gordon. "That Damned Missouri River." *National Geographic*, September 1971.

INDEX

ABOUT THE AUTHOR

Joseph J. Di Certo is the author of eight other books, including a novel and nonfiction on such diverse topics as electronics technologies, energy, and space travel. He describes *The Saga of the Pony Express* as "a fifteen-year labor of love." He has also authored dozens of articles, television scripts, and screenplays, and has composed three albums of children's music; he is presently working on a symphony. He has appeared on *The Tonight Show*, *Today*, *ABC News*, and others. A film adaptation of *The Saga of the Pony Express* is currently under contract with Dreamworks.

Before becoming a full-time writer, composer, and television and film producer, Mr. Di Certo served in the Air Force for four years as an electronics technician, after which he was a technical writer in the defense industry for ten years. He graduated from Hunter College in 1968, and in 1978 he joined CBS, where for twenty years he worked in marketing support. He currently lives in New York City with his wife, Nina. They have three children and three grandchildren.

We encourage you to patronize your local bookstore. Most stores will order any title that the do not stock. You may also order directly from Mountain Press using the order form provided below or by calling our toll-free number and using your credit card. We will gladly send you complete catalog upon request.

Some other titles of interest:

_____The Oregon Trail: A Photographic Journey	$18.00/paper	
_____Crazy Horse: A Photographic Biography	$20.00/paper	
_____Lewis & Clark: A Photographic Journey	$18.00/paper	
_____Sacagawea's Son:	$10.00/paper	
The Life of Jean Baptiste Charbonneau	(for readers 10 and up)	
_____Stories of Young Pioneers: In Their Own Words	$14.00/paper	
	(for readers 10 and up)	
_____The Arikara War: The First Plains Indian War, 1823	$18.00/paper	$30.00/cloth
_____The Journals of Patrick Gass:		
Member of the Lewis and Clark Expedition	$20.00/paper	$36.00/cloth
_____Chief Joseph and the Nez Perces: A Photographic History	$15.00/paper	
_____The Bloody Bozeman:		
The Perilous Trail to Montana's Gold	$16.00/paper	
_____Lakota Noon: The Indian Narrative of Custer's Defeat	$18.00/paper	$36.00/cloth
_____The Mystery of E Troop: Custer's Gray Horse Company		
at the Little Bighorn	$18.00/paper	
_____Children of the Fur Trade:		
Forgotten Métis of the Pacific Northwest	$15.00/paper	
_____The Piikani Blackfeet: A Culture Under Siege	$18.00/paper	$30.00/cloth
_____William Henry Jackson: Framing the Frontier	$22.00/paper	$36.00/cloth
_____The Saga of the Pony Express	$17.00/paper	$29.00/cloth

Please include $3.00 for 1–4 books or $5.00 for 5 or more books for shipping and handling.

Send the books marked above. I enclose $_____

Name _____

Address _____

City/State/Zip _____

☐ Payment enclosed (check or money order in U.S. funds)

Bill my: ☐ VISA ☐ MasterCard ☐ American Express ☐ Discover   Exp. Date:_____

Card No._____

Signature_____

MOUNTAIN PRESS PUBLISHING COMPANY
P.O. Box 2399 • Missoula, MT 59806 • fax: 406-728-1635
Order Toll Free 1-800-234-5308 • Have your credit card ready.
e-mail: info@mtnpress.com • website: www.mountain-press.com